Zaatar Days, Henna Nights

Adventures, Dreams, and Destinations
Across the Middle East

Maliha Masood

SEAL PRESS

Zaatar Days, Henna Nights
Adventures, Dreams, and Destinations Across the Middle East
Copyright © 2006 by Maliha Masood

Published by
Seal Press
An Imprint of Avalon Publishing Group, Incorporated
1400 65th Street, Suite 250
Emeryville, CA 94608

Library of Congress Cataloging-in-Publication Data

Masood, Maliha.
Zaatar days, henna nights : adventures, dreams, and destinations
across the Middle East / Maliha Masood.
p. cm.
Includes bibliographical references and index.
ISBN-13: 978-1-58005-192-7 (alk. paper)
ISBN-10: 1-58005-192-8 (alk. paper)
1. Masood, Maliha. 2. Middle East—Description and travel. I. Title.

DS49.7.M377 2007
915.604'54—dc22

2006030700

Cover design by Claudia Smelser
Interior design by Domini Dragoone
Printed in the United States of America by Malloy
Distributed by Publishers Group West

Author's note: This work is based on my travels in Egypt, Jordan, Lebanon, Syria, and Turkey from October 2000 to August 2001. It conveys my impressions of people and places as I experienced them during that time. No composites have been used. All cultural, religious, historical, and political references are my own conclusions. In the case of inadvertent factual inaccuracies, the fault is entirely mine.

*To my parents for nurturing my wings of flight,
and to my husband for allowing me to soar.*

You cannot cross the sea
merely by staring at the water.

RABINDRANATH TAGORE

Contents

A Leap in the Dark

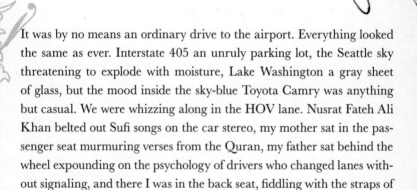

Listen, are you breathing just a little,
and calling it a life?

MARY OLIVER

It was by no means an ordinary drive to the airport. Everything looked the same as ever. Interstate 405 an unruly parking lot, the Seattle sky threatening to explode with moisture, Lake Washington a gray sheet of glass, but the mood inside the sky-blue Toyota Camry was anything but casual. We were whizzing along in the HOV lane. Nusrat Fateh Ali Khan belted out Sufi songs on the car stereo, my mother sat in the passenger seat murmuring verses from the Quran, my father sat behind the wheel expounding on the psychology of drivers who changed lanes without signaling, and there I was in the back seat, fiddling with the straps of my REI pack, trying to remember why I was running away from home.

I guess I thought it was the right thing to do and the right time to do it. If I had chickened out and waited any longer, I might have given my parents fewer headaches, definitely fewer worries, but I probably wouldn't have forgiven myself for failing to disengage from a rusty vessel of thwarted hopes before it foundered and sank. At least that was how I saw my life six years ago. I was twenty-eight and miserable. Time kept marching like an arrogant parade, taunting me with the stench of a stale existence.

No more *should haves* or *could haves,* or my personal favorite, *what if.* I was tired of going through motions that had lost their meaning. Each day had been the same as the last. I would wake up to the screams of my alarm clock and have a little war with the snooze button before dragging myself into the shower. Dressed in earth-toned suits and brown leather pumps, with a whole-grain bagel tucked inside my purse, I would head to the office to play phone tag, answer emails, and multitask, only to come home, eat dinner, watch sitcoms, and fall asleep, ready to repeat the cycle the next day, the next, and the next.

It all started out as a string of lackluster jobs after college. I worked in the tech sector, hashing out competitive analyses and returns on investment reports, for five soulless years that gave me no sense of accomplishment, no indication of what I was truly capable of beyond number-crunching on Excel spreadsheets and mapping out pie charts.

What I really wanted was to escape from routine and find new rhythms in a world that would reawaken my senses. I wanted to know the meaning of wonder and freshness, to regain the wide-eyed openness of a child. I wanted to come to terms with a truer me, a more essential self that couldn't entirely be placed amid the bullet points of my resume. So I did what had to be done. I handed in my resignation letter, cashed in all my savings, and headed to Council Travel. It was having a sale on Europe. Paris sounded nice. I booked a one-way ticket.

Then I made a little announcement to friends and family.

"I am going abroad for a while. I don't know how long I will be gone for or exactly where I will be traveling to. But I promise to stay in touch with emails and let you know my whereabouts."

They were kindhearted folks who cared for me and wanted me to be happy. So I wasn't taken to the nearest psychiatric ward. I was simply wished well and told to send plenty of postcards.

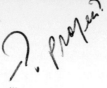
?. prayer?

"Don't forget to say your *dua!*"

My mother's words of farewell at the British Airways departure gate urged me to remember Allah in prayers. I patted my money belt for my passport and my favorite rosary. It calmed me to roll my fingers over the smooth wooden beads and mumble *Alhamdulillah* (thanks be to God), *Subhanallah* (praise be to God), *Allahu Akbar* (God is great) thirty-three times each. I had learned this ritual as a child growing up in Karachi, Pakistan, where I used to follow my mother around our house, clutching the accordion pleats of her sari like a safety blanket. But the comfort of Ammi's saris was no match for the allure of my first transatlantic flight to the United States. One day, my eight-year-old fingers let go of the silky fabric in exchange for a laminated boarding pass and a chance to visit my cousins and maybe Disneyland. I had made the trip on my own, chaperoned on three different legs of the flight by friendly stewardesses who plied me with chocolates and lollipops. My mother was surprised that a daughter so attached to her side would have readily let go to fly across an ocean to a country more than ten thousand miles away. That was all the proof she needed to say that travel was in my blood.

I hadn't tested this conviction as much as I would have liked to. Throughout my adolescence and into my twenties, I had buried my cravings for the things I loved and become a slave to practicality. I hadn't really taken any risks, and I never felt that I had achieved any goals that I could be proud of. For all my travel-worthiness, I hadn't even moved out of my parents' home and was living a complacent if dull existence in their suburban basement. I had my own car, my own phone line, and cable TV. So it wasn't all that bad, but as the years wore on, I fell into a rut and was desperate to get out.

Paris was a bumpy landing. I arrived on Easter Sunday and spent the next four days repacking my bloated bags and standing in line at the post office to ship things back home, wishing I could get my hands on a how-to manual for conducting a journey without a return date. In an effort to emulate Rick Steves, I bought an Inter Rail pass and took off for Amsterdam, then Prague, then back to France to hike in the Pyrenees, then the northern coast of Spain, then down into Portugal, and then straight to the heart of Andalusia. It was all good fun, but it was too easy. All I did was lug my pack, hop around on trains, and then march into town to the nearest youth hostel, only to meet other Americans or Europeans or Australians doing the same thing I was in a slightly different order.

Italy was my preferred playground. I worked at an organic farm in Umbria, canning and labeling jars of tomato sauce to sell on market Tuesdays. I also hitchhiked through mountain passes in the Dolomites, and once I spent the night at the house of the Libyan ambassador in Rome. Europe was an adventurous start, but I was looking for a bigger challenge, a way to test and push my boundaries.

The journey is not yet over, my inner voice said. *It hasn't even started. It hasn't even started.* The voice kept echoing, compelling me to obey its instructions. They led me to Via del Corso, where I bought another one-way ticket, this time from Rome to Cairo.

I assumed my father would applaud my decision to continue traveling. I had inherited his love of travel, and I often recalled the game we used to play on road trips—naming world capitals, with Dad playing Alex Trebek. He would break down the world by continents and regions. I liked it best when he got to the Middle East and I would get to rattle off Cairo, Beirut, Damascus, and Istanbul. The names would linger on my tongue, intertwining with scattered cultural and historical references to our Islamic heritage. I liked the sound of these names; they were more intriguing than frightening, and for the most part, unknown abstractions on a map, just as I was still an unknown abstraction to myself. I thought that by traveling to the Middle East, I might be able to stamp the place with some degree of familiarity and, by the same token, get better acquainted with little old me.

So that was my convoluted explanation to my parents from a public phone booth near the Vatican. I was right about my dad. He understood and cheered me on. But my mother only sighed and told me to come back to my senses. It gave her some consolation that my vagabond travels were inching closer to Mecca. She encouraged me to pray dutifully in all those famous Arab mosques that transfixed my attention when I flipped through oversize coffee-table books on Islamic art and architecture at the public library.

"There you can't complain about not hearing the *azan*," my mother chastised me over the phone. She was all too familiar with my flimsy excuses about not feeling connected to Islam in America. It had always remained too distant, something to create from the inside out. Now I could hardly wait to hear the muezzin's call to prayer from the Ummayad mosque in Damascus, perhaps even experience Ramadan in Cairo if the timing was right.

By all accounts, late October of 2000 was hardly the most auspicious time to be heading to the Arab world. Knowledgeable friends warned me to stay away from Israel, given the brewing intifada and its reprisals. I recalled the insistent news headlines painting grim stories about explosives, bloodbaths, and death counts. I reminded myself that I had no friends or acquaintances in the Middle East, no grasp of spoken Arabic, and no inkling of a game plan. Of course, I was scared stiff. And I was curious.

Two people living inside me fueled this curiosity, with differing agendas—my Eastern self, desiring to explore her roots, and my restless Western know-it-all self, itching for adventure. I sensed myself steering a sailboat blindfolded, feeling the forward momentum, the tug of fickle winds, unable to see the shoreline, nor even wanting to see it.

Egypt

Mother Ship

Experience cannot be created.
It must be undergone.

VIRGIL

My seatmate poked me in the ribs to point out the Pyramids below the wings. Alitalia's Cairo-bound flight doubled as a time machine, whisking me, in the span of three airborne hours, from the cafés of Piazza Navonna to the mother lode of the Arab world, claiming sixteen million residents and an intricate language of glottal stops. A smattering of applause accompanied the smooth landing.

"Ahlan wa sahlan fi misr!" Welcome to Cairo!

The customs officer holding my passport behind the windowpane glanced at my name, then my face, and made a shrewd guess.

"You Muslim girl? From Amrikiya? Why you alone? Where you stay?"

I shrugged my shoulders.

He frowned and pasted a couple of entry visa stamps, a pointy pink tongue sticking out the left corner of his mouth. A few minutes later, the man started following me down the hallway, insisting on arranging some accommodation. I shook my head and refused his help, relying on a speck of hope—a shrill female voice bouncing across the fiber optics between Rome and Cairo just a week ago.

"Yes, yes, you come to Cairo," she had bellowed into the static-choked receiver. "No worry. I have place for you to stay!"

I had picked Cairo because I wanted to travel overland in the Middle East, making a crescent-shaped loop from the Egyptian capital all the way to Turkey. It was a pretty simple itinerary that anyone could follow by adhering to the Lonely Planet guide *Istanbul to Cairo on a Shoestring*. But I wanted to be more than just a tourist. I wanted to live in Cairo for some time. That's when Dr. Nadia came into the picture.

I had pestered my cousin in Berkeley during one of the routine panic-stricken chat sessions that I conducted daily from the little Internet café next to my Roman hostel. *Please, please, please, find me an anchor over there, anyone you know. So long as I'm not empty-handed. Please, please, please!* I got lucky. My cousin had contacts. He mentioned a certain "Dr. Nadia" who might be open to renting me the Cairo apartment where my cousin's wife had formerly stayed. The very next day, I sent the doctor my flight details in an email and hoped for the best.

The airport reception area swarmed with people greeting friends and relatives. My hope had not shown up. I sank to the floor, my eyes lowering in despair and concentrating on a pair of black Mary Janes with thick side buckles. My gaze traveled up an ankle-length flannel gray skirt, past a plum-colored cardigan, toward a small, wrinkled face peering down at me through cola-bottle lenses. She was a mature woman, somewhere in her mid- to late fifties. And she was holding a stick attached to a square white board neatly printed with my name.

"Maliha Masood?"

She emphasized the *h* almost to the point of spitting out the letter in my face. It was the first time I had heard my name pronounced properly in Arabic. Back in the States, I muted the *h* and told people that Maliha rhymed with Maria with an *l*.

Nodding with relief, I held out my right hand to be pumped up and down by the flesh-and-blood Dr. Nadia, my new landlady in Cairo.

The cherry-red Mazda pierced a thick tangle of traffic. It could have been a movie set for a modern version of *Ben Hur,* in which chariots were replaced with buses, taxis, SUVs, Fiats, and motorcyles, all of them opposed to the concept of staying in their lanes and maintaining a respectable distance from the bumper to the fender. Cairo drivers showed a remarkable tolerance for mistakes that would have sparked a roadrage epidemic anywhere else. I was impressed at the deft maneuvers of Dr. Nadia, looking like a respectable grandmother yet driving like a daredevil. She clutched the steering wheel with one hand, and when her blinking turn signal failed to grab the attention of passing motorists, she rolled down the window and stuck out her left arm as a more effective ploy. At one point, she spun the car in a brisk 180-degree counterclockwise motion, narrowly dodging a scooter carrying a family of four and a group of thin, dark-skinned men running barefoot with flat disks of bread stacked on top of their heads.

The net effect was borderline anarchy. It took me back to Pakistan. I recalled myself as a ten-year-old girl, riding in the back seat of an auto rickshaw with my mother, threading our way through the congested neighborhood streets to Empress Market, where we shopped on Saturday afternoons, usually bringing home a live chicken or two. The poultry section reeked of animal and human sweat. I had developed a reflex habit of folding my handkerchief in a triangle and wrapping it over my nose and mouth, just like the bandits I used to watch on TV dramas. Men shoved past us, scratching their behinds while spitting gobs of betel-nut juice on the ground, making reddish-brown splotches that could have been mistaken for dried blood or abstract art. It was just an ordinary day at the market. I did not think of the place as unhygienic or chaotic because I hadn't yet experienced the opposite.

After we moved to Seattle, it was strange to see people bothering to wait for walk signals before crossing the streets. The local Safeway dazzled me with its polished vinyl floors and head-to-toe aisles crammed with dozens of brand-name cereals and cookies. As America sculpted me in her mold, I forgot all about shopping excursions to Empress Market, but those memories flared up eighteen years later as I was riding in Dr. Nadia's car, being driven through the frenzied streets of Cairo. They were at once familiar and foreign, brokering an uneasy alliance between my disjointed worlds of East and West.

Dr. Nadia strained to converse in English amid the cacophony of horns apparently wired to the brakes and gas pedals of every single vehicle.

"So you come to Cairo to study Arabic?"

Her eyes narrowed in oval slits of suspicion as if this might be my cover for something more sinister.

Though I told her yes, I really had no idea where or how I was going to learn Arabic in Cairo. But it gave me an official reason for renting an apartment and hanging out in the city for a few months. I didn't think my landlady would have taken kindly to the concept of aimless exploration.

Dr. Nadia glanced disapprovingly at my disheveled clothes and my uncovered hair. They were not up to her standards. When I asked her where we were going, she replied, "Al-Demerdash."

As we approached my new neighborhood, I saw the streets were lined with small shops, all with signs in Arabic. I had learned how to read and write Arabic as a child growing up in Karachi, where I was subject to weekly visits by an elderly religious scholar who came to our house every Friday afternoon to teach me the Quran. *Maulvi-saab* would hunch over the text and read aloud an Arabic phrase that I would repeat, and this is how we proceeded, he reciting the sacred verses in a singsong voice, me parroting back the guttural syllables without grasping their meanings. After my teacher departed for the day, I would scroll through the Urdu or English translations of what we had just read. Not to be able to speak or comprehend the language I knew so well in scripture felt as if I were forever in the middle of solving an equation; I longed for the day when I would apply the equal sign.

Dr. Nadia drove inside the grounds of a tall apartment complex. A dark bony man wearing a floor-length gown approached the car. Dr. Nadia introduced him as Ghuma, the building's door attendant. She barked some orders at him in rapid-fire Arabic. I noticed his kind eyes and gentle face.

"*Ahlan, Ahlan,*" he softly murmured a welcome and lifted my fifty-pound cobalt-blue backpack onto his right shoulder. Dr. Nadia and I took the elevator to the sixth floor while Ghuma followed behind on the stairs.

My new apartment featured an industrial-style kitchen, a well-furnished living room, a formal dining area, a modern bathroom, and two large bedrooms. For all this, Dr. Nadia wanted eight hundred Egyptian pounds a month, or $200. I glanced at the frosted glass windows muffling the sprawling, unknown metropolis beyond. Al-Qahirah. The victorious city.

"Well, I must go back to work."

Dr. Nadia picked up her black patent purse and pulled her head scarf closer toward her forehead. Something about how to find nearby shops for food and necessities droned in my ears, but her complicated directions failed to penetrate my woozy head. I still felt airborne, mind and body hurtling through space. My landlady gave me a look that made it clear I was on my own. She patted me on the back and jotted down the electric meter reading on her way out.

I emptied the contents of my pack and stowed them away in an old-fashioned armoire taking up an entire bedroom wall. It was a small luxury after all those months of sharing rooms in cramped European hostels. The inner left door of the armoire displayed a full-length mirror. I stood in front of it and stared at my reflection. Tired brown eyes, under a canopy of thick, untamed eyebrows, stared back. The graduated bob from six months ago had grown out into puffy black waves contrasting with a pale, colorless complexion. I stretched all five feet of my frame and inched closer to the mirror. An odd thing happened. I was looking at myself and a stranger at the same time. The facial geometry was undeniably mine. Yet I couldn't see the person within claiming allegiance to that face. I hadn't really found her yet. She was all bits and pieces when she left home, and though she tried, she couldn't piece herself together in Europe—the glue wasn't strong enough, or maybe it was the wrong kind of glue.

The apartment's silence jangled my nerves. To keep myself company, I turned on the TV and listened to a chorus of incomprehensible Arabic spewing from the mouths of news anchors, soap stars, and talk-show hosts. They looked like busy, important people who knew where their lives were heading or at least pretended to know. Suddenly, I longed to shrink myself and squeeze inside the flickering screen, to merge with the characters on set and deliver an assigned role with the requisite lines. Then I caught myself in the grip of a lie. Deep down, I knew I was here to untether myself from a life in which roles were divvied out in clear-cut packages, in which my existence was largely defined by a nine-to-five formula, by project-management flowcharts, team meetings, and web mail. I had yet to discover the components of a different sort of work that had long been neglected, the workings of how I related to myself as Maliha.

And I was convinced that this discovery had to take place in the Middle East, where I would witness up close the Islamic culture and history that informed my bloodline and, at the same time, hum along to Walt Whitman's song of the open road still serenading my ears. It wasn't so much about going back to a homeland—otherwise I could have just traveled to Pakistan. I wanted to build a new kind of home, tempered by choice and exploration, where I would have to get utterly lost before finding my way back.

You are meant to be here, I reassured myself those first few days when I was starting to feel alone and afraid in the apartment. *You are meant to be here,* I repeated as I sat down for the same old breakfast. And then the same lunch, which later turned into dinner. Bananas, oranges, little triangles of cream cheese and pita bread washed down with instant Nestlé coffee. I survived on this fare for a whole week.

Dr. Nadia rang a few times to see how I was doing. She asked if I had managed to find the shops for my groceries. Not wishing to appear the idiot foreigner, I lied to her and said I had everything I needed. I didn't tell my landlady about getting lost in the back alleys of my neighborhood, of being nearly crushed to death by a hunk of metal as I crossed a busy road where I couldn't find any shops selling food. I made do with a cubbyhole stall where I bought eggs and milk. And then I got brave. A subway station near my apartment building bore the same name as the neighborhood. Al-Demerdash. Downtown Cairo was just fifteen minutes away.

Surrogate Brotherhood

A halo of coarse, wiry hair, fitted flared denims, and a short-sleeved polo shirt. He was the first person I saw walking toward me when I was standing outside the subway station of Orabi, driven by the impulse to find a vegetarian restaurant highly recommended in my guidebook.

"Excuse me. Do you know where this is?" I asked in English.

He stopped in his tracks, blinked back surprise, and stared at a crumpled piece of yellow-lined paper scribbled with the name At-Tabie Ad-Dumyati. A perplexed look scrunched his face, as if I had asked him to name all the Nobel Prize winners in chronological order. Thick lips pursed in concentration, giving way to a little foot-tapping on the pavement to jump-start his memory.

"Yes! Yes!" he shouted like someone who had just cleaned out a Vegas slot machine. "My name is Mohammad. I will take you there."

We turned a corner and came to a busy eatery packed with locals and a handful of expats. The buffet-style salad bar looked like the kind you find in American grocery stores, except this one was stocked with fresh hummus, tabouli, and baba ghanoush. Patrons heaped food on large white plates that a clerk at the end of the line weighed by the kilo. Before I had a chance to decide, Mohammad strode to the takeout section and bought me a *fuul* sandwich, thick and gooey with crushed fava beans spiced with cilantro. I realized it would be useless to try to give him the one-pound coin jammed in my right hand.

"Come," he addressed me as one would coax a frightened child.

I munched my sandwich and followed Mohammad to what my guidebook referred to as the nerve center of Cairo—Ramses Square—a raucous hullabaloo that reminded me of a three-ring circus without the ringleader.

Noisy Vespas grazed close to my ankles. One of them was transporting a middle-aged couple. She rode sidesaddle and clutched his waist underneath the thin folds of her long black coat. Rows of street hawkers lined the edge of the road, spreading out their merchandise on blankets. There was an eclectic collection of Islamic decals, prayer beads, fake Rolexes, yellow-boxed Chiclets, Duracell batteries, and even some old Duran Duran cassettes. A teenage boy in a crew cut inserted a tape into a minicassette player.

"Very cool song!" He swiveled his hips to the familiar lyrics of "Union of the Snake." "Only ten Egyptian pounds. Special discount price!"

Mohammad and I continued walking. We paused by a fleet of buses picking up what appeared to be a tidal wave of passengers.

"What's happening?" I shouted as the wave crested into a pandemonium of last-minute farewells.

"They go to Mecca for Umrah," Mohammad told me, referring to the shorter, more informal pilgrimage that Muslims perform year-round. "You know what is Umrah?" he asked, as if accustomed to explaining Islamic concepts to foreigners. Only this time, the foreigner happened to be a fellow Muslim in Banana Republic linens.

It was a new travel twist to be in Egypt, where the familiarity of a

Muslim country clashed with my newcomer's ignorance of how to get around the place. At least in Europe, it was all just new and different. But now the newness of my surroundings came with reference points that were part of my identity—the shape of a mosque, the sound of the muezzin's call to prayer, the squiggly letters of Arabic, the taste of dried dates. I was straddling the old and the new, feeling like an insider and outsider at the same time.

Mohammad offered me a Kleenex from a pocket-size packet after I finished my sandwich. He seemed to have completely forgotten that I had deterred him from wherever he was intending to go, and when we reached another subway station and got into the same train, I began to think that our meeting was preordained rather than pure accident. It was an illusion that blurred the line between strangers and friends. I suspected the blurriness was about to disappear entirely given Mohammad's amiable talkativeness. He soon began informing me that he was twenty-nine years old and lived with his parents and four siblings. The option of moving out and getting a place for himself appeared an unthinkable luxury. When I asked Mohammad when this would be possible, he said maybe after getting married, provided his salary could cover it. He made about four hundred Egyptian pounds a month, about $100, which served the needs of his family in addition to his own.

I had never seen anyone smile as much as he did. I especially loved the way Mohammad laughed, his entire body dissolving into convulsions, like a human earthquake. He spoke English with a peculiar fervor, as if every word were integral to his speech, and some words he repeated like a chosen mantra. As the train slowed down, back at the Orabi stop, Mohammad was fixated with *incredible*. He turned to me and said, "We go to meet my incredible friend Yasser."

"Okay," I responded and accompanied him when the doors slid open.

It did not matter that this was my first evening out in Cairo and my only intention two hours ago had been to eat a decent dinner and then go back to my apartment. Detours had to be welcomed, especially when traveling. And Mohammad was promising more entertainment and adventure than anything I could have seen on TV. We rode a long escalator and merged with a throng of late-evening shoppers on a busy downtown street named "26 of July."

Mohammad mentioned the significance of the name, which was derived from the 1952 revolution of Gamal Abdel-Nasser—a "big failure" in Mohammad's opinion. Before I had a chance to ask him why, Mohammad walked into a shop to check out the aftershave collection. He sniffed and sprayed fragrances, asking me if I preferred the Paco Rabane *après rasage* or Dakar Noir, or perhaps the newest Calvin Klein. He was saving up, but he couldn't afford the designer stuff. We settled on Old Spice.

Back on the streets, we attempted to make a crossing by throwing ourselves into onrushing traffic. I instantly felt like an alien craft in a game of Space Invaders. To minimize chances of turning into human pulp, I sprinted through the sea of cars. Mohammad chose the wading strategy, grazing his knees against metal bumpers with casual deference and holding out his hand to stem the flowing tide.

We turned into a dark alley wedged between cramped apartment blocks and a boisterous cinema. The alleyway dead-ended into a small courtyard scattered with plastic tables and chairs and functioning as a makeshift café. Locals and the occasional stray foreigners played backgammon and suckled water pipes, or *sheeshas,* filled with various flavors of tobacco. A serious-looking man sat alone at a corner table nursing the dregs of his coffee and staring off into space.

"Yasser!"

Mohammad waved furiously to interrupt his friend's private reverie. A magnetic smile beckoned us to Yasser's table.

"Es salaem w'alekum," he greeted me traditionally. Peace be upon you.

"Wa'alekumes salaem," I reciprocated the message of peace.

We made some small talk, and I learned that Yasser worked as an accountant for some arcane branch of the Egyptian government and earned the equivalent of $30 a day. His tall, broad-shouldered physique, chiseled features, and chocolate-brown complexion suggested a more lucrative occupation, perhaps as a *GQ* model on a Milan catwalk. But I didn't dare mention it to him aloud as I sneaked long gazes at him when he wasn't looking my way. Yasser exuded a contemplative intensity, a refreshing change from the rather exuberant Mohammad. It was hard to believe that such polar opposites had been best friends for fifteen years.

I liked Yasser right away. He didn't pigeonhole me as a complete foreigner even when I showed him my Lonely Planet guidebook and the Arabic glossary in the index that I was trying to memorize. His grin deepened to reveal two luscious dimples.

"You should spend time learning *fushah,* proper classical Arabic," he admonished. "It will give you more appreciation of the Quran."

"Yes, but that will take forever," I said. "I just want to be able to talk to people on the streets, to buy food without pointing at things. It's so humiliating!" I recalled the horror of my first shopping experience in the neighborhood, where an entire crowd had assembled to watch my stumbling performance. It was the best entertainment they had seen in weeks.

Yasser changed the subject as if sparring to hit a raw nerve. "So what about your American foreign policy?"

"Arab countries must look more inward instead of continually blaming the West for all their problems." I said it intentionally to provoke his reaction.

"Then stop meddling in our affairs!" he replied. "Stop being a slave to Israel, stop sending them weapons to bomb Palestinian homes. America is like a child who makes messes without cleaning up!"

I was expecting the diatribe, but it was too early to get into politics. I tried to steer Yasser into more personal matters.

"So, do you have a girlfriend?"

"Well, not exactly, yes, maybe." He wavered. "She doesn't know me yet, but I see her every day at the bus stop after work. I am too afraid to say anything."

"But how will she know you exist if you don't approach her? After all, it is not *haram* to simply talk."

"You don't understand," Yasser explained. "If her family knows that we see each other, there will be a big problem. I have to wait until I have more money so I can ask her father for her hand."

"Wait a minute, wait just a little minute," I said. "You mean you haven't said one word to this girl and you already know she's the one you want to marry?"

"That's right." Yasser unleashed a grin. "It is she."

"But that makes no sense!" The analyst in me refused to believe in such simplicity. "You have no idea what she's like, her personality, her outlook on life. How do you know you will get along as husband and wife?"

"It will be okay." Yasser responded calmly. "Allah will guide me."

I sighed and wondered if love was indeed a form of divine intervention. Yasser's surefire conviction was both unnerving and admirable.

Mohammad preferred to remain a spectator to our conversation, his eyeballs darting right and left as if observing a tennis match. He ordered an apple *sheesha*, coiling the rope that extended from the wooden mouthpiece of the pipe around his neck, the water in the tall blue glass bubbling and gurgling like a noisy stream to match his long drags. Then Mohammad's face would disappear for a few seconds behind curls of smoke billowing from his nostrils and mouth. Sometimes, he would erupt into fits of giggles for no apparent reason and start shouting at the top of his voice, "Critical situation, critical situation!" When he came back from the men's room, Mohammad finished his *sheesha* and opened a pack of Marlboros.

"You want smoke?"

I shook my head and looked down at the guidebook. Yasser laughed, but not in a bad way, more like a big brother looking out for his dopey kid sister.

Somersaults

I was on my own during the days and didn't know what to do, not that there was a shortage of things to do in Cairo, whose colloquial name, *misr,* is also the official Arabic name of Egypt itself. It was like a magnet, the pull and presence of Cairo on the Egyptian psyche, and there were no two ways about it. You either love or hate the place. At first, I truly hated it. I couldn't stand the way it assaulted my senses, a hurly-burly metropolis of chaos and commotion that made all the capitals of Europe *and* Manhattan a composite of a quaint Bavarian village. But it was a different energy at night, less manic but still throbbing with life. This is when I began to like what Cairo offered.

It became an evening ritual for me to take the subway to Midan Tahrir or Liberation Square and wait next to the KFC for Yasser and Mohammad. We usually met around seven except when Mohammad had to work late. I assumed it had to do with the local Arabic newspaper, where his job was to sell subscriptions and compile sports scores. But it turned out that Mohammad also taught English some nights, which was surprising given his quirky grasp of the language; it led him to wish me "good day" at night, and once he thought I had moon rays in my hair. Yasser and I would double over with laughter while Mohammad looked on, clueless.

The three of us would walk for hours, as if scouring Cairo on foot. The city's streets teemed with hand laborers, civil servants, corporate movers and shakers, university students, mothers, merchants, and urchins. They weren't all that different from people anywhere else in the world just going on with their lives. Each neighborhood was a different

Cairo. From art galleries and trendy boutiques in upscale Zamalek to a skyline of mosques and minarets in the old Islamic quarter, the moods of Cairo layered across multiple centuries.

Some nights, we would simply hang out in the café where we had met that first night. Yasser often lost himself in a book while I pored over the school text he had lent me to learn conjugations in Arabic. Mohammad tried to help. He crossed his legs and balanced a notebook on one knee, meticulously jotting down pronouns and verbs in a clean, legible script. Then he would make up little stories to help me remember the words. In exchange, I offered to teach Mohammad American slang, but he somehow got it all wrong when he ended a phone call by saying, "See my alligator."

My new friends welcomed me into their lives with good-natured humor, never once letting me feel like a burdensome pest, even though I knew they must have been putting aside their own errands and chores to keep me company in the evenings. It was as if nothing else mattered to them, and I often wondered if it was the novelty of our impromptu friendship or some inborn selflessness that made Yasser and Mohammad so generous with their time.

Feast and Famine

Dr. Nadia had requested two months' rent up front. I wasn't sure if I would be staying in Cairo that long since I had no commitments to tie me down. I had broken away from commitments the day I left home. But as a traveler, I was constantly torn between my desire to wander without a plan and my desire to stick to one place and find a sense of rhythm and purpose. In Europe, I had chosen the wandering route, but it hadn't led to any satisfying conclusions. It hadn't satiated my hunger to learn about other cultures, peoples, places, and ultimately myself. Now I was determined to take a more structured route, because I thought it would get me Somewhere.

Just when I was craving structure, especially in the daytime, when I felt useless and guilty for hanging around the apartment with time on my hands, I found myself a job. An American expat offered me a freelance gig writing for an English-language Egyptian business weekly. I tried to get into my first article, but I failed to understand what was so exciting about mobile banking. I was more excited about other things: the shy smile of a little girl who had prayed next to me in the al-Azhar mosque, a grandfatherly shopkeeper in the Khan al Khalili bazaar revealing the history of Mamluk rulers, and the way Mohammad's eyes danced to the rhythms of an internal jukebox every time we got together. They meant more to me than the magazine's subsequent assignment to report on marketing trends in consumer electronics. So I took it as a sign to forgo journalism and try a different strategy to ground myself.

I couldn't have timed it better. Two weeks after settling in, I was overjoyed to experience Ramadan in Cairo. The sacred month of fasting and spiritual rejuvenation started with a drum roll. *Dhoom taka dhoom, taka dhoom taka dhoom.* Rolling out of bed at four thirty in the morning, I peered out the frosted window to make out a tall figure strapped to an oblong drum strolling outside the apartment complex. Day after day, the sonorous beat of this human alarm clock woke up the neighborhood to begin the fast that requires one to abstain from food and water from dawn to dusk.

It takes discipline to practice this third pillar of Islam, which I always believed was easier in a Muslim country where restaurants and cafés closed down in the middle of the day and people you knew at school or at work extended the camaraderie of fasting as a community. I hadn't experienced this since leaving Pakistan almost two decades ago. My life in the States, especially during my teenage years, had made fasting a chore. I hated being the only girl in the ninth grade who sat in the cafeteria in front of an empty plate. When my friends cut class and drove to Dairy Queen to indulge in ice cream sundaes, I made excuses to remain behind. And I almost died of embarrassment when I had to hand my gym teacher a special note from my parents that excused me "for religious reasons" from swimming in the pool or practicing five-hundred-yard dashes for Track and Field Day.

It was only at home with family that I felt remotely connected to Ramadan. We sat around the dining table and broke the fast at sundown, feasting on thick juicy dates, golden *pakoras,* or fried chickpea dumplings, and crispy samosas filled with spicy potatoes paired with succulent mint chutney. "Eat slowly, slowly," my mother cautioned when I shoveled instead of tasted the food to fill an empty stomach. Then my younger brother would face the fireplace of our Seattle living room and cup both hands behind his ears to voice the call to prayer. Importing our cultural and religious traditions to America sustained my faith as a Muslim. But a part of me always yearned for the Real Thing, when the acts of my faith were not in the minority and part of a larger puzzle of which I was but a tiny fragment.

So here I was in Cairo polishing off a platter of fava beans at 5:00 AM for the pre-fast meal of *suhoor.* As I gulped down my last glass of water, a thin ray of light ruptured night from day. The loudspeaker from the neighborhood mosque crackled to life with the dawn *adhan,* or call to prayer. My belief stirred in the soaring flight of its lyrics.

> *Allahu Akhbar.* God is most great.
> *Ashadu An La Ilah Il Allah.* I testify that there is no God except God.
> *Ashadu An Muhamadan Rasul Allah.* I testify that Muhammad is the
>   Messenger of God.
> *Haya Ala-Asalah.* Come to prayer.
> *Haya Ala-Afalah.* Come to salvation.
> *Allahu Akhbar.* God is most great.
> *La Ilaha Il Allah.* There is no God except God.

A nameless feeling, hardwired in my DNA, pushed me toward the bathroom for the cleansing ablutions. Water splashed on my face, arms, and feet, water sucked into my nostrils and swirled in my mouth in counts of three. For an instant, I recalled all the times I had watched my grandmother performing the same gestures before prayers. She once had to do them in the public restroom at the Fred Meyer store, where she dunked her feet in the white porcelain sink and held her hand on my shoulder for balance. Four middle-aged ladies gawked with a mixture of disgust and fascination at the uncouth manners of my silver-haired granny. I put on a smile and tried to explain that Muslims must be clean before they pray.

"But you don't look like a Muslim," the feistiest member of the group had pronounced, eyeing my jeans and Garfield T-shirt, her gaze continuing right down to the friendship bracelets dangling on my wrist.

I wondered what a Muslim was supposed to look like. My grandmother had finished her ablutions in the bathroom sink and asked me for a paper towel to dry her moistened face and arms. One woman glanced at the pool of water that had accumulated on the floor and rolled her eyes at her friends. They refused the cherry-flavored LifeSavers that I offered.

I kept thinking about that incident at Fred Meyer after my *fajr*, or dawn prayers, when I was lying on the living room sofa unable to go back to sleep. It had happened back in 1989, the year I graduated from high school. I grew up in America as an incognito Muslim because I did not display any overt signs of my faith. I had never worn a head scarf, not even in Pakistan, where I was used to covering my hair only for prayers and religious functions, but *hijab* as an extension of a daily wardrobe was not a part of my South Asian upbringing. The primary school I had attended in Karachi for seven years required uniforms with a folded white *dupatta*, which was a long rectangular shawl, worn across the chest in a wide V shape and safety-pinned to the shoulder to prevent the fabric from slipping. During the premonsoon summers when hot winds blew from the desert plains, I unwrapped my *dupatta* and draped it over my head and shoulders. It didn't feel as if I were covering myself in a veil. It was just a practical reflex to keep the dust and sand from blowing into my hair and eyes. Not until I came to Cairo did veiling take on a whole new meaning.

One day, I came upon a swath of pale gray georgette lying in the bottom drawer of my bedroom bureau. It smelled vaguely of incense, myrrh, or frankincense, and I found myself draping the fabric over my hair, tying the ends together with a double knot underneath my chin. I started wearing it to avoid public scrutiny, and by my fourth week in Cairo, the five-minute walk from my apartment building to the nearby subway station no longer involved curious stares directed at my formerly bare head. It was odd, the way the *hijab* made the foreigner in me instantly disappear in the streets. The sensation was the same as being an incognito Muslim in America, but now it was reversed. I was an incognito American in Cairo.

Every time I touched the edges of my head scarf, I felt a twinge of betrayal, as if I were impersonating someone I wasn't. My features blended in with those of the locals, and when they spoke to me in Arabic, they registered surprise, even disappointment, when I couldn't talk back. The visual shorthand of my veil spoke on my behalf. But whatever it said was hardly a uniform script, given the bewildering array of messages the *hijab* concealed and revealed.

Time and again, I saw giggly Cairienne debutantes in hip-hugging jeans and spandex tops that were paired with matching head scarves. If veiling represented a rebellious backlash against encroaching Western values, the backlash did not apply to their skintight Western clothing. Islamic emphasis on modesty appeared buried in the contradictory dress code. In fact, veiling seemed to go hand in hand with the fashion-conscious set in stiletto boots and fitted leather jackets who preferred lacy black scarves as a head cover.

Then I heard of a case at AUC (The American University in Cairo) in which a student insisted on attending classes in full *niqab*, or face veil, and head-to-toe black despite complaints from her professors and her own family. Most of the student opinions in the school paper were remarkably supportive of their *niqab*-wearing classmate, insisting it was her right to dress as she pleased, particularly at an institution enshrining the American value of freedom of thought.

When I visited AUC, it didn't look all that different from any campus in Southern California with its red-tiled roofs and jeans-and-sneaker-clad students, sitting in the sun, yakking on cell phones. Their Arabic was peppered with American slang, inventing terms such as, *"Yallah,* bye-bye" and "Okay, *mashi."* Most of the girls were unveiled, but as I sat down on a bench, I was joined by a sophomore in a pale green scarf speckled with black polka dots. I asked her why she wore it.

"Hijab is for God," she said in a low voice. "It is part of what God wants us to do if we believe in our hearts."

I didn't want to argue with the girl about whether the Quran explicitly tells women to cover their hair or not. If she chose to wear the *hijab* as an expression of her religious piety, then it was her right, as long as it was a function of personal choice. It would be too simplistic to label that choice as a symbol of "liberation" or "oppression." The *hijab* comeback in Cairo could be seen as the latest fashion statement among Egyptian teenyboppers, like an Islamic reawakening by former belly dancers or born-again Muslims among the Westernized elite. As a consciously created public image, veiling was both artistic and politicized, reminding me of the Egyptian movies I had seen from the 1950s and '60s, in which women with bobbed hair wore cocktail dresses and danced the tango.

As I got more used to wearing the head scarf, I began to feel freer in ambling about on my own, deriving a newfound confidence from being less visible and simply being absorbed in the endless shuffle of Cairo's street life as a budget-conscious traveler turned independent eyewitness. As I soon discovered on my exploratory rounds, the best discoveries were the ones I had least expected to see or planned to visit, such as the Sultan Hassan Mosque.

I had found it by chance one day after a long walk from the old citadel that brought me near a big traffic circle where a group of pedestrians crossed four lanes by trying to outrun a stream of oncoming cars. I watched their death-defying heroics and finally did the same. On the other side of the road stood a lovely sand-colored mosque with minarets of uneven height. I made my way toward the entrance and walked inside an enormous courtyard filled with light and air that had the effect of smothering Cairo's cacophony, in the same way churches in busy European cities became sound buffers against the street noises. As I sat down in a quiet corner facing the *mihrab*, a walled archway that indicates the direction of Mecca, toward which Muslims pray, it felt as if a lid had clamped down on my consciousness, lending the impression that nothing existed beyond the mosque's hushed calmness.

Back at the apartment, my sense of serenity vanished. I felt very alone and shut out from friends and family I had left behind. Whenever I received their calls, my emotions yo-yoed between relief at listening and talking to familiar voices and despair at having them so far out of reach and understanding. They were trying to be supportive of my travels, letting me know that they were concerned for my well-being but proud of my efforts and wishing me good luck. Once, I even got some practical help when my toilet in Cairo clogged up because of a broken flush handle, and I was able to fix the problem via a long-distance plumbing lesson from a knowledgeable friend in Seattle. I wasn't homesick, I was just overwhelmed with the uncertainty of not knowing when I would be ready and willing to return to old comforts.

Triple Jeopardy

Women who travel to the Middle East are usually on assignment. They are journalists, political analysts, anthropologists, or scholars. But to backpack through the region solo, with no official alibi, seems riskier. I sought assurance in my Muslim identity, which I thought would foster an instant bond with the people I would meet. But I failed to take into account the public reaction to my being a combination of a Muslim, an American, and a woman. Apparently, it was impossible to be all three at the same time. The head scarf complicated matters by erasing my foreign status. I couldn't get away with tourist allowances for cultural ignorance. And things got only more confusing when I persisted in observing prayer times and fasting while also heeding the call of adventure by wandering alone in the streets and getting friendly with strangers, most of whom were men.

Just over a month into my stay, when I was still getting to know Cairo, I inadvertently used a subway ticket allowing for a maximum of nine stops in crossing fourteen stations. The exiting turnstile refused to budge. I panicked and threw my weight against the metal rod. It was stuck in place. A security official watched my predicament and signaled me to step into the stationmaster's office near the platform. He volleyed heated accusations at me in Arabic that no one bothered to translate. His sidekick squatted on his haunches and smirked at me as if to say, "I know what you're up to."

"But you don't understand," I pleaded in English. "I am new in Cairo and made a mistake."

The stationmaster glowered, and another stream of rapid-fire Arabic spewed forth. The last guttural syllable of his tirade unleashed a wad of spit, the size of a dime, that hit the right side of my jaw. As I wiped off the spittle with the back of my sleeve, I caught a glimpse of my reflection in the streaky window behind his desk. Pink head scarf, gold Allah pendant, and black eyes. The realization hit me in the pit of my stomach. Now I knew why the stationmaster was raving like a lunatic. He was fooled by my appearance. It had led him to believe I was my opposite. Instead of a novice tourist, I was supposedly an Egyptian smart aleck trying to cheat the system.

If only some of my girlfriends back home could have witnessed this scene. They were leery of traveling in the Middle East, assuming that their blond-haired, blue-eyed features would set them up for a barrage of harassment. "Even if I covered my head, what difference would it make?" one friend had asked. "They would know straightaway with these!" She pointed to the freckles scattered across her face. "You are so lucky," she told me. "You can easily blend in there." Little did my friend know that blending in barred me from immunity against social blunders and against misunderstandings about the intricacies of subway-ticketing rules in Cairo. Congratulating myself for passing as a local troublemaker, I mentally prepared for my first visit to an Egyptian jail.

"Pay this amount." The stationmaster thrust a form in squiggly Arabic handwriting and drew a big circle around some cryptic numerals.

I forked over 120 Egyptian pounds (about $30), assuming it was the bribe for my freedom, but the stationmaster ordered me to sit back down. In a desperate bid, I showed him my U.S. passport and the stub of my one-way ticket to Cairo. The man stared at them as if he were hallucinating.

"You *Amrikeyi?*"

My ability to go native had clearly backfired.

"You no look *Amrikeyi!*"

His eyes started to sparkle.

"Welcome, welcome to Egypt!"

The scowling face gave way to profuse handshakes.

"You come to office every day. I teach you Arabic and you teach me your English, yes?"

He beamed like a proud papa.

"You want taxi, yes? Go with Yusuf. He get you nice clean taxi. Very cheap. You pay like Egyptian, not tourist, understand?"

I glanced at Yusuf, the sidekick who had treated me like a criminal fifteen minutes earlier. He had fallen asleep on the floor, snoring loudly, his gaping mouth an open invitation to buzzing flies.

"You will share with me some tea, yes?"

My new friend pushed a button underneath his desk. A minute later, a little barefooted boy in a worn orange sweatshirt produced two chipped glasses of steaming *shai*. I sipped the heavily sugared brew and straightened out the folds of my crumpled scarf.

Shifting Bandwidths

It was heaven to be back in Rome. A crisp fall afternoon and lemon-colored light. I was shopping in the produce market of Campo del Fiori, filling a string bag with zucchinis and tomatoes. People said *pregos* and *grazies*. I wore my Jackie O sunglasses and a brown suede jacket. I sat near a fountain and ate a rectanglar piece of pizza topped with marinara sauce and fresh mozzarella. Then I splurged on gelato, my favorite combination of hazelnuts and cassis. I took a long walk by the river and wandered around Trastevere, poking through the open-air stalls. A man sold me a maroon shawl. He had a strong foreign accent, and when I asked him where he was from, he said Egypt. "That's funny, I'm from Egypt too," I said. He didn't believe me. So I started running, faster and faster, until I was flying with my shawl turned into a cape. I flew above buildings that were squat and low like brick kilns. I climbed higher into the sky, my body weaving from right to left with my arms outstretched. I couldn't fly in a straight line. I just kept turning and turning as if someone had wound me up like a toy and threw me into the big blue void.

The dream broke off with my alarm blaring at 9:00 AM. For an instant, I forgot where I was, and then my growling stomach reminded me I was still in Cairo and I had missed my pre-fast meal of hummus and hard-boiled eggs. Maybe that man beating the drums had stopped coming by. I couldn't rely on him to rise before dawn. And now that I had overslept, there was no time to waste. I didn't want to be late for class.

Safiya's scrubbed-clean complexion exuded *noor,* a glowing sheen of inner light. A delicate flower bud of a face peeked out of the pastel-pink cotton shawl draped around her head and upper body and fastened with a big safety pin underneath her chin. My teacher leveled her eyes with mine and urged me to repeat more guttural sounds and to mimic her Egyptian accent. It was my third day into a private six-week intensive course in classical Arabic at the Fajr Language Institute. The school came highly recommended from the expat grapevine. One of the key selling points was its location in Ma'adi, an affluent Cairo neighborhood where I had experienced the thrill of shopping in a supermarket that stocked Cheerios and Nutella.

"*Enti taibana!*" Safiya admonished me for being tired.

She curled a finger and made me come up to the blackboard, which displayed a series of words with blank spaces in between to test my vocabulary. I picked up the chalk and inserted the missing letters, adding the accent marks for vowels. Safiya grinned and clapped her hands when I got eight out of ten correct. Then it was back to the textbook, as I recited words in alphabetical order, by yelling them over the roar of the traffic outside.

Lessons were tedious. My sessions with Safiya lasted three hours a day, four days a week. At least I had a newfound vocation that would prove to be useful, but it seemed unnecessary to commute an hour each way only to learn how to spell, which I already knew, and to pick up scattered bits of unrelated vocabulary, which I didn't need. Words such as *timsah* (alligator), *sehlieh* (lizard), *khiaat* (tailor), and *maes* (scissors) probably wouldn't factor into a day-to-day conversation, unless I wanted to start a business to outfit reptiles. It would have been better to take a course in *aamiyah,* or spoken Egyptian dialect. I just wanted the ability to string together coherent sentences for being understood on the streets and to buy my groceries without a gaping crowd of onlookers. Maybe that Lonely Planet phrasebook was not so bad after all, as long as I hid it under the folds of my jacket.

Right after class, I rushed to the subway. It was composed of two rail lines extending roughly forty-five kilometers from the outskirts of Cairo into the deep hollow of its belly. The long commute from the apartment to school along with trips to myriad other spots around town allowed me to get on intimate terms with the underground network. I had started memorizing most of the station names just to keep my mind occupied during the rides. Nasser, Mubarak, Sadat, Saad Zaghloul, Sayyida Zeinab, Al-Zahraa, Dar as-Salaam. The names conjured legends of history, grandeur, and struggle spanning Cairo's long-term memory.

At first, I rode only in the first two cars, which were reserved for women. The occupants ranged across a wide social spectrum: stiff office ladies in polyester suits and snug head scarves; village mothers in colorful layers of cloth; starched, uniformed schoolgirls furiously sending SMS text messages on their cell phones. They were a loquacious lot, so different from the passengers burying their heads inside newspapers or books whom I had observed in the subways of New York, Paris, or London.

The thundering train rumbled across dense particles of history in less than twenty minutes. A trip from Mar Girgis to Sadat began in Coptic Cairo, the heart of Cairo's Christian community and the most ancient part of the city, dating as far back as the 2nd century AD, when it was called Babylon by the Romans. Arriving in Sadat, one entered 21st-century downtown Cairo, complete with five-star international hotels, Internet cafés, and discos booming to hip-hop.

During Ramadan, Cairo traded its usual chaotic self for full-blown mania. Thousands of hungry, disgruntled workers raced home between 3:00 and 5:00 PM in time to break the fast at sundown. The maddening mass exodus peaked in the subway, where the women's carriage jammed with sweaty, scarf-clad, bejeweled females yakking away or clutching tiny Qurans and silently mouthing the sacred scriptures. Bodies from every conceivable angle were glued to mine. It was hard to breathe. Riding the coed cars offered little comfort with the added nuisance of male eyes gouging holes in my face. But the men were far more polite than the women, who pummeled me with their shopping bags and purses and rammed my shoulders and elbows with no apologies while shouting at the top of their lungs to someone only arm's length away.

One particular day, the subway was on the brink of becoming a madhouse. I had learned early on that without a strategy for exiting the compartment, there was little chance of getting out until the end of the line. Usually by the second or third station before my stop, I would start working my way toward the door, mimicking what everyone else seemed to be saying. It sounded like *nazla*, and I assumed it was the equivalent of asking, "Is this your stop?"

My carefully devised plan was thwarted this time thanks to the presence of a feisty grandmother standing directly behind me, her hands pushing against my back with the full force of ten bodybuilders. When the doors opened, I popped out of the train like a human projectile, nearly trampling on an elderly woman who had fallen down on the platform. She was lying motionless while people stepped around her in oblivion. I helped her get up and put her in a taxi. The normal kindness and gracious manners of Cairo's citizens vanished in the subterranean jungle of the underground during Ramadan rush hour.

The following evening, I abandoned the subway and jumped on a crowded city bus with Yasser and Mohammad. We didn't have anyplace particular to go. Mohammad's fiancée accompanied us. He had never mentioned her before, but she showed up all of a sudden when the bus stopped near the Cairo Zoo, picking up a small platoon of passengers. A green-eyed girl with a heart-shaped face climbed aboard and slipped her hand into Mohammad's. Then, to my amazement, the couple strode to the back of the bus, grabbed a seat, and gazed long and hard into each other's eyes. Mohammad loosened her *hijab* and started stroking her light-brown hair. She had one hand on his knee. Some of the older passengers glared at them and made sharp comments that were the equivalent of, "Enough already, you oversexed morons!" When that failed, they started complaining to the bus driver. He didn't do a thing. Apparently, Mohammad had bribed the driver with a five-pound note (a little over $1) to turn a blind eye. Mohammad had saved up for two whole weeks to steal a private moment with his honey in a Cairo where there was no such thing as privacy.

I thought about this incident when I was back at my apartment eating a late dinner. Though Dr. Nadia's sixth-floor rental was hardly my real home, I now thought of it as a cozy sanctuary. Compared to Mohammad and his girlfriend, I was spoiled. It hadn't always been this way. When I used to visit my relatives in India, I had to share a bedroom with five cousins. There were no locks on the doors, so I would change my clothes by standing right next to the doorway with a ready arm or leg to keep it jammed closed in case anyone tried to enter without knocking, which was the custom. The house was never silent. Even at night, when we all slept, there was the whirring air conditioner or someone coughing or snoring beside me. I would get used to it, but upon returning to the States and sleeping in my own bed, I was strangely aware of hearing myself breathing. It was a small luxury to have regained my private space. But at the same time, a tiny part of me felt the loss of some connection that happens when one is forced to live in close quarters, compromising over comforts and effacing boundaries until there is no need to preserve them.

An Old *Bawwab*

"Sabah al-kheir!" Good morning! I said to Ghuma.

He was the first person I saw every morning on my way to the Arabic language institute. Ghuma looked at me with a mixture of curious apprehension and amusement as I dashed down the stairs and shot out the building. He smiled and continued sweeping the courtyard with his tattered yellow broom. Sometimes, I would run into him in the neighborhood produce market that provided an opportunity to practice my Arabic, often doubling as free street theater to passersby. On these occasions, Ghuma refused to let me shop by myself. He didn't want me to be overcharged so he took command of hunting for tender plump eggplants and crispy green spears of okra. I stuffed a wad of bills in his hands as he bargained the produce down to pennies. Then he would help me stock up on cases of mineral water. All the while, Ghuma held on to an Arabic newspaper, neatly folded and tucked under his armpit. When once I asked to look it over, I noticed the paper was stale by five years, dating to August 1995.

Several days later, someone began to pound on my front door. I opened it to find a giggling little boy who ushered me downstairs. Ghuma, his father, sat on the floor of his two-by-four-meter room, not much bigger than a prison cell, bare except for a thin straw mat placed squarely in the center, a small mountain of clothes in the corner, a tin trunk fastened with a padlock, and a few blankets neatly rolled against the wall. A small pot of tea brewed on the samovar.

Ghuma's wife poured the steaming brown liquid into two thick glasses for herself and her husband and then opened the trunk and took something out, wiping it clean with the edge of her long skirt. My tea surfaced in a chipped white mug with the words "London Bridge" stenciled in gold. It was a touching gesture, meant to provide comfort to me as a foreign guest by accommodating my Western habits (such as drinking tea from mugs). I wondered how Ghuma's wife could have possibly internalized such a detail.

Tea was the lubricant that started my friendship with Ghuma and his family that evening. I was surprised when the normally reserved *bawwab,* or doorman, of my building began to pour out his thoughts.

"I am old man," he mumbled in English. "Yes, I am old."

It was the first time he had spoken English with me. When I asked him how he learned the language, Ghuma tugged at his earlobe.

I asked him when he intended to retire.

Ghuma chuckled. "I work all my life. I work this building for more than forty years."

I showed Ghuma a picture of my parents. His eyes lit up in smiles.

"They look like good people. They look happy people."

Suddenly, Ghuma wagged his head from side to side. "Egypt people not so happy. Rich people keep all money. *Khalas!*" He shrugged off the matter by brushing his palms from side to side, as if to say "what's done is done."

His wife poured me another refill in my mug. She sat in a corner and hemmed a dress. Their little son had fallen asleep on the floor.

I told Ghuma about my scare in the subway and the bullying stationmaster. He chuckled.

"Egypt people treat their people very bad. But foreign people *mafi mushkil!* No problem! They have blond hair and pretty white face. They no get in trouble. Egypt people give them fine service and much help. But if you no have foreign face, you make some worry. Like you!" He chuckled.

I asked Ghuma why he carried the newspaper.

"So that people think I am clever," he responded with a serious face. "I know not how to read or write."

It occurred to me that Ghuma's newspaper represented values he admired—education and smarts. It gave him a sense of dignity.

"You like fast fast world?" the old *bawwab* asked.

"Do you?"

He made a face to show he preferred a slower pace.

"Maybe you should get a car," I said in jest.

"No need car!" His voice rose in pitch. "I am simple man with simple life."

"Are you happy?"

Ghuma stretched his lips in a big smile. Two of his upper front teeth were missing.

"As long as I live in Egypt, I am happy. Egypt is my home, my life. I die if I leave. I will break in half." Ghuma cracked his knuckles to underscore the point.

He was *ibn al-balad*. Salt of the earth. The kind of person who never really fades from the populace, even when that populace surges ahead in the name of progress. On the main road leading up to the apartment complex was a billboard advertising MobiNil, an Egyptian cell phone company that envisioned "A mobile in everyone's hand." I had doubts that one of those hands would be Ghuma's. Trendy Cairo neighborhoods boasted the city's choicest clubs, offering not only the best dance night in town, but also the local Stella beer that came in light lager cans and on tap. The other Cairo had no running water, rotting piles of garbage, and overflowing sewage. This was the Cairo known to the majority of Egyptians, who did not share the rewards of cosmopolitan Westernization. Ghuma was one of the majority. But he did not seem to mind.

As he tried to explain, he was not so much against change as against the changing of principles. He had friends who feared outside influences; they were intensely conservative and suspicious of the West. They were alienated from a weak, ineffectual government dependent on foreign powers at the expense of local democratic reforms. The people were disenfranchised and ignored. So they turned to their religion and their traditions for salvation and hope.

There was silence. Ghuma fiddled with his sleeves. His face had the texture of rich brown leather. I suddenly noticed a prominent scar on his forehead and recognized it as the *zabiba* that devout Muslims earn by touching their heads to the ground five times a day year after year.

Ghuma caught me staring at his scar. He rubbed it, smiled, and said, "Praise be to Allah."

He was a man of faith, a faith that was not severed from his everyday life, but a single thread woven through his values. It gave him strength and security. It determined the way he related to people. It made him Egyptian. It held his community and his world together. This was Ghuma's Islam.

When I asked Ghuma what he most wished for, his answer surprised me.

"Nothing."

"Nothing?"

"If I have nothing, I am free. Like a bird." Then he wrinkled his brow. "But I not know bird. I know only Ghuma!" He jabbed a finger at his chest.

"So you just want to be Ghuma?"

He nodded.

As I thought of more things to ask, Ghuma took out a plastic shopping bag and motioned me to hand over my empty mug. He wrapped up the package and gave it to me.

"But it's yours," I protested.

"You keep. You like." His eyes glimmered like a winter sun on the Nile.

"*Shukrun,*" I thanked him.

"I take leave," he said. "I do more work."

Ghuma stood up. A knobby hand smoothed his long striped *galabiya,* softened like butter after years of washing.

Ramadan Nights

Given the Islamic lunar calendar, Ramadan falls eleven days earlier each solar year. The advantages of Ramadan in the late fall are the shorter days and lower temperatures, which make fasting easier. By 5:30 PM, it was already sundown and the streets of Cairo would be eerily empty, as most people were at home, breaking the day's fast with family and friends. One day, when I had lingered too long in a bookstore and couldn't get back to the apartment in time (even the subway was momentarily closed), I was led by a kind passerby in the street to a "table of mercy," traditionally set up by wealthy patrons to allow the poor or stragglers like me to break fast communally. It was in a downtown side alley where people were sitting around rows of picnic-style tables sparsely laid out with jugs of water, dates, pita, and hummus. Most of the diners were strangers to each other, and as I started to eat with them, I felt a sense of belonging, as if Cairo had embraced me in a crushing hug, like an old friend.

The fun and festivities of Ramadan started at seven in the evening and went on until three in the morning. Human traffic in downtown stores percolated with mad fervor like that of last-minute Christmas shoppers. Entertainment options offered dizzying choices with operas, plays, comedy shows, pop crooners, and fusion-jazz concerts. My favorite venue was Al-Hussein, centerpiece of the old Islamic quarter. This was the heart and soul of Ramadan in Cairo, where café-goers sat in open courtyards around the mosque, also known as Al-Hussein, or crowded inside the two-hundred-year-old El Fishawi, where I often stopped by to get my shoes shined and drink *sahlab,* a hot milky concoction flavored with cinnamon and pistachios.

One evening, I was wandering the quarter's narrow, winding passages in a sea of blurred faces until I came to a packed outdoor garden theater. Hip young Egyptians in platform shoes and flared jeans brushed arms with society ladies in silk suits and sleek low buns. Someone mentioned a Sufi concert, and I immediately bought a ticket. Being alone, I grabbed a single seat in one of the middle rows and plunged my head into an English news magazine.

"Mein enti?"

The standard query . . . Where are you from? Usually followed with a Why are you alone?, Are you married?, and How many children do you have? This time, my interviewer happened to be a handsome thirty-something man with long, curvy lashes framing eyes the color of jade. He tilted his head and peered over the article I was reading. Breezy sighs fluttered the edges of my thin chiffon head scarf.

"Ah yes, Nefertari." He nodded knowingly. "If you like history, I can give you special tour. I am archaeologist."

He produced a card. Tariq the archaeologist had studied in Italy at the University of Perugia.

"I will go on special tour next week to Saqqara. You must see the famous step-pyramid of King Zoser. It was built by the Pharaoh's chief architect in the year 27 BC."

Every time he blinked, his soft dark fans seemed to tickle my cheeks. I wasn't in the mood to explore any Pharaonic splendors other than the one hovering in the chair beside me. Before we could chart our course beyond antiquities, the Sufi sheikh took to the stage and began his performance.

His voice recalled the drama of Pavarotti's arias. The slow songs droned in tragic monotones, the rhythms mutating into higher-pitched wails, then switching to proud anthems, and then zigzagging between joy and melancholy. I couldn't understand a single word of the Arabic lyrics, but listening to their sounds made me feel the loss of something precious. With closed eyes, the sheikh rocked on both feet, seemingly anchored to an invisible cradle. Beads of sweat trickled down the sides of his face, wetting the bristles of his cropped black beard. Occasionally, the sheikh opened his eyes and flashed a delirious smile. Then he started singing louder, and I recognized some of the words praising the virtues of Allah. Al-Quddus, al-Musawwir, al-Wadud. Pure One, Shaper of Beauty, Loving One. The accolades continued. Al-Latif, al-Khabir. The Subtle One, the All Aware.

Some of the audience members were behaving strangely. The men in the front rows started jerking their heads from side to side, swinging their arms back and forth. Then they started beating their chests in unison, their faces glistening with sweat. A middle-aged woman stood up and gently twisted her upper body like a corkscrew, with her head thrown back and her palms raised to the heavens. The sheikh sang some final rousing numbers, and then he mopped his brow and stepped off stage.

After the stirring concert, the archaeologist and I strolled together through the old neighborhood immortalized in the novelist Naguib Mahfouz's Cairo Trilogy: *Qasr al-Shawq* (Palace of Desire), *Bayn al-Qasrayn* (Palace Walk), *Al-Sukairiyya* (Sugar Street). He showed me things I hadn't observed before, such as the faucets and taps mounted on passage walls known as *sabeel* that were originally constructed to provide clean water for the poor and still served as drinking fountains for passersby. Then he pointed to a high window in one of the ancient buildings and told me he used to live there. I slipped my hand in his and he squeezed it gently.

As we continued to prowl through the dark alleys, I almost laughed aloud at the reckless thought of wandering hand in hand with a man I had just met back in the United States. It was highly unlikely, unless I was asking to be molested or worse by some psychopath. It should have been the other way around, but I honestly felt safer in Cairo than I ever did in big-city American streets. Maybe my penchant for adventure, which was often a hair removed from stupidity, prevented me from sensing any danger from the good-looking companion, who was, after all, a near-perfect stranger I had happened to sit next to.

Nonetheless, I didn't see our nighttime stroll as abnormal or risky. It was just the ease of meeting people in Cairo, where a simple question on the street could lead to instant friendship. After years of struggling to connect with people back home, I found myself, for the first time ever, forging connections without any effort. And being in a Muslim society did not necessarily make it more difficult to meet members of the opposite sex. It was invariably easier because men dominated public spaces, whether it was a clandestine dance club or a Sufi concert during Ramadan. The archaeologist and I parted ways at a traffic roundabout. I lost his number on the way back.

An *Iftar* to Remember

Mohammad had invited me to his home for the fast-breaking meal of *iftar*. I met him at the subway station of Dar as-Salaam near his neighborhood. Mohammad strode up the stairs, beaming as usual. He was clutching the hand of his ten-year-old sister, Mona. She looked up toward me with the bashful eyes of a deer.

We walked through the gravelly unpaved streets. Women squatted on the roadside with carts of shiny eggplants and leafy greens dabbed with fresh village mud. It was hard to believe that an hour ago, I had been flipping through glossy art books and sipping cappuccino in an air-conditioned shopping mall in Mohandiseen, a spruced-up commercial district with high-tech office buildings and smart boutiques.

Mona, acting as my governess for the day, tied my loose shoelaces and repaired the fractured Arabic tumbling from my mouth. I amused her by jumping over puddles until the moment a honking minibus sped into my path, nearly knocking me down. Mona screamed and rushed to my side as Mohammad yelled obscenities at the crazy driver. I caught my breath and grabbed Mona's left hand as her brother held her right. On our way to the house, we stopped at a juice stall where the vendor slid long stalks of sugarcane through a machine to extract the sweet nectar.

Mohammad's father opened the door. He was an elderly man with soulful eyes and a face lathered with shaving cream that gave him the odd appearance of Santa Claus with the eyes of Buddha. We stepped into a small room that served as the living/dining area, sparsely decorated with framed verses from the Quran hanging on the wall and plastic knickknacks on shelves. Yasser, my other surrogate brother, lounged on cushions puffing on a cigarette. He winked at me mischievously, knowing that I was now on center stage as a guest from *Amrikiya* and that my audience members were keen to survey my performance.

I smiled profusely to put everyone at ease and hide my nervousness. A clattering of dishes in the back of the house sounded like a herd of elephants dancing a jig. Three girls flew into the room, giggling hysterically. They were Mohammad's other sisters, each one as different as the fingers on a hand. Nasreen, the oldest sister, seemed quiet and reserved, while Jamila, whose name means "beautiful," was excited to practice her schoolgirlish English on me. Samira, a shy teenager, talked with her eyes, just like my mother. They appraised me with the discerning air of inspecting merchandise at the local bazaar.

I noticed their carefree composure at home, a striking contrast to the steely, rigid demeanor they would be wearing on the streets, like most other girls I had seen. Gone were the scarves that wound so tightly around their faces, giving them the strict appearance of librarians. In the privacy of their home, their hair flowed as freely as the questions they hurled at me. Where did I come from? What was I doing living in Cairo? How did I like their culture? In their eyes, I was a jumble of contradictions.

She has a Muslim name and a vaguely Arab face smothered in a head scarf, but she can't form a coherent sentence in Arabic, Jamila must have thought.

She speaks with an American accent, sprinkled with slang words I can't understand, I sensed from Samira.

How can she flaunt that flagrant Western individualism that insists on going to unknown places and still call herself a good Muslim girl? I felt Nasreen wondering.

Unable to make sense of my mixed signals, they were also quick to judge, however erroneous their conclusions.

"You mean you can pray in mosques in America?" asked an incredulous Jamila. "It is not possible! I think you only have the church with too much singing."

"Well, we have the singing churches, but I can still go to the mosque for Friday prayers with my father. The imam even gives the *khutbah* in Arabic." I referred to the sermons, often feverish in tone and with enough voltage to short-circuit a small village.

"You have Muslim friends in America?" Jamila tucked her legs underneath the folds of her thin cotton dress and stared at me anxiously. "They go to mosque and wear *hijab*, yes?"

I realized with a start that some of my closest friends were in fact devout Christians and wondered how to explain the incongruity to someone whose idea of a best friend probably didn't extend beyond a next-door neighbor who was pretty much her own carbon copy. Instead, I decided to scandalize Jamila by showing a picture of my heathen friends dancing in a Seattle club. One of them had an arched back and a slightly orgasmic facial expression. To my surprise, Jamila took one look at the picture and broke into cackles, her eyes moist with tears.

"What she try to do!" she voiced between peals of laughter. "Your friend not know how to dance. I show you my cousin's wedding. I show you *raqs sharki!* Arabic dance! *Yallah!* Come!"

Jamila led me by the hand into the tiny living room. She inserted a tape recording of the requisite marriage video that every family seemed to own into the Phillips VCR. I propped a few cushions against the wall and reclined on the carpet.

A plump Egyptian bride in a Western-style white wedding gown and her equally plump groom sat like statues on the raised dais, reminding me of all the South Asian weddings I had ever attended. The camera zoomed in on their sober expressions and then panned out toward the jubilant guests stuffing themselves with rich sweets and sherbets.

Jamila grew more excited and nudged my elbow as the soft strains of the background *oud*, or the Middle Eastern lute, gave way to a pounding beat of a drum. Three middle-aged women swathed in red sequined halter bras and gauzy skirts began to wiggle their hips and breasts in joyous rapture. They tossed their raven tresses, locked eyes with the groom, and quivered their bellies. I was transfixed by the dancers' smoldering sensuality. They were utterly at ease with their bodies and exuded a bold confidence that seemed inborn. I couldn't help but wonder how different these women would look on public streets, most likely wearing the head scarf and loose modest clothing that shielded their feminine emblems. Such images were misleading. They led some of my girlfriends back home to believe that a veiled Muslim woman could not possibly know how to dance like a seductress. But I would have wagered that even five-year-old Egyptian girls were endowed with the gift of fluid hip undulations, as if music and dance flowed in their blood.

The call of the *maghrib* prayers at sunset signaled the breaking of the fast and the end of our dance program. We broke up into two separate groups because the living room was too tiny to accommodate us all. I was shocked to learn that the entire house consisted of only one bedroom that all four sisters shared with their mother while the father and son slept on the floor in the living area. The cloistered quarters couldn't have been healthy for Mohammad, but he had to put up with it given his traditional upbringing that stressed the values of family obligations and togetherness over individual independence. The kitchen functioned from an airless closet in the back of the house where the mother had prepared a lavish meal for nine.

After twelve hours of fasting, the first few morsels tasted like heaven in my mouth. I took second and third helpings at the urgings of my hosts, who would have been offended at my refusal. Jamila kept loading my plate with *fuul mudammas* (a thick tawny porridge of fava beans cooked in tomato sauce) and refilled my glass with homemade lemonade. We ate with our hands, sitting cross-legged on a bamboo straw mat.

In an Egyptian household, the guest commands royalty status and no request, however unreasonable, is ever denied. So even if I had wanted some baked brie and polenta, Mohammad's family would have hunted all over the city for the goodies. I made a mistake in bringing them some fruit as a gift. It was interpreted as an insult. No one said anything, but I sensed that I had violated a sacred code of Egyptian hospitality that had to do with pride and dignity in one's self-sufficiency, no matter how meager. My bag of oranges remained on a side shelf untouched all evening.

Little Mona pulled me by the arm and showed me her English homework. I had not realized what a frustrating language it must be for a nonnative learner. At least with Arabic, the words sounded just as they were written. Mona asked me to explain why *tough* couldn't be pronounced like *bough*. She nearly burst into tears when the ending of *transmission* rhymed with *transition* but was spelled so differently. I wondered who had chosen these words for a primary school text. And when I told Mona I was struggling with my Arabic, she shook her head with defiance and said nothing could be more difficult than learning English.

I was expected to linger, as leaving right after a meal would have been the height of rudeness to such gracious hosts. Mohammad and Yasser played backgammon while the sisters watched and plied them with tiny cups of cardamom-scented coffee. Jamila showed me how to wear the scarf that was constantly slipping from my head and nodded with approval when I got it right. Her mother pressed a small package into my hands that I dared not refuse. There seems to be an unwritten rule in every corner of the world that the materially poor are generous to a fault. Mohammad's family was no exception.

When I got up to leave, eight pairs of anxious eyes appraised my boundless freedom to go and do as I pleased. My hosts were not envious but acutely concerned for my safety. In a way, I admired their self-contained lives, rooted in rituals and traditions giving meaning and providing a strong sense of identity. It was hard to imagine Mohammad's sisters drifting through the world on endless soul-searching expeditions. They already seemed to know who they were and did not complain about the cards they were dealt. It occurred to me that the plethora of choices in the West both enriches and unnecessarily complicates life. I was reminded of my mother's observation: "You will never be satisfied. Even if you live in a mansion, you will find something lacking." I wondered if this was simply a quirk of human nature or my own shortcoming.

It was raining lightly when I stepped outside with Yasser and Mohammad. For the first time since my arrival, the air seemed lighter, cleaner. I had read somewhere that breathing in the pollution and smog of Cairo is the equivalent of smoking two hundred cigarettes a day. No wonder it gave me the impression of having a working chimney stuck in my lungs every time I inhaled. When I mentioned it to my friends, they just laughed it off, since toxins in the air were the least of their concerns.

We arrived at the subway station. I had just missed the last train and instead of waiting for another one, bound to arrive in a few minutes, I decided to treat myself to a taxi. Yasser flagged one down and negotiated the fare with the driver before I stepped inside. Mohammad assured me that I wouldn't be overcharged like a tourist. It was the going Egyptian rate. I was touched that they would go to the trouble of securing me the local rate in Egypt's dual economy, in which foreigners paid more than locals in certain cases. It seemed fair enough, because most foreigners who came to Egypt could probably afford to pay a little extra. I was on a strict budget, but the cost of living in Egypt was so much cheaper than in the States that I was saving money simply by keeping away from home. Thanking my surrogate brothers for a wonderful evening, I settled into the back seat of the cab. The driver decided to take the long way back to my apartment.

I rolled down a window and looked out into the dark night, thinking back to what my mother had said about my not being satisfied. I didn't think I was an ungrateful child, but as I got older and my dreams started to elude me, my frustrations rose. I was like the proverbial cat, wanting to go out when I was in and back in when I was out. I could never decide what to do and then just stick with my choices. I wavered between thought and action. *Is this why Mom made that comment?* Maybe what I was trying to achieve in Cairo had to do with learning satisfaction, so that I could go back home and tell Mom that perhaps she was wrong. I wished she were here with me now. She would have loved Cairo during Ramadan. In my family, I was always taught that fasting is more than an abstinence from food. It is a time for inward reflection and spiritual purification, a way to practice patience and compassion and feel closer to God. "Fasting is a training, a jihad against yourself." My mother meant jihad in the sense of striving for self-improvement, which is the inner meaning of the word. Only now was I realizing that I was fasting and traveling for the very same reasons.

Sex in the Old City

My apartment windows were always caked in dust. I had given up cleaning them. Dust was a part of life here. Gritty beige sand blew in from the desert and coated everything in sight, as if reminding you of the wilderness nestling so close to civilization. I was starting to get more comfortable with that feeling just by acknowledging that beyond the reasoned certainties of my mind lay a vast dust bowl of mystery and wonder.

It was only my third week of class at the language institute, but the alphabetical drills and fill-in-the-blank sessions at the blackboard were turning into a giant waste of time. They were not helping me speak Arabic on the streets. It wasn't a major hindrance, since most of my friends and acquaintances in Cairo were well versed in English. But I knew they were disappointed that I couldn't hold a proper conversation in their native language. I had managed to grasp bits and pieces of vocabulary and verbs to string together simple sentences, mostly by watching TV or listening to the radio. Because I wasn't getting much from formal instruction, I decided to quit the language school and just keep learning by my wits.

As the days yawned wide open again, I felt less anxious about the need for structure and let myself drift about, soaking in the city's flavors. The time capsule of Islamic Cairo kept drawing me back. I would walk along Sharia al-Muizz Li-Din Allah, a former thoroughfare of medieval Cairo and a veritable candy store of Islamic architecture. My favorite nugget was the petite al-Aqmar Mosque, decorated with stone facade stalactite carvings and ribbings in hooded arches. The street dead-ended at its northern gated entrance, flanked by Bab an-Nasr (Gate of Victory) and Bab al-Futuh (Gate of Conquest), built in the 11th century to guard the then-new walled city of al-Qahira. Next to the gates stood the Mosque of al-Hakim, named after a ruthless tyrant, according to my guidebook. I read that the mosque had rarely functioned as a place for worship. It was a prison during the Crusades, a warehouse for Napoleon, and at one point, it also served as a madhouse.

I entered the vast courtyard and walked toward a honey-colored minaret. As if reading my mind, an old custodian wordlessly led me up its stairwell, where I noticed the wall was stained with red patches. My imagination construed them as bloody handprints from one of Hakim's old skirmishes.

From my aerial perch, Old Cairo was a smog-drenched panorama of domed elegance cloaked in a maze of *souqs* named for their specialty of trade. On my earlier trip walking along the street of tent-makers, I had fallen in love with an appliquéd wall hanging of a Sufi dervish spinning in a blood-red gown. It has since hung above my bed, daring me every night as I fall asleep to dance on the jagged walls of memory. The custodian pointed to my camera and snapped a few pictures of me against the smoggy skyline of minarets.

Back in the narrow lanes, I dodged a chorus of hawkers selling thin vials of Egyptian perfume, claiming them to be hand-spun glass. A fleet of boys drifted by carrying trays of sweet black tea, their little fingers clutching rims of half-empty glasses, sometimes as many as five per hand, that they would wipe with a dirty rag for refills. I merged into a group

of women covered in long black robes and head scarves. In sp~~
eighty-degree heat, one of them wore a face veil and opaque black g~~
She rummaged inside her purse and took out a pair of sunglasses. Whe~~
she slipped them on, the overall effect was of a sea of black.

I decided to follow the women. They stopped before a cart bear-
ing heaps of lingerie. Fingers began flying through racy little teddies.
A clothesline contraption secured to two wooden poles mounted on the
edges of the cart displayed an enviable collection of brassieres, not unlike
the contents of Madonna's closet, with exaggerated conical cups and tas-
sels adorning would-be nipples. One of the members of the group picked
out a see-through nightie in iridescent pastels, a slow smile skirting the
side of her mouth. Her friend advised her to consider an ivory corset with
loose crochet work allowing for maximum cleavage exposure. She buried
the garment underneath the voluminous folds of the black *abaya*. It met
with approval when measured for size. Both women could have been
seasoned clients of Victoria's Secret.

It was hard to reconcile their candor about human sexuality with
the rigorous codes of conduct I had grown up with, ashamed and embarrassed to watch a love scene on a video or a TV show in the presence of
my family. Whenever the screen blurred with naked flesh, my father or I
would rise from the living room couch and pretend a need to go the bathroom. Even the Bollywood films we watched at the time censored mouth-
to-mouth contact. But after I discovered the contents of the *Kama Sutra*
and a titillating 15th-century Arabic handbook known as *The Perfumed
Garden,* I figured there was some sort of rift between factual accounts of
Eastern erotica and the cultural prudishness I was taught to observe.

Another customer was eyeing a hot-pink teddy. She haggled over
the price with the teenage vendor manning the cart. It amounted to a
little more than $10. Then she requested a 36D in scarlet red.

I walked over to another cart piled with bikini bottoms. It was oper-
ated by an old man with the wispy beard of Confucius.

ones are very daring," he informed me with a know-

y head scarf, he lowered his voice as if about to utter

y for show!"

ad been selling panties for more than two decades. I asked him if he never found his job awkward.

"But why?" He looked puzzled. "I do good business, especially during wedding season. And I help bring pleasure to my sisters." He swept an arm at his coterie of loyal customers. "May Allah keep them happy!"

I recalled strolling through Amsterdam's red-light district. The real-life displays of wanton female flesh standing behind full-length glass doorways had reminded me of the look and feel of a city zoo with captive creatures in glass cages.

The sage of sexy underclothes caught my eye and winked. Maybe he had read *The Perfumed Garden* or perhaps some love-drenched sonnets of Omar Khayyam. I watched the veiled vixens browsing through lacy corsets, fully aware of their God-given rights for pleasure in the bedroom. It all began to make some sense—sort of.

The F Word

I didn't grow up thinking of myself as a feminist. But the values instilled in me were rooted in feminism, and I learned them from my father. He made me believe that I could do anything I wanted, that no goal was out of reach as long as I was willing to strive for it, and that nothing stood in my way other than myself. It was my father who always encouraged me to travel, and though he shed a few tears at the airport in Seattle, I knew that he championed my leap in the dark as a means of self-empowerment. Even so, if I were to tell Dad that he was my first feminist, he would cringe at the word, associating it with self-involved women who hated men and decried housework. By the time I got to college, I was convinced that I was the antifeminist because I happened to get along better with men than with my own sex for the most part and I didn't see how cooking or cleaning got in the way of my liberation.

Most of my girlfriends held opposite views, and the ones in my gender-studies class treated me like an outcast when I expounded the merits of being a housewife. My professor told me I hadn't grasped the struggles of Betty Friedan and the second-wave feminist writers. Even though I respected their courage in resisting patriarchal demands, I was unmoved by their words. Had they known I was a Muslim woman, they would have readily endowed me with the badge of the Oppressed, suffering beneath the veil, helpless, submissive, and in desperate need of rescue from the burden of my religious beliefs. This was not my kind of feminism. I couldn't really articulate what my kind was, and throughout my college years and beyond, I gave up thinking about the fem word.

When I first met Asma, I was deep in prostration at the Amr Ibn al As Mosque. It was the last week of Ramadan, and I had taken to attending *taraweeh*, or nightly prayer sessions, in the oldest existing mosque in Cairo and on the entire African continent, built in the 7th century and named after the commander of the Muslim army that conquered Egypt. The ladies' section was packed, and I had managed to squeeze myself into a little ball to find some space, but now the woman on my right was motioning me to move forward, which I was reluctant to do because my forehead pressed to the floor was already grazing the soles of the person in front of me, who was bent in the same position at the same time.

Up and down we prostrated two more times before turning our heads from right to left as if saluting the angels sitting on either shoulder. During prayer breaks, I chitchatted with the woman who had tapped me on my rear end midprostration. She was pale-faced and thin, in her late thirties or early forties, with deep circles underneath her light-brown eyes. Upon learning I was from the States, she extended an invitation to her home for "conversation" and scribbled her contact info in my small notebook. I learned her name was Asma.

The following evening, I hailed a taxi to Asma's apartment. The driver paused near an elegant twelve-story complex in the posh embassy district of Doqqi. I had once gone there in search of an American-style drugstore and stocked up on three bottles of Clairol Herbal Essence shampoo along with Crest toothpaste.

Asma welcomed me inside the building's foyer. We rode the elevator to the tenth floor and entered a stylish apartment decorated in a hodge-podge style of Victorian chintz meets Eastern elegance. I sat on a low carved wooden chair and thumbed through Asma's collection of *Vogue* magazines. She collected stacks of them, along with thick leather-bound volumes of Islamic jurisprudence and *hadith,* or sayings of the Prophet, neatly arranged in a floor-length bookcase.

"Look at this one." Asma peered at the airbrushed photos of Christy Turlington in a backless satin number. "You think she is a liberated woman?"

I glanced at Asma's tired-looking face, her ivory cotton head scarf loosely knotted underneath her chin, and the trademark navy-blue oversized *abaya* that concealed her curves. She was clearly not trying to compete with Christy, yet her comments struck me as rather sharp, as if she had some personal vendetta against supermodels. I asked her to elaborate.

She took the magazine from my lap and started flipping pages, stopping here and there to point out skimpy clothes and excessive skin exposure. I was starting to get the message.

"It's just marketing," I said.

"Exactly," Asma replied. "These market forces in the West control women. They tell them how to dress and behave. But the Western woman is not so free! So what if she can wear a bikini and dance around naked. Is this your idea of liberation?"

"I think it has to do with choice," I responded. "It's not a matter of control."

"Very well," Asma said. "Then why does the Western world tell us that Muslim women are weak? Because we wear the *hijab?* It is not a law in Egypt! I choose to wear *hijab*. But I am not weak. I have my problems. But I am not a weak woman. Your West wants to help us but it does not understand us."

I didn't like her allusion to "my" West. I didn't own the place. I just happened to live there. But Asma's speech triggered painful memories of my high school years. Crash diets and hour-long marathons on the treadmill were the norm. I had subsisted on celery and carrot sticks and dreamed of fitting into a size 4 dress for the homecoming prom. Internalizing societal pressure to conform to a certain standard of appearance was not exclusive to an American upbringing. I thought of the Cairo hipsters in leather jackets and head scarves and reminded Asma that no society, West or East, was immune from treating women as human barometers to measure the pulse of social progress or regression. It was a universal theme.

She agreed and told me more about herself. She was raised in a well-off family, her parents were former academics, and Asma had dreamed of carrying on the profession and studied for her PhD in Islamic history in England. But she was unable to complete it after her brother died in a tragic car accident. She returned to Egypt three years ago to care for her father when he got cancer. Her mother was in the early stages of Alzheimer's and unable to support herself. The parents lived two floors above in the same building. Asma held a part-time job at a Cairo research institute, but she had forfeited her dreams of becoming a professor. It was too late, and she was exhausted enough just trying to get through each day. I felt terrible for Asma. I wanted to encourage her not to give up, but I didn't think it was my right to say anything because I hadn't lived in her shoes. I hadn't really known her struggle. I could only empathize and hope she would find solace in her heart. From everything she had mentioned, I knew that Asma was not a frail person, nor was she meek and docile just by virtue of her veil or her tendency to prefer plain clothes and wear no makeup. Living in the East did not exactly prevent Asma from exercising her mind and thinking for herself. She was as liberated as she chose to be, given, as my father always said, that one knows how to get out of one's own way. Asma's existence was not summed up in labels, be they Muslim or Arab or woman. She was who she was as a result of her circumstances and choices, like me and like everyone else on the planet.

Gender Jihad

The next time I saw Asma at her Doqqi apartment, she was in a considerably lighter mood. Her parents were doing well, all things considered. And Asma was throwing a little birthday bash for a friend. When the doorbell rang, Asma welcomed a woman carrying a Pizza Hut cardboard box. She was wearing a stylish floor-length black dress of fine jersey material and a leopard-print head scarf. Asma introduced the birthday girl, Dina, who greeted me with cheek-to-cheek pecks four times on each side. The three of us reclined on a plush Persian carpet using oblong silk cushions as headrests. Dina passed around napkins and opened a steaming box of the green pepper, mozzarella, and mushroom special. Apparently, it was going to be just the three of us at the party. I bit into a slice, chewing fast to keep up with the layers of cheese stretching into thin white rubber bands.

Dina removed her head scarf and fluffed out her curls. She told me that she had spent ten years in Europe teaching Arabic. She loved the openness and curiosity of her students, but she was also dismayed at their one-sided opinions about the Muslim world, particularly when it came to gender issues.

"But why should I be surprised?" she scoffed. "Look at what they are learning from the Western media. One day it's honor killings, the next day, wife beatings. I'm not saying these stories are not true. But my students think it is the fault of Islam. They think Islam is anti-woman. And the mass media make it worse. They don't pay attention to the cultural, social, and political dimensions that distort religious interpretations. It is so much easier to simply blame Islam."

The pizza was getting cold during all this talk. Between bites, Dina added, "But this is what we must challenge. We must show that Islam honors women. Remember what the Prophet said. Paradise lies at the feet of mothers. We have to rediscover and relearn what our religion says. We must use this knowledge as a source of strength and power."

It occurred to me just how odd (and sad) it was that the very religion credited for empowering women had also developed a reputation for shackling them.

"You are right," I said. "But how can Muslim women seek justice through Islam when Islam is used by some to silence their voices?"

Asma, who was a silent contender in our debate thus far, jumped in to address my concerns.

"My dear girl. God has given each of us the means to use our intellect to promote justice and compassion. Islam is our conscience. But we have deviated from its ideals."

Asma's convictions were based in the Quran, the primary source of Islamic principles and conduct. Now if every individual (Muslim and non-Muslim) on earth thought the same way as Asma, there would be no disagreement in Islam's attitude regarding women. But the question of who will interpret the Quran and in what context is crucial. It cuts across one of Islam's most divisive debates—official, literalist readings versus inwardly drawn interpretations of the scriptures. Depending on one's viewpoint, Quranic verses can be perceived as restrictive or derogatory (in relation to women) or liberating and respectful toward women's honor and dignity.

I asked Asma her thoughts on the divergence of opinions and their impact on Muslim women.

She smiled and said, "No religion exists in a vacuum. Even so, we are demanding equality through our God-given rights. We are seeking liberation *within* an Islamic framework. Tell that to your USA friends!"

As we ate pizza, we continued our discussion, which was our *ijtihad*, a process of inquiry and self-analysis essential in maintaining a dynamic Islam. Like all forms of intellectual debates, *ijtihad* has waxed and waned through the centuries because of shifting political and religious agendas. But it is fundamentally an individual responsibility to reason and think critically. Asma and Dina were showing me that they were used to regular *ijtihad*. We talked about the legacy of strong women in Islam, starting with Khadija, the Prophet's first wife. She had her own business and employed the Prophet to manage her affairs. She even proposed marriage to him. And Aisha, the Prophet's youngest wife, was known for standing up to her husband and speaking her mind.

I told my Egyptian friends about Razia Sultan, the first woman ruler of the Indian subcontinent who also fought in battles alongside men. This raised eyebrows and inspired appreciative chuckles of, "Go, girl!" Asma took out one of her thick books and mentioned that as early as the 7th century, Muslim women had the rights to inherit, own property, choose their husbands, and even to divorce. Dina said that when a Muslim woman marries, she retains her maiden name, and that according to Islamic law, a married working woman is entitled to keep all her earnings for herself. It is obligatory only for the husband to be the breadwinner. The wife gets to take it easier! I was confused. Surely something went horribly wrong when women's progressive status in Islam gradually eroded in practice.

Asma had slipped into the kitchen to take a phone call. So I asked Dina to explain what went wrong.

"There is no easy answer," she replied.

"Come on," I coaxed her. "Surely you have something to say about the decline of Islamic civilization."

"First of all," Dina said, "what you refer to as Islamic civilization was not a single, uniform entity. It was essentially a multicultural, multi-religious society. And secondly, Muslims themselves were not always united as a community. This has been our greatest weakness and used against us over time."

"How so?" I asked.

"Colonialism, for example," Dina stated. "It destabilized our society and made men insecure. But women paid the price. And if you really want to know, I think we are fighting on two fronts."

"And what are those?"

"Well, we have the internal oppression from our male-dominated ruling establishments as well as foreign domination in the form of economic imperialism."

"But where does Islam fit in all this?"

Dina had taken out a compact and was applying a fresh coat of lipstick. I repeated my question, to which she had a ready response.

"Islam becomes a tool to be manipulated by vested power structures." Dina looked me in the eye and added, "It is an old story."

As I watched Dina draping the scarf back over her head, I wondered what my old college buddies from gender-studies class would have thought of her, and of Asma for that matter. Would they have classified their Muslim sense of feminism as an anomaly? Asma's apartment was spotless, and she took pride in her housekeeping skills. Did that make her any less of a feminist than Betty Friedan and company or upper-class women with the means to hire domestic helpers? And since Dina looked so stylish and elegant in her modest attire, was her Islamic outlook more "modern" and therefore less alien?

It was hard to say. Asma had her share of problems at home, but not because of her culture or faith. It was part of life. And when I went up to her in the kitchen to say goodnight, I knew that I wouldn't be pestering her again with questions, because she had provided an answer. She had made me recognize that my kind of feminism derived directly from Islam and was not an aberration from it. The very act of traveling solo, of squelching fear and ignorance, was rooted in my Islamic feminist philosophy. It made me feel entitled to lead my own path and continue with the journey's jihad toward self-enlightenment.

Inner Sanctum

The bookstore at the American University stocked a fine collection of local guidebooks. I used to spend entire afternoons there poring over Egypt's maps, soon losing interest in the long vertebrae of the Nile and letting my eyes wander westward toward the Libyan border, where an uninhabited chunk of land was labeled The Great Sand Sea. I would fall asleep dreaming of silken sands squishing between my toes and a sky close enough to touch with my hand. The same dream returned to keep me company as I zapped the remote through the evening's satellite lineup on a lonely Friday night in my apartment. The local news channel announced a rise in state-subsidized bread prices. A commercial for Nescafé featured a yuppie couple flirting with their eyes at an outdoor café.

I settled on a lively talk show and brewed another pot of green tea to quell my growing restlessness. Ripped pages from old *National Geographic* magazines littered the coffee table with glossy spreads of sculpted dunes. So near, yet so far. The talk show guests were debating their favorite perfumes. I picked up the phone and called Ayman.

We had met in random fashion. I was standing outside a downtown restaurant eyeing a platter of rice, pasta, beans, and crunchy brown onions. A voice behind me offered a sales pitch in English. "It is called *kushari*. Very good Egyptian dish. You should try some." The voice belonged to a face with a café au lait complexion and eyes like black coal.

"Nice shirt." He fingered the fabric of my block-printed *kurta*.

"It's from India. They dye the cloth with vegetable colors and use a big rubber stamp to make the patterns. I chose this design."

"So you are a clothes designer?"

"Not really."

I studied Ayman's face to detect the subtext lurking underneath our cursory words. We had occasionally run into each other in downtown coffee shops, but he never had had the time to sit down with me and have a proper conversation, until now. I found out that Ayman was a tour guide specializing in the desert, and downtown Cairo was rich territory for prospecting foreign customers. I saw the way he worked, gliding up to young backpacking types and even older couples exiting posh five-star hotels, showing them some snapshots that he removed from the shoulder bag worn crosswise against his leather jacket. He didn't act like a hustler. The composure in his eyes demanded attention and respect.

Ayman promised he would take me on one of his frequent excursions to something called the White Desert. I looked it up in my guidebook and found pictures of whitewashed rocks morphing into animal shapes. A replica of the Sphinx was particularly enticing.

"It is my Bedouin blood," Ayman told me with supreme indifference when I saw him, three weeks later. "I need to keep going to the desert. It is the only place where I can think."

His eyes betrayed a hint of amusement. Perhaps he enjoyed watching me squirm under the desert's spell. It held an attraction that I could not explain. Some days after he first proposed the desert trip, I would be overwhelmed with the sense that I hadn't really touched Egypt, and the urge to physically feel the land and to leave my footprints on it was the only thing I could think about. It was like wanting to become one with a place and I was growing more and more convinced that this place had to be the desert. That night, when I called Ayman from my apartment, I nagged him until he finally relented. But instead of offering his own services as a guide, he agreed to get hold of someone else. A man called Badri.

"But why can't *you* take me?" I whined.

"Because I have to stay in Cairo for a while. It is family business."

"Great. So now I have to go with this complete stranger, and I don't even know . . ."

"We call him the desert fox," Ayman informed me with a somewhat imperious air. "All European tourists go with him. He even has a website!"

It was a slick marketing strategy and working big-time on me. "Well, can you see if the fox is willing . . . ?" The line died. My mind thrashed in suspense. *Please ring, please ring.* I pleaded with the phone while trying not to curse at Ayman in my best bazaar Urdu. He called back twenty minutes later.

"Okay. It is all arranged. You leave Cairo in two days. Tomorrow we will buy your bus ticket to Bahariyya, where you will meet Badri. He has agreed to take you for four days and three nights. We don't have a tent so you will have to sleep outside. It gets cold at night so make sure to bring some warm clothes. Oh, one more thing. Don't worry about the food. Badri will have everything. He is a very good cook."

I started to get goose bumps. So this was it. My journey into the wilderness of sand, a place of mystery and desolation, far removed from civilization, where I might just get a chance to taste something timeless. How could Ayman be so matter-of-fact about the whole thing? It may be second nature to him to traipse about in the desert every other week for years on end and to fall asleep gazing at the Milky Way, but to a first-timer like me, a four-day desert expedition was a fantasy about to be born. And I didn't want to spoil it with any distractions, namely other travelers with whom I might have to share Badri and the jeep. I insisted on going alone with the fox. Going solo incurred a hefty fee of $400 for the full share of the vehicle and gas normally split by a party of four. But it was a trifling matter compared to the delicious mingling of opportunity with timing that I was about to seize. Ayman didn't provide an elaborate itinerary. He left it to the discretion of my Bedouin guide and God's will, of course.

I was too excited to sleep the night before. The early-morning bus from Cairo lurched its way south. By noon we were in the busy little oasis town of Bahariyya. The bus halted at the small square that marked the town center. As I rubbed open my sleepy eyes, a heavyset man in a long black *galabiya* climbed in and beamed at everyone. He was searching for someone, apparently the only solo female passenger on board. The famous fox stood near my seat, flashing a set of malachite-green eyes. "Maliha?"

As we descended from the bus, one of the local hustlers tried to shove two lost German tourists our way. Badri shooed them off with a flick of his lordly hand before gesturing toward his open kingdom beyond. "Shall we go?" He seemed to be thoroughly prepared, and I delighted in his sense of efficiency and timeliness. On our way to the parked jeep, Badri stopped by a small shop and bought me a black-and-white kaffiyeh, or checkered head cloth.

"For your protection!" he explained.

The road heading out of Bahariyya unfurled as a steel-gray ribbon of paved asphalt. A sign indicated the next oasis town of Farafra, 185 kilometers farther south. I rolled down the jeep's window and wrapped the kaffiyeh around my face as a shield against the blowing sand and wind. Badri threw me a mischievous grin. He seemed incapable of looking sad and grumpy. Exhilaration rushed through me like the currents in a whirlpool as I anticipated the adventure ahead.

Black volcanic mountains, pyramid-shaped with rocks tumbling like chunks of coal, came into view and merged with a flat medley of earth and sky. Badri stopped near a crystal quarry, where I scraped a fist-size souvenir. We drove along until the sand started licking the edges of the road. All of a sudden, Badri made a swift turn and the jeep veered off the road, sliding into a blank canvas with no discernible signs. The jeep scaled the dunes, racing up and down, skidding in wide turns, and crunching its tires on the squishy sand. I felt like a rubber ball bouncing inside a vacuum.

We spent our first night near Acrobat Mountain, setting up camp in an alcove of beige boulders with arched formations that reminded me of Utah. Badri lit a fire and roasted chicken on skewers made out of twigs for our first dinner together. Afterward, he brewed sweet mint tea and plied me with dozens of tiny glasses of what he called "Bedouin whiskey." The rich, lilting voice of the Egyptian diva Om Khoulsoum flooded the still desert night from Badri's cassette player. We listened to the classic song "Inta Omri," which means "You are my life," countless times. Badri translated some of the lyrics from Arabic to English.

"The best concert hall in the world!" He waved his hand at the surrounding expanse of stubby rocks and ridges of powdery dunes. It was impossible to believe that we were less than two hundred kilometers from Cairo. My ears strained into the cool night air and I listened to the desert's silence.

It was incredibly loud, so loud that I could hardly bear the sound. And it was heavy. It filled my soul with a certain weight I could not place. When I mentioned my concern to Badri, he nodded and told me that this silence was so distressing to one European woman in a previous trek that she had to quit her journey prematurely. I wondered what it was she couldn't handle.

In the early morning, Badri was still slumbering on his thin mattress next to last night's fire. I grabbed my water bottle, some mouthwash, and wet wipes and went in search of a bathroom. Away from the camp, the land began to curve upward in a series of frozen waves. I climbed a dune, fascinated by the sight of my footprints etched in the slithery grains. Reaching the crest, I looked out into a feature-less space of sand and sky. There was no need for privacy. I dribbled water over my face and walked back to camp, where Badri was fixing breakfast—warming up flat bread and boiling water for the requisite morning tea. I spread some strawberry jam on the bread and ate it like a rolled-up burrito while Badri loaded the jeep. On our way out, tiny black rocks littered the ground like hailstones. "Flower stones," Badri called them, and he jumped out of the jeep to show me. Oddly enough, they resembled the petals of a flower, carved in intricate detail by the hand of nature. My pocket bulged as I collected them.

On day 2, we headed into the White Desert that Ayman always talked about as if it were an otherworldly planet. Seeing it for real, I finally understood why. Blinding white rock formations shaped by wind erosion dotted the landscape, giving it the appearance of an eerie arc-tic theater. As we drove farther into it, the white outcroppings began to take on surreal animal forms. I saw ostriches, camels, and hawks. Badri pointed out an elephant and a giraffe. We looked around for a good campsite and settled near a large white mound with a horse-shaped head protruding from the top. This time we were not the only visitors. As the night wore on, a dozen fires scattered around the desert. Apparently, the White Desert was getting to be a popular touristy getaway. I had even once seen a Bollywood film that appeared shot on location next to the horse-head sculpture guarding our camp.

Later that night, we were joined by Abdul, a fellow Bedouin guide and friend of Badri, and Abdul's German girlfriend. They had come over just for the day from Farafra but were too tired to drive back. Abdul talked about a group of Dutch tourists arriving at the oasis town for a weeklong safari. He was a jovial fellow and we instantly hit it off. I didn't think his girlfriend was too happy about it, and she spent most of the evening staring at her feet as if she didn't want to be where she was. Dinner was chicken kebabs, supplied by Abdul, and potatoes, crunchy and charred from roasting on the open fire. Abdul invited some nearby campers for tea, and one of them started singing some bawdy songs in French that sounded rather good given our primordial surroundings. Badri improvised the percussion by banging on an empty water drum. He kept urging me to sing some *ghazals* in Urdu but I couldn't work up the nerve.

Before going to sleep, I went for a little walk, keeping track of the passing animal shapes as landmarks. Far from excluding me, the desert embraced me. As I continued walking, I was reminded of how I felt when I danced tango, that somehow everything was aligned right within me. There was perfect balance and harmony. And knowing that this state of equilibrium would dissipate as soon as the music stopped and the lights brightened made me relish it all the more. I would go on dancing and feeling somehow betrayed that I couldn't hold on to this moment beyond its finite duration. It seemed so unfair, even cruel, that this balanced self didn't settle into my everyday life. She was more of a casual visitor, and I often wished she would stay longer and make me at ease. Maybe that's what the White Desert was trying to do that night, reacquainting me with an old and cherished friend.

I overslept the next morning and found our guests had already departed. Badri mentioned that Abdul might be driving to Siwa from Bahariyya and had offered me a passage if I were interested. But I couldn't think so far ahead. The desert was teaching me to live moment to moment, making only the present count because the present is all that exists.

I had read somewhere that the worst insult to a Bedouin is a refusal to be under his obligation. So I accepted Badri's welcome to desert life. It was a rough but cordial existence. I tried to help out with the daily rituals, easy work such as rolling up the bedding and preparing tea, while I watched my guide making bread by hand twice a day and digging up firewood when there appeared to be none. I never saw Badri shirk a piece of work even when he was tired and needed to rest. Nor did he complain about what we lacked in provisions; he was always grateful for whatever we had to eat. Sometimes I caught him wiping away the sweat on his brow with the edge of his tasseled kaffiyeh and the smile of a contented man. I envied his constant cheerfulness. *"Enti mafsoota?"* he kept asking me. Are you happy?

On our third day, we headed toward the Libyan border, entering the cusp of the Western Desert that branches out into the Sahara. An immense wilderness unfolded and held me captive. We discovered a plain with no visible limits. Only our jeep tracks indicated any signs of life, carving deep incisions in the chocolate-brown sand. This time Badri found a fabulous campsite. We scaled the ridge of a long dune and inched down into a hollow depression flanked by boulders as if they were curtains.

It was still midafternoon. After we set up camp, I went exploring and felt as if I were getting drunk on light and space, the headiness of just being able to breathe, just being alive. I started playing a little game, walking backward in the sand just to watch my feet leave their imprints. As I kept moving, I sensed my borders shrinking, getting smaller and smaller until my mind dissolved all its rationales, theories, prejudices, and fears, leaving behind an emptiness, which was not a void but a type of wholeness I had never experienced before.

Later in the evening after dinner, Badri and I took a long walk together, barefoot in the cold sand. His shadow roved next to mine and we walked without talking much. I asked him only how he managed never to get lost in that vastness. He simply said, "Learn to read the stars, the language of the sky."

I threw my head back at the black dome sown with tiny silver sequins that appeared permanent and ageless. As I continued staring at the stars, I began to see my journey as a process rather than a destination. The insistent need for structure to give it a necessary weight faded into oblivion, replaced by a more surefire desire to trust in the unknown, to travel as a nomad whose only compass is intuition. A line from the Quran chimed in my head. *Everywhere you turn is the face of God.*

On my last night in the desert, I slept on top of a cold sand dune. There was no trace of any other human being. Not even the slightest wind, just a great stillness as if time itself was suspended. I was totally exposed and vulnerable to the infinite space around me. A space without walls, furniture, or restrictions, a space studded with hundreds of self-reflecting mirrors, with nowhere to run or hide from myself. Everywhere I looked, there was only me. The sound of my breathing and the soft thuds of my beating heart compelled me to fully absorb my solitude and revel in it.

Was this what the desert's silence was all about, a coming back to myself? Maybe that explained why it was so hard for me (and others before me) to listen to that strange silence, because it was a reminder that ultimately we are alone. No one can live our lives for us. You can seek empathy and help, but in the end, you have to fend for yourself in your own skin, mind, and soul.

After watching the sunrise, I ran down to the camp to wake Badri. He had already started packing and was ready to head back into civilization. By late afternoon, we were suddenly pulling into the main drag of Bahariyya. The desert was eclipsed from reality. I was speechless and numb with emotion. Badri shook my hand and put me on the last bus to Cairo. I sat in the back row and waved at the desert fox until he shrunk into a black pinpoint. A slow triumphant wave washed over me, and I felt certain that I would never, ever repeat the experience I had just had. Even if I went back to the desert, it would be a different kind of high.

I slept it off through the entire bus ride. Someone was shaking my shoulder and shouting, "Ramses." For a split second, the name meant nothing to me. I flagged a taxi to reach the apartment. It did not really have a street address. I told the driver "al Demerdash" and then rattled off a series of landmarks we had to pass to get closer to the building where I was living.

Sliding Doors

After I experienced the desert, it became impossible to settle back down into the urban rhythms of Cairo. The bleak signs of winter in the middle of December had sullied the city from its initial brilliance. I no longer spent much time with Mohammad and Yasser, for whom my desert expedition had reinforced the wide gulf between my privileged Western upbringing that could afford the luxury of wanderlust and their humbler lifestyles that could scarcely contemplate the thought of vacationing outside of Egypt someday. It was easy to dismiss all this when we shared laughs over political cartoons and ate hummus and hard-boiled eggs for *iftar*. But deep down, we all knew that we came from very different worlds and would probably never be able to switch sides.

On the dawn of the new millennium, I found myself in Upper Egypt, clambering amid Pharaonic ruins in the Valley of the Kings and farther south in Abu Simbel near the Sudanese border. The sudden barrage of tourist madness irritated me, and though I had avoided group tours like the plague, I signed up for a week-long felucca excursion on the Nile. All the while, I couldn't shake off the sensation of feeling like a deep-sea diver surfacing for air, but this air was so different from the one I had known for two months. I hadn't interacted with foreigners until I came to Luxor and Aswan on the guided tour, and I found the experience oddly discomfiting now that I finally had emerged from my hibernation into the mother lode. That hibernation had given me the self-reliance and confidence I needed to restore my questing spirit. I was ready for new adventures in the Middle East and my curiosity shifted into high gear when I returned to Cairo and retrieved a three-day-old email.

It was from Bea. She had provided her flight arrival number from Madrid. I did a quick calculation and realized that my Australian friend was somewhere in Cairo at this very moment. We had exchanged some instant messages about meeting up in Egypt during my stay, but I didn't know precisely when she would show up. So it was a huge surprise to find her already landed and waiting for me to greet her. Good old Bea! But I hardly knew her at that point. We had met in a youth hostel in Paris, when I was fresh off the plane from Seattle. In the three days we had spent together, I knew we were kindred spirits.

Welcome to the mother of the world! I wrote her back.

My inbox received an instant reply. *Where have you been hiding?* We agreed to meet downtown, at the Nile Hilton, in an hour.

There was no mistaking her. Thick cascades of dark wavy hair, a serene composure that did not believe in anxiety, oversize black-framed glasses slipping down that perfectly sloped Italian nose. She was the same as I had remembered.

"Bea!" I yelled. "What a surprise!"

People in the hotel lobby swiveled their heads in my direction.

She smiled that maddening smile of hers that could melt the heart of a brutal dictator.

"Oh, you know how it is. I got fed up with Spain. So I thought I would come down to see you in your new digs. You look great, babe. Very much at home in Cairo, eh?"

I recalled a little joke we had shared in Paris of "doing the Middle East together." Is that why she was here, to turn the fantasy into action? I was hoping she would. And I didn't mind at all teaming up with her. It wasn't some kind of ironclad rule that I *had* to be alone to find myself. The essential point was to keep on traveling, to keep on moving and seeking. I had been on my own for nearly nine months since I left home, and I was longing for some company. Bea wouldn't be in my way. In fact, she might even help me see better.

"I am so glad you are here. Care to come to the Sinai with me?"

"You know I would, babe," she said. "And then on to Jordan, Lebanon, Syria, Turkey, maybe even Greece. I told you anything is possible if you set your mind to it. Just think of all those adventures waiting for us!"

"Yeah, and what about all the hassles? Two single girls traipsing together in the Arab world. A very male world, don't forget. We will invite trouble everywhere we go."

I was just playing devil's advocate.

"Oh, hush up. You always worry so much. Just have some faith. Nothing will go wrong. And if it does, I'll be right by your side. What more could you want?"

Her declaration was confirming my own percolating thoughts.

"You'll have to teach me about the culture, all the dos and don'ts. I won't be like those ignorant tourists who wander into mosques wearing short skirts and singlets."

I smothered a smile.

"We'll have a blast!" said Beatrice, my newfound comrade and partner in adventure.

"Inshallah," I muttered, hoping our guardian angels heard my plea.

She stayed in my apartment for two weeks, during which time we amassed tourist visas for our future ports of call and did some sightseeing. It was Bea's first time in Egypt, or anywhere in the Middle East. I took her to all my favorite places in Cairo, showing off the city like a proud parent, not yet comprehending its tenuous grip on time. There would be no more Ghuma and his silent morning appraisals; Ayman had disappeared into the vastness of his desert, but not before giving me a piece of it to hold on to in the silent chambers of memory. I never knew what happened to my archaeologist dream date, but the recollection of our nighttime walk through the old city still smoldered my blood. As for Mohammad and Yasser, we really were joined at the heart, no matter how wide our differences. I would miss them all terribly.

Bea and I left Cairo on a chilly January morning. Dr. Nadia came over to the apartment to say good-bye. When she asked me where we would be staying in our future destinations, I shrugged my shoulders in ignorance.

Mohammad and Yasser came with us to the bus station. They were unusually quiet and kept their eyes fastened to the ground most of the time. Mohammad looked as if he would burst into tears at any moment. Yasser's face was soaked with sadness. He seemed to say, "Don't go so soon."

"I will email you all the time," I said in consolation. "Besides, Dahab is not so far. You could always join us for a weekend there. I am not going to the ends of the earth, *wallah!*"

"But it just won't be same without you," said Mohammad. "Remember all our walks, remember that day at the pyramids when you fell off your horse, remember the *iftar* at my house?"

"Yes, yes, of course I remember all the fun we had. How can I ever forget? You've both been like my own brothers."

The bus driver unleashed a volley of honks. "We have to go!" I shouted, nearly collapsing under the weight of my luggage.

"You look like an astronaut!" Yasser poked fun at me for old times' sake. I waddled with two heavy backpacks fastened front and back.

We must have said *maasalaama,* or good-bye, at least a dozen times. Mohammad's moistened eyes couldn't hold it in any longer as big fat tears rolled down his rugged face. I smiled bravely while fighting the gulp in my throat.

"Don't forget to write to us," Yasser shouted. "And be careful of those Bedouins in Dahab!" he warned ominously.

Bea and I watched the two best friends waving madly at us. They diminished into spots the size of faraway planets as the bus speeded up.

Dancing in Dahab

We headed south, crossing the vast Sinai Peninsula. The landscape was barren and tremendously old, as if nothing had changed since the beginning of time. Sinewy red mountains rippled in every direction. By sunset, Bea and I reached Dahab, a beach town perched on the shores of the Gulf of Aqaba. About a dozen foreigners staggered off the bus, and we followed them into the back of a pickup truck that would take us to the only accommodation in town, according to the driver. A place called Camp Bishbishi.

The following evening, Bea and I strode through the main thoroughfare. Touristy shops advertised elaborate headdresses worthy of Cleopatra, glitzy belly-dance costumes made entirely out of red sequins, and jewelry with colored stones of dubious origin. Ignoring the sales pitches and stares from the shop vendors, we headed toward a row of restaurants strung along the seafront. An insistent waiter urged us to try the local *karkaday* tea made out of hibiscus flowers. He gestured toward the cushions and rugs scattered in place of tables and chairs, allowing customers to lounge and eat at the same time. The pungent smell of marijuana added to the mellow hippie ambience. I couldn't help but notice that most of the patrons were Western foreigners. A beachfront espresso stand up the road looked more inviting.

Bea and I sat on barstools and observed a head with a baseball cap worn backward furiously working a red Lavazza machine transported right out of Piazza Navonna.

"You wanna cap?" the voice belonging to the head spoke. The face was boyish, with chubby cheeks and pouting lips. His name was Waheed, beach café operator by night and part-time diver by day. We shared cigarettes and ordered two more caps, or cappuccinos.

By 1:00 AM, we were still perched on our stools, smoking and guzzling caffeine. Waheed turned out to be a dance fiend after hours and coaxed us into a nightclub operating from a palm-thatched hut on the beach. It became routine for the three of us to boogie through dawn.

Instead of going back to Camp Bishbishi, Bea and I would sleep on the beach. Waheed provided coarse woolen blankets and then rolled himself up like a mummy on a nearby mattress. He wanted to stay with us "for protection." Once I woke up at two in the afternoon and found a dark bearded man snoring next to me. Our esteemed protector was nowhere in sight. Neither was Bea. Then I saw the two of them approaching, carrying platters of food. Waheed threw some water on the stranger by my side, whom I vaguely recognized as Abdu, the bartender from the club. He woke up with a start and unleashed a funny little laugh that emerged from his nasal passages sounding like a long, overdrawn snicker. Bea started imitating it to perfection.

One afternoon, the four of us decided to go on a picnic in the nearby hills. Within half an hour, we had spread out blankets and cushions on a barren patch of earth surrounded by serrated hilltops. Waheed's many talents included the ability to spot wild herbs and fashion joints by rolling the stalk and sipping it like a straw. He also knew how to whistle twenty different ways and sulk like a four-year-old. Abdu, on the other hand, turned out to be surprisingly practical and improvised a fabulous lunch in primitive conditions. He used twigs for skewers, on which he laced potato cubes. A half-broken water bottle functioned as a kettle. Bea and Waheed were getting quite chummy, feeding each other charred potatoes. They soon wandered off, leaving me behind with Abdu.

I raced him toward a boulder and began climbing a steep path for a sunset view of the Red Sea. It was the color of indigo ink in the dimming twilight. Abdu lit a match and used it to illuminate our way back down. We heard a familiar whistle as we got closer to the ground, and then a hysterical voice shouted, "But that's crazy, I can't marry you!"

Bea came up to me breathlessly. "Thank God you are alive! We thought you two fell off some mountain. And now something terrible has happened!"

"What's wrong?" I held on to my fraying threads of calmness.

"We were just kissing and this policeman saw us. He was disguised as a Bedouin and had followed us all the way and hid in the bushes while we were eating. Now he wants to take us to the police station, and Waheed insists we must get married to prove that he wasn't taking advantage of a helpless foreigner. But how can I just marry him just like that? I'm not even a Muslim!"

Waheed was clutching his forehead and muttering to himself in Arabic. I was mad at him for not keeping a tighter check on his libido and equally frustrated with Bea for not being more careful about amorous embraces in open view.

We scrambled into the back of the alleged police officer's truck while Abdu trailed behind in the jeep. Waheed kept clutching his head in both hands and shaking it back and forth. Upon reaching Dahab, I steeled myself for the impending trip to the nearest police station. Instead, the vehicles stopped at the beach, near the grass-hut nightclub, and our Arab hosts waved the officer a cheery good-bye.

"What's going on?" I nearly pushed Waheed down to the sand.

"Nothing." He had the sheepish look of a shoplifter caught red-handed.

"They probably paid him off to keep his mouth shut," Bea jumped in, having regained her usual composure.

Waheed did not dispute her conclusion, so I figured that this was indeed the case. A thought flashed through my mind that maybe the whole thing had been a setup, like those insurance scams that happen in the States. If so, I couldn't see how Waheed had benefited from the incident. There would be no trip to jail or walk down the aisle.

But the romance continued as we hung out in Dahab for another week and Waheed trailed after his Cleopatra like a lovesick puppy. He even proposed marriage again. Bea mulled it over, but she couldn't envision a lifetime of brewing espresso on the beach for sunburned tourists.

On our last evening, I surprised Bea by arranging a group excursion to Mount Sinai. A van full of hardy foreign backpackers honked outside Camp Bishbishi at midnight.

We began climbing by two in the morning with groups of pilgrims chanting and singing hymns. I got a sugar low halfway up and would have fainted if it weren't for a kind Frenchman who gave me some bread and jam. Bea had gone ahead, and I found her shivering at the summit by dawn. An eerie hush descended as we all waited for sunrise. Then I saw it, a wafer-thin line creasing the horizon. The sky swelled with yellow-orange streaks turning brighter and brighter. A carpet of mountains unfurled around us, glowing red fire. We snapped pictures to freeze a moment of eternity.

Jordan

Treading Water

Savages we call them,
because their manners differ from ours,
which we imagine to be the height of civility;
they think the same of theirs.

BENJAMIN FRANKLIN

Waheed insisted on seeing Bea and me off in style. We climbed into his Land Rover, leaving Dahab for the nearby seaport of Nuweiba, which appeared desolate save for the gleaming white catamaran berthed in the harbor. I shuffled toward the terminal with my astronaut luggage. Bea tried to lend a hand, but she was dragging her own weight with Waheed glued to her left arm, murmuring in her ear, and occasionally throwing her the pleading have-some-mercy look of a man sentenced to a firing squad.

The official at the ticket booth glanced at our passports and pointed out a separate building where we paid ($45 apiece) for the sea passage to Aqaba. A horn boomed from the catamaran. Waheed pledged his love to Bea one last time before we turned our backs and climbed aboard. It was a comfortable passage—an almost soundless slicing across the turquoise waters of the Gulf of Aqaba.

"Yordan, Yordan," a scruffy teenager selling Pepsi bottles out of a stained rucksack tapped my slumbering shoulder to signal our new port of call. A conga line of passengers inched toward the ship's gangplank. I sat as if welded in place, brooding over the loss of familiar faces now abandoned in Cairo and the supreme comfort that comes with having known a place and owning a small share in it.

"Missy stay on boat?" The Pepsi hawker was picking up candy wrappers and other waste strewn on the floor of the now-empty cabin. I couldn't help berating myself for having left Cairo too soon. Movement was foremost on my mind. The act of physically moving or displacing myself through time and space seemed to be integral to new discoveries. But now I wondered if there were two kinds of movements, one having to do with motion and the other with stillness. Perhaps if I had remained still in Cairo, I would have moved more.

There was moving to do all right. Bea stirred awake from her nap, her squinting, sleep-laden eyes making her look as reluctant as I felt to rise from my seat. "Come on, you," she mumbled.

We stepped outside into harsh sunlight. A pair of porters in slate-blue one-piece pajama suits were tossing luggage into a wheelbarrowlike contraption. Bea and I handed over our packs. An open-air bus ferried us to the arrival terminal. Even though I had secured my Jordanian visa in Cairo, it took Bea less time to receive a visa on the spot than for me to convince the immigration official that I already possessed one.

"To where you go?" he asked us in a mocking tone. We had been asking ourselves the same question for the last hour.

Two single females backpacking through the Middle East, for no motive other than pleasure, might as well wear sandwich boards advertising in bold letters the snickering clichés they endorsed. CAUTION! FLIRTING WITH DANGER. INNOCENTS ABROAD. HARBINGERS OF IMPENDING DISASTERS. Inoculation demands strong doses of common sense, a reptilian thick skin, and generous applications of spontaneity tempered with prudence. Bea and I were determined to rely on all of the above to map out the contours of our travels. We were beginning to realize that our gender proved advantageous in bringing out the protective side of locals, who were at first either horrified or simply amused at the sight of our enormous backpacks clunking with hiking boots and plastic water bottles. Bea, with her razor-sharp instincts, urged me to throw out my Lonely Planets. She claimed they made me analyze the journey rather than experience it. But I still clung to my precious guidebooks as safety kits in case we lost contact with the forces of serendipity.

As the last round of stamps pounded across our passports, I threw the officer a weak smile and rolled my eyes heavenward to indicate that someone else was in control of plotting our direction. Outside the terminal, taxi drivers prowled in a slow circle with their cabs, reminding me of eagles hunting for prey. One of them offered to drive us into town.

"Bikam?" I asked how much it would cost.

"As you wish."

The cabbie had brooding jade-colored eyes and appeared to be around our age.

"I take you to nice place on beach with fire and fish!" he volunteered in heavily accented English and produced a laminated business card with the logo of a busty mermaid.

I stared at the mermaid's cleavage, her yellow wavy hair, and considered the fire and fish. It seemed an offbeat destination for a first round of exploration in a new country. Another taxi approached, immediately dismissed by the green-eyed cabbie. He had made up his mind that we were his next customers. I glanced at Bea and she nodded in affirmation. Our packs were secured with a rope on the roof of a white Toyota Corolla serving as the taxi. We were off to Mermaid Camp.

An old man smelling of the sea was snoozing in a hammock next to a dying fire. He wore a khaki safari suit, and the panama straw hat shielding his face kept rising and lowering in tune with his heavy snores.

"Take no notice of him. He is always sleeping," bellowed a voice. It belonged to a tall, raffish-looking man with a New York Knicks cap and a plaid flannel shirt paired with frayed blue jeans. He inched toward us with the wary gait of a housecat in the open air.

"My name is Khalid. I am the owner of this place. So my brother brought you two here. He seems to have a way with the ladies. You have your pick of any of these tents." His arm swept a showy arc.

"We have dinner in an hour. The old man caught some fish today."

I liked Khalid's directness. Within minutes of our arrival, Bea and I were plopping down on two mattresses with tattered wool blankets—the sudden Spartan style made my Cairo apartment seem like a mansion. After a brief rest, we gathered around a sandpit of roasting fish and surveyed the new faces. Our host, Khalid, reincarnated as a modern-day sultan in J Crew attire, sprawled on cushions with a long-legged blonde curled under his arm. He spoke good English, having lived in a former life in America, where he had met his Minnesotan girlfriend, Karen, the girl under the arm playing footsie with him. The old man from the sea had disappeared into the kitchen and Ahmed, the taxi driver/brother, hunched in a corner, throwing furtive glances at Bea. We were the only guests at the camp.

I asked about the other travelers. Khalid threw back his head and laughed with scorn.

"They are afraid to come now. They think we are savages and terrorists, so they stopped coming. So many tourists before. Australians, Germans, French, Spanish, even Americans. I take many people to Wadi Rum and Petra. But now the season is dead. The intifada killed our business."

"Well, it didn't stop me from coming," I reminded him. "I am not afraid."

"Fear, what is fear?" he shouted. "If you fear life, you might as well stop living."

Khalid's words boosted my confidence. I felt more empowered that I had made a wise decision to abandon my fears and give in to my wanderlust. Though clearly, fear had seized most would-be travelers. One of the most popular destinations in the Middle East, Jordan had suffered a dearth of tourists after the September 2000 Palestinian uprising in the Occupied Territories. Rumors of Petra disguised as a ghost town defied credibility. And here in Aqaba, only locals appeared to frolic in one of the best diving spots in the world, with crystal waters rich with marine life. Encouraging serendipity to strike, I proposed to Khalid that he take us on a weeklong excursion to Wadi Rum. In Arabic, *wadi* means valley, and to be in Jordan and miss out on this particular *wadi* would be like visiting Arizona and skipping the Grand Canyon. Besides, Wadi Rum was desert territory, my favorite kind of place. Khalid whooped with joy and started planning our caravan.

Red-Earth Living

Three days later, the gang from Mermaid Camp—Khalid, Karen, Ahmed, and a heavily bearded man named Saba—were all set to accompany Bea and me to Wadi Rum. After cramming the back of a dusty pickup truck with essential supplies, we left Aqaba by midmorning. An hour later, we were already driving in the open desert. I hadn't realized its proximity to town. Saba, our designated driver, led us into a world of mulberry-colored sands and serrated cliffs that appeared like a third-grader's first attempt in art class to draw a landscape.

It was delicious to live in the open air again. We spread our blankets near the fire and talked in hushed whispers. That first evening, a bony old man visited our camp. He played a handmade violinlike instrument, coaxing out notes with a low, falling cadence. He sang ancient songs with a voice crackling like a fresh fire. When he was tired of singing, he would talk in halting English.

"My father know al-Lawrence! He come to Wadi Rum many time with Arab army."

"He was fine man al-Lawrence! He help Arab peoples. But he no win. He no strong."

Khalid was sitting nearby. I noticed him smirking and shaking his head. "Lawrence was a British officer. He was never one with the Arabs."

"But he was on their side, right?" I chimed in. "During the Arab revolt. Didn't he try to band the tribes together to defeat the Turks?"

"A masterful effort. And where did that get us in the end? Did we get the freedom we were promised? Those treacherous Brits let us down. End of story."

Khalid was getting worked up. I tried to get the old man to play some more music. But he was tired and trudged back to his camp.

Cool gusts of wind flapped the kaffiyeh wrapped around my head to keep away the fine sand particles that inevitably lodged in the skin's hidden crevices. After an early dinner, I lay flat on my back, mentally saluting the canopy of constellations that Lawrence must have gazed at in his time. It was amazing to think of the immense distance between me lying on the desert's surface and the stars above. I recalled my father telling me when I was a child that even the closest star was three to four light years away, the amount of time it took for light to travel from that star to my eyes. Then Dad would remind me of the speed of light, 186,000 miles per second. He shared my fascination about what was out there in the universe, what we could barely imagine, much less comprehend, beyond numbers.

As I looked back into time, three years or longer, I wondered if my father was lifting his head at the Seattle sky when he came home from work or if he was too tired to bother. I felt pangs of guilt for being so free, for no longer having the responsibility to go to an office and sit at a desk for eight hours or more a day and then repeat the pattern over and over. There never seemed to be enough time at home to do other things besides work. Even when I tried to find a balance, it was hard to sustain. And I had gotten so fed up with it that the only way out was to yank the cord and simply run away.

Was I still running? I didn't think so. I had learned in Egypt, especially during my time in the desert there, the impossibility of running away from myself. It simply couldn't be done. And as I thought of my dad and home that night in Wadi Rum, I knew that I would be returning with a different outlook, one that made me less anxious about getting trapped. I hoped that whatever lay in my future would make me embrace rather than resist change.

The next day, we drove farther into the desert to collect rocks. The ground here revealed less sand, but hard, red earth with beds of exposed minerals strewn about, a geologist's paradise. All around us, rocky walls, pockmarked with wind erosion, rose like skyscrapers. We saw rusty, amber-colored cliffs, their edges sometimes drooping like melting sheets of honey. We stopped for lunch near a rocky embankment, and I immediately raced off toward a bevy of arches. Khalid's girlfriend, Karen, who appeared to share my enthusiasm for climbing, followed. On my way, I found a rough stone with orange streaks and began grinding its edges to produce a fine red powder. Ecstatic with my discovery, I collected the residue in an empty photo canister. Later at our lunch spot, Bea and I had the gang hooting with laughter as we dabbed the powder on our cheeks and foreheads, looking frightful but playful in our Bedouin makeup.

Saba showed us how to make sandy bread. After he lit a fire, he scooped out some flour and moistened it with water to make a thick paste, adding a pinch of salt. He kneaded the dough into a thick disk and dropped it on a glowing bed of embers. Once the heat sealed the outside layer, our expert baker dug a hollow pit in the sand and buried the bread, piling on more hot sand and embers until they accumulated in a small dome. The bread cooked underneath this dome, and when it was done, Saba unearthed what looked like a charred pizza crust and brushed off the loose grit of sand and ash. He gave us each a piece that tasted both soft and crunchy. Then he made a salad of canned tuna, tomatoes, and yogurt that we mashed with our fingers, scooping up the mixture with thick slabs of bread and chunks of fresh onions.

Suddenly, from seemingly out of nowhere, a group of camels began to arrive on the scene, surfacing like sea creatures from out of the sand. At first, they came in pairs, two, four, six, and then dozens more emerged as silent spectators to our desert picnic. I asked Khalid if they were wild camels or part of a domesticated herd. He didn't really know, but he remarked upon the Bedouin love and respect for these magnificent animals. They symbolized patience. I was tempted to take pictures, but my camera remained untouched. The camels treaded gently over the landscape in slow motion. Perhaps they were not so much moving but floating with an immeasurable lightness. I detected an unmistakable sense of freedom in their movement that churned my senses with envy and fatigue.

As I continued to watch the wandering camels, I began to realize that my soul-search was not meant to be a plan to activate; it was an organic discovery, a by-product of my curiosity to be open and alert to people and places along the way. I was no longer as anxious about finding something to do to ground my travels. Spontaneity would be my only guide.

During nights, our camp became the meeting ground for some neighboring Bedouin men. Their mannerisms were more composed and guarded, almost mysterious, compared to the bubbly joviality of my Arab friends in Egypt. Upon arriving, the Bedouins draped themselves in regal poses on the woven straw mats we used as carpeting and silently appraised us with their intense dark eyes. Lest I take them for desert nomads, Khalid indicated their rather worldly lifestyles. He told me that one of the men had a German wife and another had a web-design business and led tours to Wadi Rum on the side. They all lived in town and drove SUVs and were used to hanging out with foreign tourists. It was nice to know that our Bedouin visitors had come out to the desert for the same reason as us, to unwind.

Dinner consisted of a communal pot of chicken stew, prepared by Saba, whose culinary skills raised his standing to that of the most valued member of the Camp Mermaid lot. The usual round of hot tea followed. Someone fired up a *nargileh* and passed it around. Ignoring the hygienic consequences of puffing from the same mouthpiece as a dozen strangers, I took the requisite drag. We sat around a large circle with a fire dancing in the middle.

Our Bedouin visitors apparently loved to sing. Their boisterous concert of what were most likely folk songs sounded rather raunchy, despite the incomprehensible lyrics. The men sang with a heated fervor, raising and lowering the guttural syllables and doubling over with laughter at the end. It was refreshing to be with people who did not take themselves too seriously. Bea and I chimed in with our own disjointed voices at the chorus and fell into a kind of trance as we repeated the same melody. After much eating, drinking, smoking, and singing, all the men suddenly rose to their feet.

Their movements exuded poise and controlled energy. The men were dancing not so much for their pleasure, but for *ours*. They were showing off their manliness in a desert version of Chippendales. And when they summoned Bea to join them, I scarcely knew what to expect.

She was dressed in one of their voluminous black robes that shrouded her from head to toe. A tight circle knitted around her. The Bedouins began shuffling their feet back and forth, clapping their hands, and growling in a way that barely sounded human. Bea held up a stick as though it were a mast underneath her covered figure and glided back and forth, her dancer's flair making her movements fluid and graceful. At one point she reminded me of a teepee on wheels. The gender divisions seemed to melt away, almost as if they were never there to begin with. It was all so nonchalant. The men lined up next to each other leaned toward Bea, the sound of their claps and growls harmonizing, then speeding up, faster and faster and faster.

I was surprised at Bea's composure. She didn't seem the least bit perturbed by the situation, as if it were second nature to her to be dancing in the desert darkness surrounded by a group of Bedouin men, enacting some sort of primitive ritual. My Aussie friend continued her shadow dance, hidden from view by the heavy material, yet somehow electrifying in her presence. The performance subsided when one of the men collapsed on the sand and asked for a glass of water. Bea lifted a corner of her robe and gave me a broad wink.

Later that night, alone with the stars and desert skies, I took out a flashlight and peered at my map of Jordan. Wadi Rum was no more than a tiny dot on its southern fringes. Having experienced the actual size and scope of that dot on the map gave me more perspective, a sense of inner satisfaction to know of an endless space where you can walk for five hundred meters and lose all sense of direction, a remote space closed by curtains of rosy red cliffs from the weight of the world, a simple space that stripped the bulkiness of life, if only for a moment.

Windows to the World

My favorite verse from the Quran reads, "We made you into different nations and tribes, so that you may know about one another." It has always made me aware of the importance of celebrating differences as a way to understand others and ourselves. And travel allows this to happen almost by necessity. Not only was I getting more and more adept at making friends with strangers, I was also starting to realize the value of these friendships as more than just random encounters that made me less lonely. My friends were cultural windows to another world that was no longer abstract, but that was an intricate tapestry whose textures and colors I was getting to touch, feel, smell, hear, and see up close. And it was this sensory knowledge of living in a culture and among its people that allowed for real meaning. It was the traveler's privilege, even a blessing, to come away from a place and know its moods and shapes with a far deeper intimacy than the most passionate scholar with an encyclopedia in his head or the pundits whose expertise, for all its sanctified authority, may not necessarily measure up to the immediacy of eyewitness accounts.

Bea and I had set up a new base in the Jordanian capital of Amman. Though only three hundred miles east of Cairo, it seemed to be in a completely different hemisphere, given the decidedly mellower characteristics that made me wonder if the place had been sedated and told to behave itself. Part of this might have to do with Amman's vertically stacked layout on seven hills. Bea and I were staying in a budget hotel at the lower rungs of society in what the Jordanians referred to as Downtown Amman.

Here we could eat dinner for less than $1 and buy Marlboros at wholesale prices from Bedouin women squatting on the sidewalks with their makeshift cardboard shops. One of them was an elderly grandmother with elaborate face tattoos. She had added to her collection of cigarettes a medley of chunky tribal jewelry draped on a strip of cloth. Her helper was a teenage daughter, who doled out change while breastfeeding her baby boy. Just as we were leaving their little pavement shop, the young mother asked me for some American nail polish.

If we chose, we could have also climbed into the hills to upgrade our existence to Safeway, McDonald's, and Pizza Hut and mingle with rich, Ivy League–educated Arabs who wore Diesel jeans and drove shiny imported cars complete with GPS and Dolby acoustics. But we preferred the scruffier reality of Downtown, with the little boys peddling bread and cake from trays perched on their heads, and the roadside juice stalls where a cocktail of fresh kiwis, oranges, and bananas accompanied mournful discussions on the latest crisis in the Occupied Territories next door. The intifada escalated in intensity every day, and the Arab media pulled no punches in their coverage of Israeli brutalities and American compliance.

"How would your neighbors back in *Amrikiya* feel if their homes were bulldozed in the middle of the night?" Some of the old Palestinian refugees asked us this when we sat next to them in the broom-closet-size juice bar and sipped our fruit cocktails every morning. One of the men showed me his house key, worn like a locket around his rubbery neck. His eyes were numb with pain.

Some days, I got the impression that we weren't really doing anything in Jordan. But I didn't mention this to Bea because I knew she wouldn't agree. By the time we had left Egypt, it was already clear to me that Bea couldn't care less if we had an action plan or not. And unlike me, Bea wouldn't have gone on a guilt trip for "wasting" time nor would she care to justify her wanderlust by asking for structure and productivity. I envied Bea for this. While I didn't intend our Jordanian foray to be nearly as intense as my Cairo immersion, I still wanted things to happen, things that would teach me cultural lessons and deepen self-knowledge. Bea wanted the same, as does almost every other traveler. The crucial difference between Bea and me was how she didn't demand changes, she just let them evolve. I couldn't figure out her secret, but a part of me was convinced that my friend must have been a Buddhist monk in a former life, because she was always so calm and unperturbed, as if her mind had never known the taint of doubts or misgivings.

"Now don't you feel better?"

Bea was asking the obvious. She had succeeded in making me do what I should have done months earlier—shedding my baggage in the most literal sense of getting rid of some stuff I had been lugging around for more than half a year. I had emptied out all the contents of my humongous pack that, according to Bea, weighed more than I did. Two piles were on the floor, one for the absolute essentials, the other for the throwaways. It had to be done, and since we had nothing better to do in

Amman, at least not yet, this is how we spent our evenings in our hotel room. Bea seemed to have mastered the art of traveling light, one of her many practical skills that I was sorely lacking. And I was also glad that she was a light sleeper, unlike me, who would have dozed through an earthquake.

One morning, Bea woke me up and claimed that someone had been in our room the night before. We couldn't be entirely sure since nothing was missing, but she was convinced she had heard keys jangling and seen the shadow of a man near her bed.

"You were just dreaming," I said.

"I'm sure I wasn't," she countered. "Someone was there and it gave me the creeps."

"Let's not dwell on that," I said. "If it happens again, we will move to another hotel."

"What do we do in the meantime?"

"We look for some breakfast!"

We wandered about and stumbled upon a no-name café just around the block from the hotel. It was run by Iraqi immigrants and appeared to be a local watering hole where men drank strong cardamom-scented coffee and burrowed their heads inside Arabic newspapers for the greater part of the day. Not a single woman was in sight, but a waiter immediately cleared a discreet corner table where Bea and I sat down to a hearty platter of hard-boiled eggs, olives, and salty white cheese. Sometimes, the men around us would break out in excited discussions, banging their fists on the table and challenging their opponents in a game of verbal Ping-Pong. A small tea cart stood just outside the café entrance where a sweet-faced man ladled milky-brown concoctions into thick glasses. I caught his eye, and he came over with two steaming beverages.

"My name is Amer." He extended his hand and sat down at our table. "Your breakfast, it is good?"

"Delicious!" Bea responded.

Amer smiled as he held her gaze. "You are nice girl with clean heart."

I liked the way he put it so simply. Bea murmured some thanks and went back to her eggs.

"First time I see you, I think you are my sister. You look so much like her. Here, see picture."

He took out his wallet and showed us a black-and-white passport photo of a twentysomething girl who did bear an uncanny resemblance to Bea.

As we ate, Amer told us that he worked six odd jobs around the city to make enough money to send home to his family in Baghdad. His father's death had forced him to quit his engineering studies. When I asked Amer if he wanted to go back to Iraq, his eyes welled in tears and he scuttled back to his cart.

The café became a morning fixture for a week, mostly because of Amer, who came to be known as our kindhearted tea merchant for refusing to accept any money from us. It would have violated his code of honor and pride. Sometimes he would help me decipher the crumpled Arabic news magazine spread across the table. But I preferred to listen to Amer than to read the daily headlines.

He often launched into monologues that sounded rehearsed, as if he had practiced them over and over in private conversations with himself. Amer talked about his sister. It turned out that she had married an Englishman and gone to live in London. But she was not happy. I asked Amer why. He rocked his head from side to side, eyes fixed on his fingernails.

"My sister no like England. She find small job but not same like Iraq. In Iraq she have mother, sister, brother for nice talk and laugh. She miss family too much. She say family more important than money and big house."

"Doesn't she have any friends?" Bea asked.

"Friends in England not same as home. They are too much busy. They do only job."

"But you still want to go to America?" I asked. "To find work?"

"It is my wish. Maybe come true, maybe not."

He mopped his forehead with a checkered black-and-white kaffiyeh draped around his neck.

"America good country. People very kind. I go there to speak good English. Maybe I get job to wash dishes in American restaurant. I work very hard. You help me, please?" Amer fixed his gaze on me as if I were a fairy godmother.

I felt bad not knowing what to say, not being able to do anything besides just listen to a man pining for a better life, vacillating on the jagged edges of hope and despair. The manager frowned when Amer was away from his tea cart for too long a stretch. Customers grew impatient for more *shai*. Amer resumed his post behind the little cart. I watched him brewing his beverage with Zenlike mindfulness.

Peekaboo

Though Bea grew up in Australia, her ethnicity was Italian and South American. I would never forget the exact moment I had laid eyes on her in the Paris hostel. She had been sleeping in the bunk below mine, and I had climbed down from my bed early one morning to fetch a glass of water. Then I saw her lying awake, her hair a tumble of black waves, her silky nightie exposing creamy smooth alabaster skin. Even before I knew her name, I was instantly taken with her high forehead and wide-set dark eyes, her long neck, chiseled nose, and full lips; they were all so perfectly proportioned. As we got to know each other in Europe, I had a feeling that Bea's physical beauty would be a distinct advantage if and when we ever traveled together. Men (and women) would be drawn to her like flies, and we would hardly lack for company or attention. She had already left one smitten Waheed back in Sinai. And now in Amman, Bea was the talk of town as soon as she donned the head scarf.

I hadn't encouraged nor discouraged her from wearing one. But as soon as she had arrived in Cairo, Bea had taken to the *hijab* for the purpose of blending in, and not only did she blend in, but she looked downright stunning in the veil. This had consequences every time we set foot outside our Amman hotel.

For starters, the men's eyes were glued to our faces (or more precisely Bea's). The men would audaciously walk ahead of us and turn around to steal another glance. Not only men but women were intrigued by my friend's looks. Many of them would ask her if she were Arab because her sharply drawn Latin features fringed with the head scarf made her appearance disconcertingly Middle Eastern, more so than mine. Most of the time no one would believe that Bea was a foreigner, and I stifled a laugh knowing full well how that felt.

One day, Bea and I tried a little experiment. We walked out with our heads uncovered, but this produced no difference in the local stare-athon. It was the very opposite of the austere anonymity I was used to from the States and Europe, where people didn't gawk at you in the streets unless you gave them good reason to, and even then, it was nothing more than a curious turn of the head and then it was back to doing their own business. Here in Amman, public scrutiny by a group of attentive fans was a bit of a nuisance, but also rather touching. I figured they were just trying to say, "Yes, you are here and your presence matters." Bea's attitude was even simpler. Instead of being a Nobody back home, a woman could feel like a Hollywood celebrity for a day by strolling along the streets of Downtown Amman.

The old Roman amphitheater was our favorite afternoon hangout. Tourists drifted in and out, climbing around the perimeter and shouting at each other in a linguistic stew of German, Japanese, Spanish, French, Italian, and American slang.

The old security guard welcomed Bea and me on our frequent trips to the theater as if we were estranged family. *"Ahlan wa sahlan, ahlan wa sahlan!"*

Offerings of tea, biscuits, and oranges appeared from his small caretaker's cottage near the gated entrance. He warned us to keep away from teenage hustlers and freelance tour guides parading around the theater. I had seen them in their leather jackets and gel-slicked hair. They didn't seem inclined to wage jihad against America so much as be consumed by its mystique.

"Hey there!"

A cute teenage girl approached us. She shoved a camera into my hand and asked me to photograph her group of friends. I got into the act and ran up and down the steep stairs as if doing a photo shoot for an Arabic version of *Vogue*. The girls needed no encouragement to show off their poses in front of the gathering male audience. One of them crossed her legs, allowing the slit in her ankle-length skirt to reveal a shapely calf with fashionable tights in a herringbone pattern. Her dark sunglasses slipped to the tip of her nose, and she puckered her lips as I snapped the shutter.

"Take some more, more!" the teenage girl shouted from the top of the stairs.

I finished off the roll as she made her way down and retrieved her Minolta.

"Thanks for the pics. They'd better be good!"

She reached into her shirt pocket and took out a tube of lip balm, uncapped it, and rolled it on her lips. I noticed her purple paisley bandanna and frayed blue jeans.

"So, what are you guys doing here? Are you teachers or something? I kinda thought you might be folks from one of the embassies. But you don't look the type. You guys seem way too mellow."

Her accent was so authentic. If I simply closed my eyes and listened to her, I would have thought she was a Valley Girl. It turned out I wasn't so far off the mark.

Her name was Leila. She was transplanted to Jordan when her parents moved back. Before that, she had lived in Calabasas, California, in Los Angeles County for ten years and gone to an American high school. Leila had played on the girls' soccer team and driven down to Baja on weekends. She missed watching *Oprah*.

"It must be a big change for you to live here," I managed to say.

"Yeah, it was pretty scary at first. I mean I couldn't go out by myself anymore. I had to be chaperoned by my cousins and aunties. We live up in the hills, which is not that different from the States. Well, it's not quite the same but I could handle it okay. Then I *really* wanted to go back to L.A. to see my friends again. But my dad wouldn't let me go. He wanted me to stay here to learn about the culture and all that crap. He refused to pay for my plane ticket and even took away my passport. I was pretty pissed. We fought about it *all* the time. He started freaking out every time I watched *Friends*. He didn't want me to be contaminated by American culture anymore. So he got real strict. Not like back in L.A. He was *real* cool there. I got away with tons of stuff. But here I can't do much. It's been two years now. And I got no other place to go."

Leila winced and smiled at the same time. She sat down on the stone stairs and tucked her legs sideways.

"Well, Jordan is not so bad. I mean surely you can have fun here and not feel so restricted," Bea said. "Look at us. We are traveling around by ourselves and so far, so good."

"Yeah, but it's different for you guys. You don't live here. You're not Arab. So you're not accountable in the same way that I am. You guys are considered foreigners. You can skip the rules that we can't. It's not the same."

"Do you think all foreigners are the same?" I asked.

"Sure, why not?"

"I don't think so," I countered.

Bea raised her brows as if to prevent me from starting an argument, an argument I would most likely not win with somebody such as Leila, whose upper-class upbringing gave her license to wear whatever she liked, including tight jeans and *hijab*less hair. It was rather funny that Bea and I were dressed far more conservatively than Leila was, though we were the foreigners who apparently had no rules to observe. Were we making a big deal for nothing, wearing loose garments and covering our hair, making all this effort to blend in when we didn't really have to? I couldn't be sure if it was a matter of cultural respect or a dogged determination to obscure our foreign status and perhaps transform ourselves as different people, to play up the illusion that travel affords in inventing a brand-new self. Maybe it was a combination of all those factors.

Leila was scribbling something in a notebook. It turned out to be a website for an online dating service. "It's my own business," she announced. "Now I just have to get people to sign up. But my cousins are afraid. They don't want to end up with some goon who looks like Freddie Krueger!"

"That's a fantastic idea. Do you really think it will take off?" Bea asked.

"Sure it will! I'm not doing anything wrong. It's just a way for guys and girls to meet and check each other out. How else will they ever get married?!"

I told Leila about the marriage ads in Indian and Pakistani cultures. These were serious proposals emphasizing academic degrees and skin colors.

Leila laughed. "Let me tell you guys something." She leaned her face closer to ours. "The girls here are not as goody-goody as they look."

"Is that right?" Bea and I both chimed in.

"They just do everything in secret." Leila said. "That's what I can't stand. The sneaking around. The lying. The deception."

"But isn't that normal?" Bea asked. "That's what happens when people have trouble accepting change."

"BCD," I pitched in.

"What's that?" Leila and Bea chorused.

"Behind Closed Doors."

"And what does that mean?"

"That's what people do in Pakistan," I replied. "Well, not everyone. Only the ones who can afford it, the rich upper crust. They drink and party and do whatever the hell they want. And no one can say anything because they have immunity."

"Money talks!" Bea said.

Leila giggled. "I'm gonna stir things up!"

Cultural Diplomats

Few of us would have the urge to travel to foreign destinations if we claimed to know it all. Even if we do know a thing or two, travel allows us the opportunity to test that knowledge, to see how much of it is true or not. Before I traveled to the Middle East, I had preconceived notions about what the people would be like. It couldn't be helped, since neutrality is not my strongest suit. Despite all my better judgment, I was equipped with biases. For one thing, I hadn't realized that the East wouldn't be distinctly East but an amalgam of Eastern and Western influences.

One day, Bea and I slipped into a bohemian-looking café with a rather creative menu in English meant to accommodate English-speaking, non-Arab patrons who were not expected to take the trouble to become acquainted with the local language. Customers could have their choice of "mashed potatoes cornered by yellow cheese," "pearls of couscous chased by bold tomatoes," "wicked eggs," or "dainty fish cutlets cooked over a fine fire."

Not in the mood for taking any chances with wicked eggs or dainty fish, we simply ordered cheese toast and *shai bin sukur,* or sugarless black tea. A duo of fresh-faced college boys eyed us from a corner table. The duo dodged my gaze, but I caught one of the two repositioning his chair for a better look when he thought we were not aware. They kept shifting their heads up and down, pretending not to let us know that we were the object of their attention. Paying for our food, Bea and I left the café and strolled down the main Downtown thoroughfare on our way to mail some postcards. Our admirers tailed us about a half block back. I quite liked their perseverance.

They were waiting for us when we came out of the post office.

"'Scuse me," said the tall one with black curly locks.

He rolled his head in circles and fiddled with his shirt collar as if trying to work up his nerve.

"Err. . . ." Another roll of the head. "Can we eat you?"

Bea and I exchanged smiles.

The request was clarified. "You like chicken *shawarma?*"

Having already eaten, we declined the *shawarma*, though it was bound to be tasty stuff, and settled for some coffee instead. In the next instant, the four of us piled into a taxi and headed into the hills high above Amman. The café occupied the ground floor of a modern high-rise. It had the look and feel of the corner Starbucks back home. We all ordered cappuccinos and waited for the scintillating conversations to begin.

"You are from where?"

"America."

"Australia."

"You are tourists?"

"Well, not exactly," Bea responded. "We are just traveling around. You know, seeing the sights, getting to know the people."

"You mean like cultural diplomacy!" Salim, the shorter of the duo, with a stronger grasp of English, coined the phrase. "It is so sad. Americans know so little about our culture, and we know little about yours except what we see on TV."

"Well, not every day in the States is like a scene in *Baywatch.*" I tried to steer him away from the one-sided views he must be receiving.

Salim wasn't buying it. He rattled off his favorite episodes of *Baywatch* and asked me how many times I had roller-skated on Venice Beach. In addition to *Baywatch,* he was also a fan of Joey, Rachel, Phoebe, Ross, Chandler, and Monica, talking about the made-up lives of *Friends* as if they were his very real next-door neighbors.

I had the sudden urge to hire Salim as the spokesperson of American public diplomacy to win Muslim hearts and minds.

"The other day in the chat room, this girl from Texas asked me how many camels I had and if I slept in a tent. I mean does she really think I'm sitting here on my own camel sending her instant messages?" Salim turned to me with a pained expression.

"Do you realize that the things that interest that Texan girl sound as ridiculous to you as your impressions of America based on a few TV shows sound to me?"

"It is so sad. There is ignorance on both sides. I see it at university whenever we have visiting foreign students. They are expecting to live like Bedus in the desert. They find it hard to believe that we have highways and mobile phones with GSM technology, even better than the ones you have in USA!"

He had missed my point. The issue for him was U.S. ignorance of Arabs. Arab ignorance of the United States was not so important. The spokesperson was hereby fired.

"But how can anyone change their attitudes if they don't know any better?" Bea jumped in. "I mean if it hadn't been for my Lebanese friends back in Sydney, I would be just as clueless about the Mideast as your friend in Texas. But I certainly wouldn't judge the entire place based on what I saw on the nightly news. That's just buying into propaganda!"

"Exactly!" Salim banged a fist on the table.

A tall blonde with smoky green eyes sashayed by our table. She wore leather pants and a halter top. The boys stared hard. Bea and I stared harder.

"That's how the girls dress in Beirut!" Salim said knowingly. "You won't need your *hijab* there!"

His friend with the inventive English cleared his throat. "Err. . . . My name is Ali. Please, may I say something?"

"Shoot," I said.

He looked confused. "You want me to shoot? But why?"

I laughed. "Shoot also means 'go ahead.' So go ahead."

Ali cleared his throat again. I couldn't really understand what he was trying to say, but he got more excited, and then he pointed to a newspaper ad featuring a bearded, half-naked Tom Hanks. Ali was a big fan of the famous American actor, and he wanted to see *Castaway*, his latest film playing in Amman. It would be an "experience" to see Hanks marooned on a tropical island. Upon learning I was from Seattle, Salim mentioned how much he had enjoyed *Sleepless in Seattle*. Wasn't that also with Tom Hanks? And who else? Oh, yes, Meg Ryan. She was one of his favorites. I told him I had liked her in *When Harry Met Sally*. He hadn't seen it, but he jotted down the title in his little black book.

It was hardly surprising that they harbored so much curiosity and interest toward America, in spite of the sensationalists and fearmongers who brand Arabs and Muslims as anti-Western. With their mobile phones and web chats, our Jordanian friends were clearly steeped in a globalized world. They were living proof that Islam and the West were not so diametrically opposed. Yet the stereotypes persisted on both ends.

I thought of the U.S. news stories on the Middle East I had often seen. They inevitably included footage of Muslims in prayer, usually men, accompanied by snippets of the muezzin's call. Even when the story had nothing to do with religion, it emphasized religion. And this incessant depiction of communal devotion conveyed the impression that the only thing Muslims do in their waking lives is engage in religious rituals. This alienating depiction portrayed Muslims as strange people with odd habits and reinforced their differences from the average non–Muslim American. The media never seemed to mention collegiate Jordanians partial to Hollywood blockbusters. There was not even a hint of the Yassers and Mohammads of the world, who not only prayed but also worried about job security, doctors' bills, and saving up for college tuition. Were they not meant to exist or was their existence not meant to be publicized?

"So what's the first thing you would like to do in America?" I changed the subject.

"See a baseball game," Salim responded right away.

"I want to meet real American cowboys!" Ali replied with a giddyap motion.

Bea and I declined to see Tom Hanks. He might have ruined further adventures.

Thank You for Your Emotions

Sometimes, the urge to be a tourist creeps up like the slow-burn guilty pleasure of devouring an entire pint of Häagen-Dazs in one sitting. It's easy, available, and beckoning, so why not go for it? As travelers, we feel the burden of responsibility. We want to find places that no one else has presumably seen, to seek the truth (whatever that means), to stretch ordinary experiences into tales of epic adventure. In general, we like to take ourselves far too seriously, and I admit no shame in being a culprit. For some reason, Jordan did not inspire the traveler in me. I didn't feel any deep emotions, any mind-shattering revelations during the two weeks we were there. It was as if Bea and I were migratory birds, resting ashore before flying off to new lands. One day, we decided to wing our way to the Dead Sea.

Having declined the invitation to go there on a guided excursion with some German tourists from our hotel earlier in the morning, we were now left to our own devices. I had remained firm in my resolve to stay away from group tours, having had my fill in the feluccas and tombs of Upper Egypt. Besides, I did not think it would be too difficult to find our own way to such a well-known locale in a country as small as Jordan. Bea was in full agreement. When it came to the logistics of getting to and from places, she valued adventure over convenience. I couldn't have found a more ideal travel companion.

The hotel manager told us to go by minibus. When I asked him which one, he shrugged and upturned both palms in the air before getting reabsorbed in the soccer match on TV. We walked outside the hotel and drank our usual cocktails at the juice stand. When I thumbed through my guidebook and uttered the words "Bahar al Mayyit" to indicate Dead Sea in Arabic, the man behind the counter scribbled some directions on a napkin. Following his squiggly letters and arrows, we took a taxi and got off near a busy traffic roundabout. A fleet of minivans came and went every few minutes. We hopped on one rather indiscriminately.

It was full of local families and some Bedouin men carrying live chickens in their bare hands. They all scrutinized us in that manner of intense curiosity that often made me feel like a specimen in a petri dish. I repeated "Bahar al Mayyit" to the driver. He nodded and motioned for us to take a seat in the fully packed vehicle. We squished ourselves into the narrow aisle. I leaned against a rolled-up carpet, tall enough to hide the identity of its owner. Bea sat in the lap of a grinning toothless lady who was trying to look comfortable. The bus careened forward and dipped into a low valley. Both my ears clogged up. About half an hour later, the minibus driver vaguely pointed his finger in the direction of the sun and halted on the roadside to let us off. The Dead Sea was nowhere in sight.

A thick patch of needlelike bushes extended along the edge of the two-lane road like a protective wall. We walked straight ahead, inches away from the steady stream of vehicles whizzing by at breakneck speeds. The late-afternoon sun duly heading west indicated the sea to be on our right, just beyond the bushes, but there appeared to be no pathway to reach it. So we cut through the bushes.

"Ouch!"

Bea dislodged the nasty thorns from the back of my thin cotton pants.

"I wish we had gone with those Germans," I mumbled, sucking at the blood oozing from my thumb. "Are you sure this is the right way?"

"Sure it is!" Bea's enthusiasm remained undeterred. "I can see some water up ahead."

I peered at the horizon. It yielded a gray sliver of nothingness through a spindle of spiky desert plants.

"But where is the mud? I don't see any mud."

I wanted to look like the creature from the Black Lagoon, coating my body with the therapeutic minerals of the famous Dead Sea mud that I had last seen advertised in a swanky Parisian spa. Here we could have the real thing at no cost.

We continued to pick our way through the bushes until a clearing emerged. Bea and I staggered onto a patch of sand curbing the mass of a comatose sea lying straight ahead. It was the color of a pigeon's gray wing.

"Well, look at that. We finally made it," I gushed with relief.

We removed our shoes and approached the shoreline. Gentle waves cruised back and forth in their eternal rhythm and we sat down to watch them.

"Look, Bea. The sea is breathing," I remarked.

My friend, who had grown up along the beaches of Sydney, smiled. "It feels good to be near water again. I hate being landlocked."

"Me too. Water is so liberating. Like the desert with its wide, open spaces. Just you and the elements."

"Hmm. That's going a bit far. I mean you didn't come all this way to be alone, did you?"

"Of course not. But I can't stand routine. That's why I wanted to leave home. It was getting too predictable."

"But you can't live your entire life jumping from place to place just to keep it new and exciting. At some point you have to build stability and find a home base," Bea said.

"I do want that. But I'm still searching for a place to put down some roots. Maybe that's why I started this journey," I mumbled to myself.

"So what do you do in the meantime? Until you find this Shangri-la of yours?" Bea probed.

"I guess I keep afloat. Kind of like treading water."

"But you can't even swim!" Bea burst out, quelling her laughter so I wouldn't get offended.

"Why does that have to matter? I tread water in my own whirlpool of thoughts. It gets hard to keep up sometimes."

"Well, I guess you could say that, in a manner of speaking."

"Thank you, my dear. Now let's do some more exploring."

We walked farther along the shore and noticed a cabanalike area where men and women were sunning oiled bodies on chaise lounges and sipping drinks. A few walked around in white bathrobes.

"So that's the main entrance. The driver should have left us off there," I said, somewhat peeved.

"Yeah, but look around. They all seem to be foreigners," Bea pointed out.

Suddenly, I was glad that we weren't with them, though we clearly belonged to the same group. A few yards ahead, some Arab men were enjoying a barbecue picnic, lacing food on skewers and holding them in the flames of a beach fire.

"Don't talk to them," Bea whispered in my ear. "Just walk quickly without looking their way."

We were halfway across their line of sight when the cutest and youngest member of the group came up holding out a plate of smoky chicken kebabs. "For you. Please join us. We have plenty of food."

A trio of smiling faces echoed the invitation and gestured us to come forward. They were all cousins from Amman playing hooky from school. We described our trip in the minibus and our encounter with the thorny bushes. This drew raised eyebrows of admiration, as if audacity alone were a triumph.

"Just like Indiana Jones!" little Ali exclaimed, popping the air with an imaginary pistol.

When I whined about wanting the famous Dead Sea mud, one of the cousins led me by the hand toward the water's edge, where he scooped up chunks of gooey black stuff and dabbed it on my face.

"Close your eyes. It is very salty." He proceeded to slap my cheeks softly as I began to relax and enjoy this unexpected facial with a complete stranger.

Once again, I marveled at the ease of making friends in such far-flung posts of the world. It was getting to be a habit, and since I was not accustomed to such effortless ways in forging friendships back home, I suddenly felt like the class nerd who had turned cheerleader overnight.

"My name is Abbas," he said softly, and I could feel his intense gaze even with eyes screwed shut.

"Okay, you are free now," he murmured, and I stared into a pair of coffee-brown eyes framed with huge horn-rimmed glasses.

"We should go see the others. They must be waiting."

Squeals of laughter greeted my black gooey face. No one could fathom why someone from America would come all the way to Jordan to play with some dirt.

Bea snapped a close-up of my mask and pointed out a group of local women floating in the sea fully clothed. "I don't think your mud bath will go any farther south!"

Based on the mounds of black fabric surrounding the women like a silky parachute, I had to agree.

"Who wants to go swimming?" The cousins were stripping down to their swim trunks, revealing slim brown bodies and chests matted with soft dark hair like bird feathers.

"I can't swim!" I said.

Bea rolled her eyes and reminded me of the salt content of the Dead Sea.

"There is no way you can drown. Not even if you try."

She had worn her kaffiyeh as a sarong and knotted her T-shirt, under which I could still make out the straps of her lime-green bikini top. Our head scarves were nowhere in sight.

Abbas came up and took my hand. "Do not be afraid. I will show you how to float."

The rest of the gang were already bobbing like human corks. A blazing sunset etched their silhouettes in champagne-colored light.

"*Yallah!*" I gingerly approached the water. It had the warmth of a tepid bath that was about four hundred meters below sea level and the lowest point on earth. I waded farther until my skirt plastered around my hips like wet clay.

Abbas cradled his head behind his arms and floated nearby. "It is easy. Just throw yourself back. Come on. I will catch you."

But I couldn't do it. The water felt heavy as lead, but when I tried to lean back against its magnetic pull and my feet started losing contact with the ground, I would panic and abort the movement. Even if I did let go and allow my body's natural buoyancy to take over, I couldn't figure out how it would be possible to stand upright again. My only claim to fame is a probable listing in some almanac of underachievers as the only person in the world unable to float in the Dead Sea.

Hussein, a lanky nineteen-year-old with matinee-idol looks who had gone to school in Saudi Arabia and looked a bit princely, pointed out Israel just on the other side of the shore. I asked him if anyone had ever managed to swim across.

"It is not impossible," he said, then added, dark eyes flickering dangerously, "but they would shoot you these days for even trying."

I threw a glance at Bea floating on her back with closed eyes. A crowd of onlookers had gathered on the beach; the women appeared to be snickering and pointing fingers at us. It was the same bunch we had seen earlier frolicking in the water in their flowing robes. Judging from their open-mouthed gapes, our modest bathing attire did not meet the benchmark for decent public exposure.

Back on land, the boys changed into dry clothes in the fading light. I couldn't find any traces of the live studio audience, members of which had probably rushed back home to entertain family members with scandalous stories of wet T-shirts and other X-rated horrors. They certainly would have had a fright at the sight of me sitting in Abbas's lap in the cramped little Volkswagen. I think he was more embarrassed about it than I was. His face flushed a deep pink during the entire ride back to Amman. We stopped at a posh hotel to clean up. A lobby of well-heeled Arabs nearly fainted in shock at the sight of my mud-streaked clothes and greasy tangled hair as I headed straight for the nearest washroom.

It was not the first time I realized the importance of class in Middle Eastern society as *the* crosscutting definer of all social interactions. This cultural aspect remains severely underestimated in the Western media's one-dimensional depictions of veiled Muslim women and bearded mullahs. The hotel guests who balked at my peasant skirt and flip-flops probably had more in common with East Coast bluebloods than with the downtrodden underside of Jordanian society to which we clearly belonged. It did little to bolster my confidence when Ali, who had lost one of his shoes, was hobbling on one foot in the lobby with holes in his T-shirt.

Half an hour later, we were back in Downtown Amman, just in time for dinner at the local KFC, where a steady trickle of local families dined on Colonel Sanders chicken wings. Hussein ordered a generous round of chicken drumsticks, french fries, and Coca-Colas.

"That's funny. I didn't think you ate so much junk food here," I said in some surprise. Our friends guffawed and stuck out their bellies to show the effects of globalization and multinationals.

"If you think we eat falafels and hummus all day, think again," said Hussein. "We are not living in the Stone Age anymore."

"But falafels and hummus are so delicious here! Why on earth would you want to eat garbage such as that?" I pointed to a tub of greasy french fries.

"It tastes pretty good to me. Here, take some more chicken."

Clearly, the forces of globalization had entrenched roots in both West and East, the only difference being that the East did not benefit from the luxurious timeline of adaptation the Western world had enjoyed. Out here, globalization appeared like a fast and furious thunderstorm during an August heat wave. It appeared in the form of four-wheel-drive Land Rovers parked outside Bedouin tents in the middle of the desert; it wound its way into the altering palates of Hussein and company, stripped clean of their hummus pedigree.

We finished off the evening by heading to some mineral hot springs just outside the city. This time I didn't have to sit in Abbas's lap, but we were still squashed together in the back seat of the car. I asked him what he did for a living.

"I am a low-level engineer," he said.

"Well, I'm sure you'll get promoted," was all I could say.

Abbas smiled ruefully. "It is not so easy. Many of my friends are depressed. They have university degrees but they cannot find jobs. The Jordanian economy is suffocating their hopes. I had one friend. He was very smart but he was also very angry. He started going to this mosque and joined a political Islamist group. He thought it was a way to get back the honor that Muslims and Arabs have lost."

It turned out that Abbas had tried out one of these groups. He was luckier than his friend, who had volunteered as a suicide bomber and succeeded. Abbas came to his senses and dropped out when the group started getting too radical. I asked him to explain.

"They wanted me to stop shaving and throw away my jeans. It was getting to be a cult. I was starting to lose my mind. But remember this," he added. "Extremism is not just unique to Muslim countries. It is the result of negative conditions in society. Look at Russia before the Bolshevik Revolution. It was in chaos because of social problems."

"So we need another Islamic revolution?" I asked. "Like what happened in Iran?"

"I'm not saying that."

"Then what?"

Abbas tensed up. "We need something. I just don't know what it is."

I recalled similar conversations with Yasser back in Cairo. He often talked about Islam's "Double Curse," in which extremist Muslim ideologues justified brutality in the name of religion, thereby bolstering suspicion and alarm against Islam. The pluralistic, compassionate, tolerant attributes of the faith fell by the wayside. They didn't even seem to matter, much less exist, as the Muslim/Arab world gained publicity in the West only when a car bomb exploded or some fanatic gunned down another innocent civilian. According to Yasser, there were many different types of Islam in the Arab world. There was Islam as a spirit. Then there was the Islam made by governments and mullahs. There was an Islam of the poor and desperate. And there was also Islam as a power trip. I wondered where Abbas would eventually find a balance in this spectrum.

We arrived at the hot springs. At midnight the place was packed with rowdy teenage boys showing off their buff bods to their female friends decked out in low-cut swimsuits, a glaring contrast to the starchy marms who had sneered at our heathen ways on the beach just a few hours back. The bewildering range of conduct according to dress and mannerisms among Arab women never ceased to astound until I reminded myself that it was mostly a function of class, under which system the wealthier set could afford exemption from tradition. But I didn't have to come all the way to Jordan, or anywhere else in the Middle East for that matter, to know this.

I had been acutely aware of class differences ever since my childhood in Pakistan, where my best friend in school was a hip eleven-year-old who spent summer vacations in London and knew how to groove to "Staying Alive." Her parents threw swanky parties where the women wore sleeveless blouses and the men drank beer. They employed a crew of servants, and whenever I visited their house, it was impossible to fetch even a glass of water without someone handing it to me. On the other end of the scale, I was also friends with my baby sitter's daughter, who donned the burqa in public and wouldn't dream of wearing makeup. So I had grown up presuming that class had a lot to do with the way Muslims responded to religious and cultural practices, including the way they dressed.

Some of the brassier kids catcalled us until Hussein threatened to bash their brains on the rocks. I hitched up my skirt and waded in the moonlit mineral waters. Curls of hot mist plowed the air, making it feel like that of a Buddhist shrine. Bea was lying flat in the shallow pool with reams of her jet-black hair spread out like a peacock's feathers. Ali had crept up behind and started raking his fingers through them, exuding a sensuality far too mature for a ten-year-old. I caught a glimpse of Abbas chain-smoking in a dark corner, trying hard not to look in our direction.

On our way back from the hot springs, we were serenaded with the first snowflakes of the season. It was a bit surreal given our earlier excursion in seventy-degree bathwater. Hussein mentioned the roughly thousand-meter gain in altitude, which seemed to explain the sudden climate change.

He was driving ten miles an hour, hunched over the steering wheel like an old man as a hail of Styrofoam seemed to dump from the sky. The car's broken wipers caused Hussein to roll down the window every few seconds and make a small clearing in the windshield, his closed fist acting like a broom. We were nowhere near our hotel.

I glanced toward Bea sitting in the front seat, drumming her fingers to Amr Diab's latest hit yelping from the car radio. The music video, in which boy meets girl, they fall in love, girl snubs boy, boy falls apart and belts his pain out, heightens the lyrical melodrama. I often thought it would make a good corrective for a CNN after-hours show in which Arabs are not just terrorists and martyrs, but jilted lovers with broken hearts. Hussein started tapping the dashboard with his left hand in time to the beat. Bea was doing her best sitting-down shimmies.

The car veered into the oncoming lane. For a minute, I thought we were going to drive straight into some approaching headlights. Then Hussein pulled over to the side and cranked up the volume as more of Amr Diab dribbled into the frigid February air. It was three in the morning, the air was freezing, and our clothes were still damp from the hot springs bath and the Dead Sea dip from eight hours ago. The boys got out of the car and danced in the middle of the empty road, hands upturned and fingers snapping. Bea and I joined them. Abbas turned out to be quite a good dancer, his hips arching up and down with practiced ease. I didn't think the Muslim brothers would have approved.

A bright winter sunrise greeted us upon reaching the hotel. It would be embarrassing to walk inside and evade the questioning looks from the management for our all-night absence. Hussein's car screeched to a dead halt in the alley near the hotel, waking up Ali gently snoring in my lap. He rubbed his eyes and looked up at me.

"Thank you for your emotions," Ali said softly and fell back asleep.

The morning after the snowy dance fest, Bea and I decided to leave Jordan and travel to Syria later that day via *servees*, or shared taxi. Our tea-merchant friend, Amer, walked us to the station with eyes anchored to his feet most of the way. A stubbly forest sprouted across the lower half of his face. It was a face I had grown to like and respect, a face I would probably never lay eyes on again. It had been a brief friendship, yet it flared with meaning and worth. Why, oh why, was it so much easier to bond with people here? Would I be able to do the same when I returned home? Would I find my old friends impossible to talk to? Maybe they wouldn't be so different. Maybe I would have changed.

A silver Mercedes SUV doubled as a communal taxi. Amer unloaded our packs and placed them gently in the trunk as if they contained the fragile pieces of his heart. Then he bolted across the street to buy some falafel sandwiches rolled in old newspapers that he thrust in my hands.

It was futile to protest his generosity. When I tried to stuff a few dinar notes in his front shirt pocket, neatly rolled up like a cigarette, Amer recoiled as if touched by burning coals. He simply smiled his sweet, serene smile. In parting, we jointly recited the "Aytal Kursi," a long Quranic verse that I have had memorized since the age of eight.

I translated the Arabic in my head. *His throne extends over heavens and earth and He feels no fatigue in guarding and preserving them for He is the Most High, the Supreme in glory.* The words wrapped around my shoulders like a cozy shawl.

Amer's eyes did not cloud with tears as mine did. They shone with an inner brilliance that was trying to tell me something. After we climbed into the taxi, I scooted over to the window and rolled down the glass to stare into those eyes for as long as possible. But I couldn't decode their message. The vehicle speeded up and we lost sight of Amer and his light.

Syria
(Damascus)

Playtime

Do not be satisfied with the stories that come before you.
Unfold your own myth.

Rumi

Crossing borders makes me wrestle with conflicting emotions. Acute loss for what I leave behind and a surge of excitement for what lies ahead. It's hard to reconcile the two. I feel like splitting myself in half and living on both sides at once. But that would be like running in place and going nowhere. In travel as in life, borders must be crossed.

Our driver was a bushy-haired Lebanese who swapped his cigarettes for my U2 cassette tapes and insisted that Beirut, his last stop, was where we should really be going instead of the provincial backwater of Damascus.

"You have no fun in Sham. Only *Mukhabarat,* secret polis!"

The driver moved his index finger across his throat to drive the point home.

"In Beirut you have party all night. Many beautiful girls!"

He wriggled his hips while steering to remind us that our chosen destination was a clear mistake.

For a minute, I was tempted to give in to the PR campaign for Beirut. Bea threw me a wink as if to say, "What are we waiting for?

Let's get a move on to some big-time fun." But she knew as well as I did that Damascus had to come first, given the looming expiration date on our Syrian visas. Two hours later, we found ourselves in line at the border checkpoint getting our passports stamped to enter country number three.

It was well past sundown as the Mercedes taxi cruised into the city center of Damascus. Bea and I hadn't a clue where to bunk for the night, but our driver made the decision and dropped us off at the Hotel Merhaba, insisting that it was a "good, clean place, suitable for ladies." We decided to take a chance on what appeared to be the Syrian version of Motel 6, not entirely shabby, but more partial to traveling salesmen than two single girls lugging tanker-size backpacks. The head scarves were confusing and the lack of male chaperones downright scandalous. Our entrance into the small lobby with its tattered posters of Alpine villages and snowcapped mountains caused a group of middle-aged men to halt in midsentence as if someone had pressed a pause button on their conversation. Undeterred by their inspection, I approached the hotel manager, who was squinting at me through thick black-framed glasses reminiscent of Woody Allen's 1970s look.

"You want room? We have no ladies staying. You want how many nights? You want sleep only?"

We presented passports and traveler's checks.

"It is only for sleep?"

Bea faked a yawn.

"You sleep together? Same same?"

Now it was my turn to yawn.

"I give you nice double room. For sleep only."

It was perched above a cacophonous street lined with a few garish red neon signs, lending the impression that we were either living above a brothel or were in one. The bathroom across the hall reeked of open gutters. In making use of it, I had to wrap my scarf over my nose and hold my breath for ten seconds of olfactory torture. Surely, the centuries-old system of chamber pots or the squatting hole in the ground was better than the modern-day unflushed toilet.

The fan in our room was cranked to full speed and Bea had already collapsed in bed. I unpeeled her leather boots and loosened the tight jersey head scarf ensemble she had taken to wearing lately. It was hard to believe that we were finally in Syria, a country considered by some to be one of the most troubled in the Arab world, a favorite poster child of state-sponsored terrorism and all-around oppression, according to the U.S. government and the State Department travel advisory in effect. But I knew nothing about its politics or history at the time. The Syria that had long seized my imagination was a place of handcrafted *ouds*, ornate mosques, and bargains galore in the marketplaces.

After a short nap, Bea and I ventured outside the hotel. Two short blocks away, we spotted an INTERNET sign lit up on a marquee. It was the last thing I had expected to see. According to the travelers' grapevine in March of 2001, Syrian censorship had not fully embraced the unrestricted flow of digital information. But there were also news reports about the country's new president, Bashar al-Assad, who was apparently a modern Arab leader, partial to downloading tunes by Phil Collins. To find out for ourselves the open or closed status of the World Wide Web, Bea and I climbed a steep set of stairs to enter a room no bigger than a broom closet. It housed four desktop computers and two middle-aged engineers who offered us Nescafé with condensed milk and pointed out the back-door entry to the government-blocked Hotmail site. I read a five-day-old email from my dad requesting some Quranic wall hangings and prayer rugs in nice simple designs.

Dad seemed to think Middle Eastern *souqs* would be quite a different experience from the bazaars of Karachi—not as congested and more flavorful with history. I hadn't thought of Karachi as unhistorical, but compared to the great capitals of the Middle East, it was a neophyte. Damascus happened to rank as one of the world's oldest continuously inhabited cities, with some traces going back as far as seven thousand years. And during the 7th and 8th centuries, Damascus was the center of the Ummayad caliphate under Islam's first dynasty.

Though I wasn't consciously seeking out all this history, an implicit reminder of it hovered in the backdrop that was part of my roots, and it felt good just to be near that past—not vicariously as I had been in the public library flipping through books on Islamic art and history—but up close in living sounds and colors. I dashed off a quick reply assuring my father that all was well. Then I turned toward Bea, who was on her third cup of Nescafé and apparently quite refreshed.

"Let's do some exploring, eh?"

We waved good-bye to the engineers and stepped back out into the streets. I suddenly felt the grumbles of my empty stomach.

"Food, Bea, food."

"No worries. We shall find some."

At 10:00 PM, Damascus was bustling but not half as frenzied as Cairo nor devoid of a pulse like the spruced-up parts of Amman. Already we were noticing a major regional difference in that staring was not a full-time spectator sport. Heads still turned, but the appraising eyes appeared more distant, whether out of politeness or aloofness it was difficult to know. We walked over to a juice stand where bunches of bananas, oranges, carrots, apples, and pomegranates dangled from the ceiling like Christmas ornaments. The juice man looked our way inquiringly, his lack of English matching my ignorance of proper Arabic. Relying on my patchwork of vocabulary retained from TV commercials and occasional flips through the dictionary, I strung the word for banana, *moz*, next to milk, *halib*. This effort produced thick, luscious banana milkshakes for the equivalent of about eighty cents. We ordered two more apiece and called it a satisfying dinner.

Home Away from Home

Two days later, Bea and I were wandering around the district of Saroujah and noticed a cobblestone-paved alley that looked inviting. A shop of musical instruments was visible a few yards ahead. We walked toward it and continued walking until an unassuming glass doorway appeared on our left. It was slightly ajar, as if beckoning us to enter. The sign above it read AL-RABIE HOTEL. A lanky man at the front desk with cinnamon-colored skin and a curly mustache drooping over his lips offered tea and a packet of menthol-flavored Marlboros. I noticed an elegant indoor courtyard with inlaid tiles in shades of coral and jade, relics of the old Damascene mansion now converted into a humble haven for backpackers. It was home at first sight. We chose a small room tucked in the back for maximum privacy, furnished only with two single beds and a table between. It opened out to a cozy sun-drenched private courtyard with a tiny porcelain sink in the corner. The cost amounted to a negligible $2.50 apiece per day.

We moved in early the next morning. It was a relief to leave Hotel Merhaba. The manager with the Woody Allen glasses accompanied us outside. He was about to hail us a cab when Bea edged closer to the edge of rush-hour traffic and let out a piercing taxi whistle in her demure black veil.

"Allahu Akbar!" The elderly driver attested the glory of God as he stopped for us. We struggled to squeeze into the cab with packs worthy of tackling Everest. Then our cabbie floored the gas pedal, plunging us into a maelstrom of buses and minivans stuffed with passengers. A uniformed police officer was directing traffic by standing on what appeared to be an upside-down bucket. We whizzed past little stalls selling dried fruits, nuts, and plastic knickknacks, perfume shops, electronic shops, and grubby signs advertising medical specialties such as hematology, anesthesia, and a dubious "ladies repair."

"Allahu Akbar!" The taxi driver braked near a quieter back street to let us off. Then he touched a CD dangling from his rear-view mirror and recited the prayer inscribed on it. We gave him a big tip and heaved our pack-strapped bodies in the direction of the cobblestones.

No one was at the front desk. We wandered inside the hotel's courtyard, where a small-boned teenager was down on his hands and knees, feverishly scrubbing the tiled floor with a ragged sock worn over his hand like a mitten. He paused at the sound of our footsteps and turned his head toward us.

"Merhaba!" Charcoal thick eyebrows rose with curiosity.

I mentioned the empty reception hall and inquired about our room.

"My cousin is away at market. But he told me you are coming today. Your room is ready." He stood up and pointed out the way that we would know so well in the days to come.

Ahmed was the all-around helper of the al-Rabie hotel, and Bea and I soon developed a fierce friendship with him. He showed us the neighborhood bakery with the crunchiest sesame bread, the little *fuul* shop where the owner was always asleep, and the best place to buy fresh *labneh* (thick yogurt cheese) and *zaatar* (ground sesame seeds laced with thyme). Ahmed's hands were always busy scrubbing, polishing, or cleaning something, as if they did not know the meaning of rest. Despite his nineteen years, he was already a hardened soul, carrying the burden of supporting himself and his two youngest siblings after his parents had died. Ahmed dreamed of securing a work permit to look for a job in Beirut. His daily schedule alternated between working at the hotel, which brought in $3 a day, and attending classes at a state-run college where he was studying French and history. When he first heard my name, Ahmed chuckled with appreciation.

"Don't you know what your name means?" he asked.

"It means salty."

More friendly laughter. "Who told you that?"

"I looked it up in the dictionary." I was getting somewhat irritated. "Remember I can read Arabic? It says salt next to my name."

"You are much more than salt," Ahmed replied with a now-serious face. "Maliha stands for prettiness, sweetness. It's about goodness!"

It was news to have so much responsibility bestowed by a name.

"I like your name as well," I told Ahmed.

"It is only small name."

"But you are not small."

He stood on his tiptoes and walked around in a little circle.

"What was that for?"

"I wish to be on high mountain place so I don't feel so small."

"Ahmed, you are not small. You are big in your heart. And that's what counts."

"So it is all how you say, okay?"

"A-okay."

"In Arabic, we say *mashi*."

"*Mashi, mashi*."

When I returned to my room and lay in bed, I thought some more about Ahmed. He was so young, yet at the same time almost ageless. I couldn't put my finger on it exactly, and maybe I was getting carried away with character analysis when I had no basis for judgment. But there was a certain quality about Ahmed in which it was not necessary to know all the intimate details of his life to know him as an individual. It had been the same way with Yasser and Mohammad in Cairo. Though I had known them for only three months, it felt more like three years. Our closeness was not a function of time; it was something else, something I hadn't quite experienced with my friends back home, where I would spend years and years trying to get to know them and still not knowing beyond what they chose to reveal.

Maybe the difference was in the layers. Ahmed seemed to have fewer to peel compared to my Stateside friends. And it wasn't because he was any less complex than they were; it was just that Ahmed did not need to hide himself as much. It seemed a rather courageous thing to do.

Unlike Ahmed, I didn't have the guts to remove some of my masks. Even if I had wanted to, it was nearly impossible back home, where the pressures of work and other responsibilities made it necessary at times to add more masks, if only to cope. It seemed easier to get rid of them abroad, and I recalled from my days in Europe how Americans there seemed so much freer and happier, as if they had seized the right to enjoy life and bring out the inner child.

I wanted to be this way, but it was difficult given the yawning chasm between my life on the road and the life I had left behind. And not being able to bridge this chasm made me feel stranded in no-man's land. I tried to think of Seattle now and then, but my mind drew a blank. The person I used to be there had dissolved into memory. Family and friends appeared to exist on another planet. I tried to picture their faces but they appeared grubby and out of focus. I couldn't really picture home anymore. And when I tried to, all I got were glimmers of a past life, seen in the yellow tinge of old photographs. It was the same for Bea. When I asked her why she had left Sydney, she would simply say she needed a change. But we both knew it was more than that. As if by tacit agreement, Bea and I didn't talk much about why we were traveling. What mattered most was the day-to-day existence that was our only reality at the time.

Act One, Scene One

A pile of old mattresses was stacked in one corner of the little courtyard outside our room. I used to hop on them as if they were a makeshift park bench, with my journal in one hand and a cup of steaming black tea in the other. Bea would often still be asleep, but I would think about her as I wrote. She had inspired me so much with her grace and her innate sense of trust. In some ways, Bea seemed so much more comfortable in the culture than I was, even though it was less familiar to her. She donned the head scarf with eagerness instead of questioning its merits as I often did. She seated herself in quiet back corners of mosques while I prayed. People assumed she was Muslim, and we didn't feel the need to contradict them. In our hearts, we were soul sisters, united in our adventurous spirits and supportive of each other's weaknesses and strengths. Bea kept encouraging me to let go and just allow things to happen. Together, we doubled the intensity and serendipity along our path.

The old city functioned as the daily stage set. The standard route from al-Rabie to its walled entrance near the citadel was never short on entertainment. After crossing a busy four-lane roadway near the hotel, we hit a bird market with shrieking winged creatures inside cages that their owners paraded in a sleepwalking trance. Some days, we cut through an appetizing bazaar specializing in animal intestines that promptly earned the nickname "Slaughter Street" for its rows of camel heads, sheep entrails, and cow tongues displayed as neatly as seasonal produce at a farmers market. Restaurant entrances were decorated with carcasses of meat hanging on huge iron hooks. Butchers with blood-splattered shirts and sharp knives hovered around their choice merchandise, some of them giggling at our careful attempts to avoid stepping on furry bits of ears and tails scattered about the ground.

The entertainment steadily increased as streets gave way to crooked lines of honking cars, many of them vintage American Chevies sporting sleek new paint jobs. I squinted to make out a two-toned Bel Air, followed closely by a humongous DeSoto, looking more like an art deco exhibit on four wheels. A beat-up old Pontiac rolled by with its owner wearing dark sunglasses, playing an old Fairuz song in the tape deck. For a country that Washington condemns as a state sponsor of terrorism, Syria's apparent love affair with old-fashioned American automobiles seemed deliciously ironic. For a moment, it felt as if we had fallen through the cracks of yet another time machine.

It was fun to meld with the crowds on the streets. They invariably swept us along in their tireless tide, and we found ourselves moving with the current. This current was taking us toward the central passageway of the Souq al-Hamidiyeh. Streams of people were going in and out. Their faces were a kaleidoscope of Kurdish, Armenian, Greek, Circassian, and Turkic ancestry, weaving a collage of charcoal-black hair with strands of ginger or chocolate brown, and caramel-glazed skins serving as canvas for eyes the color of minerals such as amber, lapis lazuli, emerald, and onyx. The women's eyes glinted, like water at the bottom of a well.

Bea and I linked arms and waded inside the *souq* determined not to breathe a word of English. Our plan fizzled out thirty seconds later as shopkeepers beckoned us to try on a lovely *jelbab* and "only just look" at sterling silver jewelry. One man tried to sell us the carcasses of giant birds with their wings extended in perpetual flight, and we heard snakelike hisses from all sides to "change dollars."

Ignoring all merchants clamoring for our attention, we inched toward the Roman arch leading to the Ummayad Mosque of Damascus. The passageway gridlocked, smashing bodies together into human sandwiches that rekindled memories of Ramadan rush hour in the Cairo subway. Earnest salesmen continued chanting the mantras of their trade, and soap-size bars of sunbeams poked through the corrugated iron rooftops.

Pausing for a drink at a juice stand, Bea and I managed to stand apart from the hordes and breathe a little. Soon after we merged back into the bottleneck, a man came out from one of the side shops and immediately appointed himself as our escort. His slanted Mongolian-looking eyes and spiky goatee gave him the appearance of an enigmatic gnome. He introduced himself as Wisam and suggested a tour of the historic *souq* that was in all likelihood the original shopping mall. Bea and I followed

Wisam into the back alleys spiraling behind the Ummayad Mosque and where the focus of my attention swung like a pendulum.

I wanted to buy some sumac, a Middle Eastern spice with the red-purplish dye and the taste of sour cherries. But a shopwindow display of Islamic calligraphy caught my eye. One step farther, I fell in love with a tribal-looking navy woolen jacket with swirls of embroidery on the cuffs. Then Bea pulled at my sleeve to point out trays of silver rings and chunky Bedouin jewelry. I had meanwhile slipped into the calligraphy shop to buy a tapestry hand-stitched in golden thread with all ninety-nine names of Allah. Back outside the shop, a trio of little boys dazzled me with some artsy prints of Quranic verses in stylized lettering and arabesque borders. The boys toting the merchandise were no more than seven or eight years old, and one of them was wearing a red T-shirt with the words CALIFORNIA GIRLS.

Bea and I sat on the pavement and began raking through the pile for the best picks of holy verses as if raiding a table of half-price cashmere sweaters at Nordstrom's anniversary sale. Abandoning frugality, we ended up buying the entire lot of cards from our young merchants. They split the equivalent of $5 among themselves, each of them licking his fingers and counting the notes with the rapt attention of a bank manager.

We found Wisam leaning against the door of the jewelry shop, urging us to enter. I chimed, *"Alatule, alatule!"* It was Egyptian slang for straight ahead that had served me well with Cairo taxi drivers. Bea muffled some giggles in her scarf, pointing out Wisam's funny little walk—more of a slouch, with an exaggerated drag of the right leg alternating with a quick two-step shuffle of the left. He appeared to be in his midtwenties and seemed rather partial to black sneakers with three-inch platform heels. They made his skinny legs look like those of a malnourished chicken. All this time, I had forgotten about the sumac. When the spice market came into view, the orgiastic riots of color and smell failed to arouse my overloaded senses.

Wisam understood a bit of English and spoke not a word of it, while I was able to patch together some rudimentary Arabic phrases for survival on the streets. I realized how spoiled or lucky I had been in Egypt and Jordan, relying mostly on English to communicate with my friends. Nonetheless, this sudden language barrier was largely irrelevant thanks to Wisam's creative ways of self-expression. He excelled in using body language, to which he would attach words to communicate his feelings and thoughts. To a passing observer, it might have appeared that we were constantly engaged in a game of charades.

At one point, Wisam crossed his arms over his chest and waved his hands slowly. It dawned on me that he was implying a bird, but the word was different, something like *hurriya*, and he kept flapping his hands and looking at the sky.

"He looks deranged," Bea whispered in my ear.

More hand-flapping and sky-gazing.

"Freedom!" I shouted with the glee of an escaped convict.

"Ahh, ahh!" he nodded and clapped his hands.

Sometimes, it would not be so simple to comprehend Wisam's pantomimes. When he ran out of options, he wrote down the word on a piece of paper, and I would whip out my pocket dictionary to find its meaning. Wisam didn't seem to mind. He was a patient and encouraging teacher, never mocking me for being an ignorant fool unable to understand his native tongue, but forcing me to *listen* to the language in the classroom of everyday life.

Act One, Scene Three

"*Hawkawati*," I read aloud from my guidebook. The Arabic name for storyteller fascinated me. But for our new friend in Damascus, the object of fascination centered on the guidebook itself. Wisam could scarcely believe that somebody had actually taken the trouble to catalog the jumbled maze of narrow alleys in the *medina,* complete with little maps pointing out the locations of old *khans,* or caravansaries—formerly shelters for trading merchants and their cargo—now functioning as chic art galleries of abstract village scenes. His eyes crinkled with amusement as he led Bea and me to a café where a man with a red tasseled fez was reading aloud from *One Thousand and One Nights* as a live *hawkawati.* We sat at a corner table and watched his animated performance.

Wisam stepped out, returning with a slim boy with gel-slicked hair and tinted sunglasses. Ziyad worked at a handicrafts shop across the street during the day and after-hours as an enterprising tourist guide. His English was flawless, but it sounded rehearsed and artificial compared to Wisam's authentic, incomprehensible Arabic. And he spoke in an exceedingly formal manner, often "petitioning our kindness" for this or that. The effort seemed to dilute his personality, causing us to know little about him.

"Will you take more te-eea?" Ziyad's singsong Syrian accent made the last word of every question soar like a bird.

As Bea and I guzzled more chamomile tea, Ziyad invited us to a birthday party later that evening. He mentioned it as soon as Wisam had left the table, scribbling the address on an old sales receipt before heading back to work and cautioning us not to breathe a word of it to our self-appointed personal city guide and chaperone. Bea thought it was prudent since Wisam seemed to be the possessive type. I wouldn't have known either way.

Later that day, Bea and I slunk out of al-Rabie at 11:00 PM dressed up in our best party clothes. As a special favor, Ahmed had given us the key to the front door so we could slip back in undetected by his cousin, who was usually sprawled asleep on the floor of the reception room. We hailed a cab to Bab Touma, the Christian quarter of the old city with a smattering of trendy nightclubs. Ziyad was eating at a falafel shop near the entrance and urged us to try the chicken *shawarmas,* apparently the best in the city, according to the born salesman. A steep flight of stairs led to a basement club reserved for a private bash. We stayed up until dawn dancing salsa. On the walk back to the hotel, a muezzin chanted the first call of prayers from a nearby minaret, his voice quivering slightly as if under water.

The following evening, Wisam accompanied Bea and me to Beit Jabri, a historic house dating to the years of the Ottoman Empire and now converted to a chic café patronized by hipsters in black turtlenecks and fashionable Damascene grandmothers smoking water pipes. It had a separate room for Internet browsing and a staircase leading to a balcony where modern-day Juliets could spy on their would-be Romeos. A waiter came to take our order, scribbling into a notepad with an extended pinky. He looked suspiciously like a Spanish matador with his tight high-waisted black trousers and Brylcreemed hair. All that he needed for the final touch was a red bolero jacket on his superstraight back.

We listened to the soft strains of the *oud* wafting from the middle of the room, where the musician perched on a stool, his dexterous fingers plucking a rainbow of emotions—sadness, joy, misery, elation, regret, surprise, satisfaction—fusing into the hypnotic rhythm of ocean waves. He played by closing his eyes, head slightly bent, and swaying in a lost reverie. On subsequent nights, he sang old folk songs, the long arias mingling with self-styled expressions of deliberate ennui and the sweet smell of tobacco smoke.

The Mad Hatter's Tea Party

Each day in Damascus began ripe with possibilities, unleashing the heady mystery of travel in which the unknown is not a rational fear but a craving for a moment-to-moment high. Severed from the trappings of home, the traveler thrives on this suspended state of intoxication but at the same time desires to combat feelings of alienation. It invariably becomes second nature to develop a hyperawareness of everyone and everything in a place, no matter how trivial.

One afternoon, after an extensive shopping spree, Bea and I sat down to rest at an outdoor café next to the Ummayad Mosque. We listened idly to the babble of tourists swapping opinions of regional differences and the latest horrors in the *souq*.

"Watch out for those merchants in Cairo's Khan al-Khalili bazaar; if they know you are American, they will eat you alive for those greenbacks."

"Istanbul men are generally slimy, and Turks on the whole are not to be trusted."

"Iranians are terrific hosts with refined manners."

We heard the usual allusions to depraved perverts who grab body parts in crowded streets and unanimous affirmation that all Middle Eastern men consider foreign girls to be nonstop sex machines, no better than the *sharmuta*, Arabic for whore.

Wisam came by looking rather haggard. A frail wisp of a man trailed behind. He wore a faded dark-brown corduroy blazer with elbow patches and clutched a newspaper under his armpit. Wisam introduced him as Mahmoud, a journalist friend with a strong command of broken English and French. He showed us his credentials in the form of a laminated press card featuring a sallow-faced youth with bulging fish eyes. I tried to engage him beyond *bonjours,* but Mahmoud wasn't very communicative for a newspaper man, answering all my questions with a monosyllable *oui* or *non.*

Only his eyes talked. They were saying things about Bea's profile, aquiline nose, and curvy lips sharply illuminated in the late-afternoon sun. I was used to playing sidekick to my friend's magnetic beauty, which often compelled people to treat us (more accurately her) as royalty. Once, when we had walked into a photo shop in Amman, the shopkeeper's first action was not to fetch my film but to extend his hand with a closed fist toward Bea's nose so she could smell and comment on his new choice of perfume oil.

A few more rounds of tea followed as the café filled up with patrons. Mahmoud invited us for tea at his home later in the evening. Wisam led us there, navigating a circuit board of *souqs* and alleys to which no map could do justice. We entered an immense courtyard with a dried-up marble fountain now functioning as a rather extravagant lavatory for visiting pigeons. Two raised platforms with a frieze of Arabic poetry scrolled across walls once painted a shimmering turquoise and speckled with bits of mother-of-pearl inlay. A jute rope strung between two lemon trees sagged under the weight of an old tribal kilim and jockey shorts in shades of canary yellow and fire-engine red. There was no sign of Mahmoud, who clearly had neither time nor money to restore the decaying elegance of his bachelor pad. Then we saw him waving to us from the second-story veranda that ran along in a semicircle above the courtyard.

"Welcome, welcome! *Bienvenue, mes chers amis.*"

He was wearing a crisp white linen shirt and blue jeans. I noticed how his nostrils flared when he got excited, like a French winemaker about to taste the year's first vintage.

Mahmoud ushered us into a small living room decorated with magazine cutouts of old British cars and Swiss chalet mountain posters. We sat on a velour sofa pockmarked with cigarette burns. Our host handed out pistachios and sunflower seeds and put a Fairuz CD in his boom box. I told him how I had nearly wiped clean a small music store near the hotel that was selling pirated copies for fifty Syrian pounds, or $1 a pop.

"You like Arabic music?" He smiled and fished out a couple of cassette tapes. "For you. Present from me."

Bea coughed and pointed out Wisam, who had sprawled along the floor with his eyes closed, hand held to the forehead.

"Maybe he had a rough night," I surmised.

"You know, there is something about him that I just can't figure out." She had one of her pensive looks. "He seems nice enough, but I get the feeling that he is hiding some terrible secret and it's killing him inside. And the way he treats me sometimes is downright vicious. Do you know, the other day he nearly broke my arm in the *souq* when I refused to go back to his shop. I don't know if I can put up with that Jekyll and Hyde routine of his much longer."

Wisam woke up and fixed his eyes on Bea and then on me as if to ask, "What has she been saying behind my back?"

Mahmoud brought into the room a small kerosene stove on which he placed a rusty aluminum kettle. He told me the house was more than five hundred years old. When I asked him how he had acquired it, he deliberately ignored the question. I noticed stacks of yellowed newspapers piled three feet high in one corner of the room. A framed picture showed a European-looking woman and a brasher, younger Mahmoud holding hands in front of the Eiffel Tower. He followed my gaze and held it for a few seconds before pouring out the steaming tea into shot glasses. It had the tart tanginess of *karkaday*, or hibiscus-flower tea, that I had first tasted at the seafront restaurants of Dahab.

"*Alors,* what have you see in Syria?" Mahmoud asked in a jovially.

I told him about our visit to Ma'alula, a small village near Damascus where Aramaic, the language of Jesus, is still spoken. It was a charming place with Mediterranean-inspired sugar-cubed houses stacked against a cliff and an ancient church carved into mountain flanks. We had met a friendly mother-and-daughter team who invited us home for lunch.

"*Très bien, très bien.*" Mahmoud gushed in praise of Syrian hospitality and urged us to take more tea.

Bea asked him the burning question about the woman in the photo.

"She was my *femme,*" he said. "But she only want money and fine dresses. She leave me for rich *monsieur* from Aleppo. But I never forget her." His sigh ruffled Wisam's hair. I noticed he was leaning against the sofa playing cat's cradle with his shoelaces.

The sofa was big enough for only two people, so I slid off to the floor, leaving Mahmoud to cozy up next to Bea. She was wearing her famous sea-green *hijab* ensemble that had already caused five heads to turn earlier in the day. I figured that Bea's *hijab* produced more or less the same effect as Carrie Bradshaw's sexiest little black dress. Mahmoud's cupid-struck eyes said it all. But he was trying to play it cool by puffing on his Gauloises and making blue rings of smoke. I was on my fourth cup of tea and asked for the bathroom when I noticed Bea's hand, speckled with green polka dots.

"What's wrong with your hands?"

"Nothing's wrong with my hands, silly. Why do you ask?"

"Well, something is wrong with your hands. Did you make the bed this morning?"

"What?"

"Yeah, and what about that parakeet I wanted to buy? I want something in rusty brown. You know, like that old Chevy we saw."

"What??!!"

"Wisam, where's Wisam?"

"He went out for some cigarettes. Mal, what the hell is wrong? You're acting really strange."

I started laughing uncontrollably and pointed my finger at Mahmoud. "Look, there goes the sultan on his shiny white horse."

Bea joined in with the laughter. Soon, we were making faces at each other and cackling like idiots. I would start to say something only to have the thought disappear from my mind, as if someone stole it or shredded it to bits.

Wisam returned with a pack of Marlboros and some small newspaper bundles. He didn't seem to have gone mad like us but remained withdrawn, determined to win the title of the world's foremost Brooding King. His friend was busy unwrapping the pita, hummus, and olives from the newspaper rolls.

"*Min fadlik.*" Mahmoud gestured to the food.

"I'm not hungry. I want to fly on an elephant." I was serious.

"Pas de problème. But first you must eat."

"La!"

"No *la.* Eat!" He stuffed a wad of bread and hummus in my mouth. It tasted like brick.

The next thing I knew, we were in a cab on the way to my doctor's appointment. I didn't know how much time had passed, or how we escaped from Mahmoud's house. All I knew was that Bea was in charge. Thank God her mental faculties were intact.

"Don't you remember he bought us some chocolates near Bab Touma? Just before we climbed into the taxi to get to your doctor?" Bea tried to jog my memory.

"Chocolates, what chocolates?"

She fished out the empty wrappers from my coat pocket, but still my mind drew a complete blank.

A few days ago, I had been afflicted with an atrocious abscess on my stomach. Ahmed had called a doctor, who came to our little room at al-Rabie and performed some minor surgery to open the fluid-filled sac. He had asked me to come to his office every other evening for a week to change dressings. That night was no different—thankfully, Bea remembered the appointment and we arrived on time. As I was stretched horizontally on a vinyl bench with a pack of gauze taped to my tummy, Bea sat across from the doctor's desk and told him in a matter-of-fact way that we might have been drugged. He nodded and said nothing. We made it back to the hotel in one piece. The next morning our limbs had turned into lead.

"My arms!" Bea wailed.

"My legs, something's wrong with my legs!"

It was no small matter getting to the sink when I was feeling like a prisoner with chains on my feet.

Bea was trying to do jumping jacks, and it made my head spin just watching her. I finally gave up and crawled back into bed. It was awful, not knowing if I would be able to walk like a normal person again.

"Come on, you," Bea kicked off the covers. "You can't stay like that all day."

"What do you suppose is the matter with us?"

"There's only one way to find out."

No one was around the reception room. Ahmed had gone to school and left us a tray with some apples and a packet of digestive biscuits. We ate a bit and somehow dragged our ailing bodies to the waiting stage set.

Wisam was chatting with some friends near the *souq*'s entrance. They all gave us the usual visual inspection, taking in my pajamas that were inside out and the clumps of mascara tattooing Bea's face. We had kept on our *hijab* only because we must have slept with the scarves plastered to our heads. I was in no mood for exchanging pleasantries and pulled Wisam by the shirtsleeve. His tall, lean figure functioned as a pole to lean on.

"*Lesh? Lesh?*" I kept asking Wisam why as the crowds parted to make room for my chaotic veering.

"*Haram,* Wisam, *haram,*" Bea was trying to tell him that whatever had happened was wrong, shameful.

Wisam was clutching his head and muttering in unintelligible Arabic. At that point, we did not have enough evidence of his exact role in last night's doping tea party. And we weren't about to get any evidence, given my lousy Arabic that prevented me from either accusing him or demanding an explanation. Tongue-tied and bewildered, Bea and I watched Wisam spewing a torrent of anguished words with some snatches of *afwan,* meaning sorry, and then he uttered the word *hashish.*

"Oh my god."

So we were not crazy after all. An iota of common sense would have revealed that unlike normal *karkaday* tea, the liquid was not a transparent red, but dark and opaque like red wine. I also would have noticed that our dear friends had not touched their glasses while I had consumed six helpings, twice as much as Bea. No wonder I had blanked out. Back at the doctor's that evening, I registered a more coherent complaint. Given our current symptoms, he guessed we had been slipped something similar to Valium. Then he wrote down the name "Obervale" on a piece of paper. The pharmacist confirmed it was a common sedative.

So what were we to do about it? Going to the police would have likely landed Mahmoud in jail or somehow thrown suspicion on us. Because of the language barrier, it remained unclear at this point if Wisam was an accomplice or even the mastermind behind the whole scheme. We just wanted some straight talk from his friend who had invited us into his home and betrayed our trust. I couldn't tell if I was angrier with him or at myself for having fallen for his ruse.

The next day, Mahmoud was a wanted man. Bea and I planned to confront him with the aid of a mismatched threesome—Ahmed (furious about the incident and ready to roll up his sleeves to deck the bastard who had tricked us); Ziyad (more concerned about the bad publicity that would get around the *souq* if we handed the bastard over to the police and tourists stopped coming to the handicraft shop); and Wisam (who may or may not have been part of the plan but definitely had to answer for making us meet the bastard to begin with).

Upon our setting foot in Mahmoud's neighborhood, rumors flew to our ears.

"They are saying Mahmoud is not here, that he might be hiding, because he is afraid of the police," Ziyad translated.

"Let's go get him," I said.

Bea and I barged into the familiar courtyard trailed by our bodyguards, determined to protect us with their manly courage in case of any bloodshed. I hoped only that they were not armed.

"Mahmoud, Mahmoud!" All of us yelled in unison.

Not a trace of wind blew. He hadn't even cleared the clothesline with the carpet and jockey shorts. A cat was yowling in the background as if announcing an impending brouhaha. All of a sudden, I noticed a white-shirted blur dash across the veranda.

"There he is!"

"Mahmoud, *descendez-vous!*"

"*Yallah!*" The bodyguards transformed into GI Joes and raced up the stairs, issuing strict orders for us to remain in place. We heard an awful clattering of pots and pans and some foul-mouthed curses in Arabic. Ten minutes later, there was absolute silence.

"Oh, god. I think they killed him," Bea whispered.

The suspense was unbearable, so I tiptoed up the stairs, slowly sliding against the wall and looking out the corner of my eyes, just like those TV detectives.

Instead of gory body parts, I saw orange peels. They were all sitting on the living room floor munching tangerines that were apparently some kind of peace offering. Mahmoud had dark circles under his eyes and looked as if he hadn't slept for days. He refused to meet my gaze, and when Wisam tried to help him stand up, he flinched as if touched by fresh hot embers. I noticed his eyes were tinged with yellow and racing like a pair of trapped mice inside the sockets.

"Please tell him we are not going to the police. We just want to talk to him. That is all." I issued a joint statement that Bea and I had agreed upon earlier.

As if on cue, she peeked inside the room. Then we all watched in amazement as Bea glided up to Mahmoud and took his hand in hers and held it tightly.

"Mahmoud." Her voice was soft and soothing. "*Ana asif.*" She was saying sorry. But whatever for? For not letting him touch her and upsetting his grandiose plan? For being smart enough to get away unharmed? If that whole incident had been some sordid idea of a practical joke, he had really lost it.

The man said nothing but stared at her as if in a trance.

"Mahmoud, just say you are sorry," she urged him to confess.

His mouth was sealed.

"Why did you do it, Mahmoud? Why?" I had lost my patience and looked toward our bodyguards for encouragement.

Ziyad spoke to him in his sing-song voice. I think he was asking him to simply own up to what he had done and ask for forgiveness.

Mahmoud waved his head side to side like a stubborn three-year-old.

"I did nothing, nothing."

"Rien?" I asked.

More head-waving, and then he started sobbing violently.

"That's it. I give up. He's clearly guilty but too scared to say so." My eyes scanned Bea's for approval.

She looked sad for having been betrayed, for having trusted a stranger/friend so easily. But trust was our strongest protector. If we had started our journey with suspicious minds, it would have perpetuated a cycle of fear and isolation. There would have been no Mohammad and Yasser in Cairo, no adventures with Waheed in the Sinai, and certainly no Dead Sea picnic with a friendly trio of cousins in Amman. To trust strangers in a strange land ultimately means trusting yourself to exercise good judgment. Failing to do so does not make you a victim. It only strengthens your radar of intuition for preventing future mishaps. Not expecting any or building an iron shield of protection from the elements is tantamount to traveling inside a cocoon. One might as well have never left home.

We left Mahmoud's place with a couple of tangerines and a whole lot of mixed emotions. On the way out of the courtyard, Wisam was saying something rather long-winded. Ziyad translated that he was asking us not to think badly of him, that he would be terribly hurt if we held any grudges against him when he just wanted to be our friend and show us a good time. As if to prove his point, Wisam was extending a dinner invitation at his house the following night.

"I think we need a break from house calls. Don't you?"

I turned toward Bea, who nodded in full agreement. But she still had that wistful look that comes with disappointment.

Ziyad had to get back to the shop. Though we hardly knew him, he seemed to be a decent fellow, his English skills had been valuable, and he did volunteer as our bodyguard. Even if it had been mostly for the sake of his PR image, at least he was there for moral support. He waved us a cheery good-bye.

Bea and I walked slowly with Ahmed in tow. The old city had lost some of its old charm. None of us talked on the way back to the hotel, each lost in his or her own thoughts. Even though Mahmoud had endangered our lives to some extent, I mostly just felt sorry for the man.

"I think you let him off too easy," Bea spoke up.

"Me? What about you? You're the one who was trying to apologize to him. That was gracious!"

She shrugged it off. "What else could I do?"

"It wouldn't have mattered anyhow," I said. "Even if he did confess, he wouldn't have had much peace of mind. That man is suffering as it is, what with his wife having left him and the way he lives all alone in that derelict mansion with no one to look after him. I would call that punishment enough. Why torture him any more?"

"You do have a big heart," Bea said.

"It's not that. I just don't like playing judge with someone else's life."

"Well, with that attitude, you would be sacked off the bench even if you were a real judge! You would be pardoning all the rapists and mass murderers!"

I laughed and then we were quiet again. Part of me was still unresolved. I had wanted Mahmoud to come clean, and his obstinacy bothered me. He hadn't trusted our discretion the way we had trusted his hospitality. Maybe he had good reason to if he had been duped before. He was like everyone else, a product of his conditioning, and this is how I had to view his twisted behavior and be able to forgive him. My compassion for Mahmoud reminded me of a story I had read about the Prophet Muhammad and the garbage thrower.

A woman wanted to take revenge on the Prophet because he was telling people to stop worshipping idols. So she started throwing garbage on his head every time he walked past the roof of her house. Much to the woman's disappointment, the Prophet did not say anything nor did he get angry. He simply continued to walk down the same street and though the woman continued with the garbage-dumping, the Prophet did not bother to pick an alternate route to avoid her. One day, the woman did not show up on the rooftop. The Prophet knocked at her door and the woman allowed him in even though she feared that he would punish her for what she had done. Instead, Prophet Muhammad told the woman that he was worried about her, and upon learning how ill she was, he asked her if she needed any help. The woman asked for some water. He gave it to her and prayed for her health. This made the woman feel guilty, and she apologized for her mean behavior. The Prophet forgave her and started coming to her house every day to clean it and to feed the woman until she was back on her feet again.

It was an inspiring story. And though it's not easy to practice kindness, especially to those who have harmed us, I thought the Prophet's empathy toward that woman was a way of holding back judgment, which is really not in our hands but in the hands of God.

We were nearing the hotel. The al-Rabie sign was dripping wet. It had started to rain, and I was glad to be sheltered and safe again.

Matters of the Flesh

On my first visit to the Louvre, I was transfixed not so much by the *Mona Lisa* but by Jean-Auguste-Dominique Ingres's *Turkish Bath,* featuring a slew of nude damsels lounging in misty pools of steam on slippery marble floors. They were alluring, mysterious women, catering to the Orientalist-inspired visions about the sensual East. Ever since sighting that painting, I had wanted to visit a Middle Eastern *hammam,* or the public bathhouse, that promised an instant gateway into this slippery, sensual world.

One morning, Bea and I ran into Ahmed in the back streets of Saroujah. He was carrying thick slabs of sesame bread as big as pizza crusts. Killing some time before his shift started, we strolled through the neighborhood, talking too much and not paying attention to where we were going until the street dead-ended near a small mosque. Adjacent to it appeared a public bathhouse with the name Hammam al-Warda, meaning "flower." We had no intentions of going in, but Ahmed grinned and told us to wait outside for a minute as he disappeared into an underground cellar.

"It is all arranged," he reported. "You each pay three hundred Syrian pounds for a full massage and wash. Anything else is extra money," Ahmed added, raising his thick eyebrows for emphasis.

"I guess there is no harm in going in."

Bea's insouciance clashed with my reluctance about undressing in front of strangers, which rehashed painful memories of seventh-grade locker rooms, peeping Toms, and showers without screens. Then I remembered the seduction of Ingres's bathing beauties, and their languorous sighs lured me inside the hole in the wall.

A woman with a jet-black mane and eyes like lit coals was smoking clove cigarettes and speaking in fast Arabic on the phone. She banged down the receiver and looked at us inquiringly.

"You want wash, yes?"

Bea fished out the agreed-upon sum and handed her the notes. The woman, apparently the manager on duty, waved it aside with clucks of her tongue.

"You keep until finish."

She pointed to a separate room, where we stripped down to our underwear and then entered the moist steam room to lie head to toe on the cool stone platform.

The bathing chamber had creamy marble walls and a row of brass spigots where women, young and old in all shapes and sizes, were mixing hot and cold water into plastic containers and splashing themselves with ladles. A heavy-limbed but sweet-looking woman with a fuzzy mustache motioned us over and proceeded to scrub my back with a coarse loofah in a sawlike motion that released dreadful black shavings of dead skin cells. Then she lathered me with soap while keeping up three simultaneous conversations with some of the other bathers without missing a beat. I sat on a wooden stool and rinsed off by the spigots, luxuriating in the feel of warm water cascading down my back. No one was staring at me, and I began to feel less and less embarrassed about communal bathing in the nude. This *hammam* was nothing like a seventh-grade locker room. Bea dunked her head under the spigot of cold running water. Then we just sat on the floor and combed each other's hair. My attentive helper offered us crispy lettuce leaves from a wet plastic bag with her soapy hands on our way out.

After bathing, we wrapped ourselves in thick cotton robes and lounged on plush ottomans that were set on a raised platform in a hexagon pattern. Sweet mint tea and a large fountain bubbling in the middle of the salon perfected the languorous atmosphere. We watched a woman in front of a large mirror applying henna to clumps of her gray hair with a large paintbrush. The other customers consisted of middle-aged Syrian women and a group of French tourists. I recalled my one-time experience in a day spa back in Seattle. It had a three-month-long waiting list, and when I finally got there, the cool, efficient service that sequestered me in solitary flotation tanks and rainforest rooms left me strangely dissatisfied. The *hammam* in Damascus functioned as a communal gathering place for women to let their hair down, to gossip and giggle like teenagers, and to forget about their demanding husbands and mothers-in-law for a few furtive hours. The bathing services seemed incidental to the social interaction.

Before we headed back to the changing room, the fuzzy-lipped woman who had helped me bathe approached us with a tube of sticky honey-colored paste. She gestured at my hairy legs. I had no choice but to sit back and let her do what she wanted to do. She worked swiftly, using her thumb to spread the wax and peel it off. My robe was hanging open, and the waxing lady knelt by my side as I lay on some cushions. Soon, I felt her hands beyond my legs, tugging off my panties.

"Nadeef!" she kept saying. *"Nadeef!"*

I figured it was either some kind of a compliment or a reprimand, though later on I learned that it just meant "clean." I refused to submit to more waxing torture, not of that kind, not in front of all those people. Bea was laughing her head off. The French tourists looked horrified. And as my commanding helper turned more aggressive, I was forced to yank her hand away from my crotch. She looked sad, as if I had bruised her feelings. I was only trying to save my own hide and not get too carried away with the whole *hammam* experience of unself-conscious nudity. I had actually enjoyed the bathing part of it, in which all our bodies sort of blurred into each other, making fewer distinctions between shapes and sizes. It had made me comfortable just seeing other women in the buff who weren't the least bit ashamed of their physicality. But I had to draw the line somewhere.

Bea chided me for chickening out. She said it would have been the cheapest Brazilian wax in history and I should have taken advantage of it. I told Bea it may have been dirt cheap, but I still had some prudishness to preserve and I wasn't about to suffer and scream in front of total strangers, not to mention a gawking group of French coeds. Bea's take was that it was just a harmless old *hammam*. Harmless, indeed. I had learned that it was a place where slippery sensuality merged with torturous beauty rituals, all in full public view. Some things were best done in private chambers.

Later that evening, Bea and I accompanied Ahmed to visit his eldest sister and her family in an older part of town. The taxi let us off near a cramped alley where children were playing soccer with a tennis ball. One of them screamed in delight and promptly climbed over Ahmed's back like a feisty squirrel.

"This one is Fadi. He is very naughty," Ahmed informed us as Fadi's tiny hands clamped over his uncle's eyes in an attempt to blindfold him. We ducked inside a concrete building and climbed five flights of stairs to reach the apartment.

The door was flung open. A shrill female voice screamed in Arabic, presumably to two rowdy toddlers chasing each other in endless circles.

"Mustafa! Besma!" their mother shouted, but no one was listening.

The game continued until someone tripped and started bawling. We left our shoes on the landing next to a dozen other pairs. Fadi, still perched on his uncle's back, yelled, "Mama, Mama!" to announce our arrival.

A striking woman with shoulder-length wavy hair, black as a raven, welcomed us inside. She wore a loose-fitting sleeveless cotton dress and wiped her flour-smeared hands on it before shaking my hand.

"So happy to meet you," she said in a lilting accent. "My name is Rabia." A schoolgirlish giggle followed. She didn't look a day over twenty-five. We were ushered into a spacious room devoid of all furniture except a Phillips TV and a small trampoline. A stack of pillows against one wall served as the seating area, where Ahmed had already staked out a comfortable position, stretching out his legs and lacing his hands underneath his head. It was nice to see him so relaxed after all that running around he did back at the hotel.

Rabia motioned for us to sit down. Instead of disappearing into the kitchen as my mother used to do whenever we had guests, she summoned her teenage daughter with the glamorous face of a made-up model to get us some soft drinks. When I asked Rabia how many children she had, she motioned five with her fingers and pointed to her slightly bulging tummy to indicate another on the way. Then she spoke to Ahmed in fast Arabic sprinkled with mischievous laughter.

He smiled his trademark Cheshire smile. "My sister says she and her husband cannot keep their hands off each other. It is not easy to keep control."

I asked if they were newlyweds, which triggered loud guffaws from her end. Apparently, the couple had been married for seventeen years.

Rabia said something else in Arabic. Ahmed groaned and shook his head. She poked him in the ribs to translate.

"My sister says that Arab woman likes too much sex. She says that in Islam you get reward for having sex. If you are married." He clarified the crucial point.

"What about Eve and the forbidden fruit?" Bea asked no one in particular.

"The Islamic version doesn't single out Eve for falling from grace. That means Muslim women are not carrying the burden of original sin. They are responsible for their own actions," I responded.

Rabia's eyes darted back and forth as she tried to keep pace with our conversation. But our English must have strained her ears as much as her rapid-fire Arabic did ours. She uttered a lengthy passage to Ahmed, who nodded his head several times in agreement before he faced us to translate.

"According to my sister, if a Muslim husband fails to satisfy his wife, he will be taking away her rights."

"Rights, what rights?"

"According to my sister, a Muslim marriage contract is about the husband and wife only having sex with each other. So this makes it a duty on both people to keep each other happy."

I was impressed that Rabia was so well-versed in such matters. Judging by the satisfied look on her face, it seemed that Rabia's husband was fulfilling his matrimonial obligation. We met him later in the evening when he came home from work and collapsed on the cushions, a great big bear of a man with a booming voice and a handlebar mustache. He teased his wife with obvious affection, and she wasn't above the occasional swat on his behind as a playful gesture. Ahmed told us on the way back that the couple had eloped as high school sweethearts.

Act Three, Scene Two

The days rippled with energy. Even doing our laundry was not a mundane chore. We took turns washing and scrubbing in the little porcelain sink of our private courtyard. Bea carried little plastic bags of detergent that she had carted all the way from Australia, while I relied on the local soap. There was no clothesline, so we would drape soaking-wet socks, panties, and shirts over the backs of chairs and on the railings of our beds. One day, there was great excitement when Ahmed announced the arrival of a brand-new washing machine. We followed him up some stairs to al-Rabie's rooftop, where I often ventured during sundown just to listen and tape-record a beautiful rendition of the call to prayer from the neighborhood's muezzin. Ahmed pointed out a metal tub attached underneath a motorized contraption that moved from side to side when he plugged it into a crumbling wall socket. Given the weeklong waiting list for use of the washing machine, we stuck to our sink.

So there was plenty of action in Damascus, only it was *everyday* action—the kinds of tasks necessary when you live someplace. Bea and I weren't like the few casual backpackers we'd run into at our hotel, usually in town for a couple of days on their way to somewhere else, not staying in the city for two entire months as we had. And by the end of our stay, I wanted desperately for something big to happen. It wasn't something I could picture or articulate, but I knew that I would recognize it as soon as it came my way.

Meanwhile, I went overboard with my list of remaining historical sights to visit. I wanted to see the Azem Palace, earlier the residence of the governor of Damascus, now a cultural museum, and a gorgeous 18th-century Damascene house known as Beit Nizam, and the old Hijaz station, start of the train line built by the Ottomans to transport pilgrims from Damascus to Medina. There were not-to-be-missed tombs of the Muslim conqueror Saladin and the great Sufi master Ibn al-Arabi. There was also a postponed side trip to Palmyra. It wasn't Bea's style to be running around with a full agenda. But she kept pace with me, occasionally hinting that maybe we ought to slow down and just sit tight for a while. That was the last thing I wanted to do, because it would have given me too much time to think. And there was something bothering me. It had to do with Bea.

I was feeling somewhat neglected, living in my friend's shadow. Eight times out of ten, she was the star attraction. I didn't mind at first because her arresting presence made it easy to meet people and befriend strangers who were always brimming with curiosity and helpfulness. They would pay me some attention, throw in a *salaam* or two, maybe praise my baby-talk Arabic, but it was really Bea they wanted to flaunt their English with and to impress. She did cut a dashing figure with her *hijab* and Latin looks.

As I had gathered from the fan club in Amman, the veil was a bit of a vanity boost for Bea, making her good-looking features even more pronounced, often inducing cases of public admiration that were probably not so common on the streets of Sydney. I still had mixed feelings about wearing the *hijab* when the focus on outward appearance alone became society's benchmark for Muslim piety. It was more of a cultural uniform, though I had learned my lesson in Cairo's subway about the drawbacks of blending in.

Now I was starting to analyze the subtle language of veiling. In my mind it was no longer an outright dismissal of female sexuality, because the very act of covering the hair was accentuating its hidden appeal. Just as some women unveil their bodies to highlight their sexuality, veiling could also be interpreted as sexualizing a woman by shielding or protecting her attributes from the public's gaze. Whether or not Bea read so much into it was a matter of some debate, which we never hashed out.

She really was a vision in her veil. I had no problem with people's appreciating this, but I was beginning to tire of getting shoved to the side like a pair of worn sneakers in deference to my friend. Bea's antenna had picked up on my irritation, and she told me to get over it. She said it was actually a compliment that people ignored me. It meant that I did not stand out as a stranger. Familiarity tainted my name and my face. But this level of supposed intimacy did not stand to the test whenever I opened my mouth.

In many cases, I felt obligated to know Arabic, and my lack of fluency drove a wedge when language took precedence over religion as a social bond. Even though less than 20 percent of the planet's 1.6 billion Muslims are Arab, I sometimes got the impression that those of us for whom Arabic is not a native tongue are somehow lesser qualified as Muslims.

"I have to pee," Bea urgently whispered into my ear.

Squeezed between a sudden madness of bridal dresses and drapery in a narrow covered alley, I was wrestling through bits of tinsels and taffeta, trying not to get run over by a parade of voluminous women in black hurtling through the arm's-length passage like careening bowling balls.

There was no such thing as public bathrooms in the *souq*. Out of sheer desperation, we stumbled into a hairdressing salon. A chubby balding man rose to his feet and opened a back door.

"Please, welcome to my home. You find *hammam* inside. No problem, no problem."

We climbed up steep stone stairs that led to a second-story house hidden within the confines of a graceful courtyard.

A stocky woman with strawberry-blond hair was dozing in a rocking chair with a sleeping infant.

"Mama, Mama!" A naughty-looking boy sped across the room and clambered in her lap.

He pointed his finger at us and said, *"Shoof,"* as if to say, "Look what Daddy brought home from the market!"

She smiled at us graciously, as if accustomed to having foreigners wander into her house in search of a bathroom, and said something in rapid Arabic.

Her husband laughed and translated, "She jokes I bring you here as my future wives!"

It would certainly provide a way to prolong our Syrian visas without hassling with the immigration officials. We made use of their mosaic-tiled squat toilet, equipped with a pressurized rubber hose to wash the private parts with the left hand (one of the reasons why toilet paper is nonexistent in most Muslim households). A dinner invitation promptly emerged. Children streamed into the room, inspecting us with eyes wide as saucers. The mother smiled and gestured toward them with arms open wide and then bunched up her fingers to poke at her chest. "Mine, mine, all mine," she was saying. I was astounded to learn that at twenty-seven years of age, she had already given birth to a brood of eight.

Dinner was a sumptuous spread of *mulukhiyyah* (dried spinach leaves cooked with chicken), rice mixed with fava beans, salty black olives, sheep's milk cheese, and fresh-baked pita. We sat in a large circle over thin cotton bedsheets protecting the handwoven carpets and ate with our hands. They had invited some friends over—a middle-aged couple, him with graying wavy hair, her with a frizzy cap of curls—who sat on the sofa and appraised us in that pregnant silence that accompanies the contented chewing and swallowing of a good meal. The children were remarkably well behaved, wiping clean their plates and carrying dirty dishes to the kitchen, scooping up the sheets with fallen bread crumbs. A precocious seven-year-old girl allowed me to look over her long-division problem sets. We ate bowlfuls of creamy pistachio-flavored ice cream. It came from a famous ice cream parlor that Bea and I had sighted on our first day in the *souq*. It seemed like years ago.

Curtain Call

Two days later, a call came through to our little room.

"There is a man named George who wants to talk to you. He says it is urgent." Ahmed's voice sounded a bit funny on the receiver.

I could almost picture his curly-lipped sneer and the question-mark eyebrows shooting straight up his forehead. It was strange to receive a local phone call. We were so used to direct face-to-face contact in our everyday encounters.

"Hello?"

"Yes, hello. This is George. We met the other night at the Shabaan house."

"The what?"

"Our friends, Mr. and Mrs. Shabaan. You were eating dinner with the family."

It was news to hear a name associated with our kind hosts. We had simply dubbed them the *hammam* house.

"Yes?"

"My wife and I would like to invite you and your friend to have dinner with us. We live not far from your hotel."

"Weeell, we might have plans tonight. . . . " I closed my hand over the receiver and hissed at Bea. "It's that older couple from the *hammam* house. They want to meet us for dinner."

She shrugged her shoulders and went back to doing her nails. I took it as a yes.

"Yes, that would be fine. Where should we meet you?"

"Just come to al-Merjeh square. I will pick you up. Shall we say in half an hour?"

I hung up the phone slightly puzzled.

True to his word, George was waiting for us next to a steel-gray Peugeot sedan.

"Merhaba, merhaba. How smart you look!"

We all shook hands.

"Where is your wife?" I asked.

"Oh, she is fixing dinner at the house. She is very excited to meet you both."

We hovered outside the open car door, where we were treated to a strong whiff of George's aftershave.

The house was near Jabal Qasiyun, the modest-size mountain overlooking the city, with a summit teeming with overpriced-food hawkers and café stands. Madame Miriam was standing near some plants. She was a tall woman with an auburn-tinted afro and wore tight black jeans and a red-and-black striped turtleneck sweater stretching to midthigh. She pecked her husband on the lips and thrust a bunch of mint leaves under my nose.

Their home had the cold mustiness of an old graveyard. It was strewn with used Christmas wrapping paper and bottles of unopened wine, suggesting a temporary shelter rather than a lived-in sanctuary. Some dusty pictures on the mantelpiece of a teenage boy with enormous sideburns and bellbottoms provided the only clues of a past. They were a Christian couple, evident from the silver cross pendant around Miriam's neck and a tattered reproduction of *The Last Supper* hanging in a gilded rococo-style frame.

George brought a tray of champagne and peanuts. He reminded me of Donald Duck with his protruding behind that waddled from side to side.

"What are we celebrating?" I asked.

"Tonight let us celebrate life!"

Miriam popped a cassette tape in the stereo and tried to teach Bea and me a traditional *debke* dance. We all stood in a straight line, with our arms overlapping each other's shoulders, kicking legs in the air and stomping heels as in Irish step dancing. I couldn't get the footwork right and pursed my lips in frustration, causing Miriam to double over in laughter and collapse on the sofa. But she laughed from the mouth only, not the eyes, which looked sad and empty as if mourning a tragic loss.

George had disappeared into another room and called us in a high-pitched voice. "Oh, girls, come and take a look!"

We went into the bedroom and faced a queen-size mattress scattered with some velvet pillows and a leopard-print blanket. Behind it draped a string of tiny light bulbs flashing in red, rather like a ritzy motel sign. George was going through a small suitcase of clothes. His wife unleashed a girly giggle and pulled open the top drawer of a bureau. Bea and I exchanged glances and watched the couple as sheer nighties and baby-doll dresses began flying around the room.

George came up to me with a see-through red teddy. "How about you try this on? It would look rather nice on you."

The man had to be joking. I felt a tinge of panic, just a tinge, and I willed it to go away. Maybe they were celebrating Halloween, Syrian-style. And it was none of my business to wonder why.

I turned around, and to my astonishment, Bea was slipping a pink

Goldilocks frock over her clothes. Miriam did up the back buttons and started putting on makeup, a scarlet lipstick and black liquid eyeliner. She came up and slowly kissed my cheeks, deliberately aiming close to the lips. Her vacant eyes implored me to stay and join in with the fun.

I was starting to think this was more than just trick-or-treating.

Bea had clearly caught the spirit. I found her sitting in George's lap, tweaking his wig of frumpy black curls as he fidgeted with his high heels and a faux-fur muffler. I grabbed my camera. But instead of loosening up, I began to get scared that we were stuck in a situation that wasn't going to be so easy to escape. It may not be as innocent as a dress-up party. *What would we have to do? Would they force us to do something we didn't want? How would they react if we refused? Would there be any weapons at their disposal? A knife, a gun, some kind of homemade booby trap to make us stay put?* My mind spun in paranoia.

Suddenly the lights went out, and Miriam's face appeared ghostlike above a glowing candelabra. She sat down next to me on the sofa and held my hand tightly in hers.

"I go to my village next week. Why don't you come? It is near Hammah, where they have the *noria*, the waterwheels. Very beautiful village with river and mountains. You meet my family. They teach you more Arabic."

I said nothing and cast my eyes downward to watch a flickering shadow.

"Your friend, very nice girl. You very nice, too. Such lovely eyes."

I continued staring at the shadow and tried to loosen my hand from her grip.

"My husband and I, we try new things. But Syrian people very afraid. They are not like us. In America, many different people. You meet, you like. But here it is very hard."

Her tone was soft and sad. It was the tone of a child lost in the wrong crowd, longing to break free. I wondered how we were going to get out of this little snare. They were just getting warmed up. What would happen when the real fun and games started?

"Listen, Miriam. My friend and I are not what you think. This is not for us."

She looked surprised. "But when I saw you together, I thought that you and her . . . very good friends." She pinched my ass. "I asked my husband to call you so we know you better. It is nice fun. Nobody hurt."

"Sorry, but we are not interested. Please tell your husband that we want to go home."

"No! You must stay. Please. You cannot leave me." Her eyes were begging.

I got off the sofa. Bea had slipped off the pink frock. Her face was flushed, and for the first time, I noticed a ruffle in her normally placid exterior. She had just rebuffed George.

"Where is he?"

"He went out to pick up some friends. I think they are coming over to the house."

"We'd better dash out before he comes back. Did you say anything to him?"

"I couldn't stop laughing when he put on that black negligee and slipped on his high heels. I think he was a bit embarrassed after that."

Poor Miriam. She started sobbing softly as we gave her a quick hug, grabbed our jackets, and bolted out the door.

Dual Anatomy

We slept until noon the next morning. Ahmed had slipped a note underneath the door. He had a free morning and wanted to take us to Sayyida Zeinab, a Shiite mausoleum/mosque just outside of Damascus that I wanted to visit. We seemed to have missed out on the opportunity. I could have blamed George and Miriam for keeping us up so late, for kidnapping us and bringing us to their house to have some kinky adult fun, but I didn't. It wasn't really their fault, unless one can be faulted for being human and fallible. Actually, I felt a particular kinship with the crossdressing couple. They were living a dual identity, having to shield their private quirks for publicly acceptable roles. Though I have no such secrets to hide, I do understand duality. It seems to be the thesis of my life.

It's a tiresome job, and sometimes I wish I didn't have to do it, that I could just ignore the whole thing and be less self-absorbed. But when you live in fragments of identities, how can you avoid the need to feel some wholeness? Even so, I wouldn't want my life to be a single tidy integer. I prefer an identity fraught with messy decimal points and broken fractions. They give me a certain texture, a certain density that I'm used to carrying, without which I would feel hollow and empty.

This was why I resonated with our friends from last night. Their desire to practice an alternative lifestyle was part of their inner texture; it made them different and added to their complexity. Even though I couldn't share that lifestyle with them, I appreciated their individuality. It was not about judgment in my book. It was about empathy and humanity. And I revel in being human. It means I am not perfect, that I have flaws, weaknesses, and bad habits. I embrace them all even as I try to fight them and change them, knowing that no matter how hard I try, a human being is all that I am and will be.

"Come on! We're gonna be late!"

I dashed over to the little mirror above the washbasin to secure my slippery black scarf with more pins, nearly knocking over Bea. "Look at you! That *aba* is positively stunning. You could pass for a Syrian woman."

She twirled around like a model for full inspection. Her scarf, lightly embroidered on the edges in a beige crisscross pattern, was tied behind her head, accentuating a smooth, tight jawline.

"No worries, babe. We'll make it on time."

"Wisam said Friday prayers start at one and it's already half past noon. We'll have to fly to the mosque at this rate!"

"Aren't we meeting him at his house? It's just near the Citadel."

"My camera, where's my camera?" I tore through a small mountain of clothes in our room.

"Relax, girl. It's in my bag. You gave it to me last night when we started running down the highway for that minibus."

"That was a lucky escape. George must have been livid to find us gone."

"Poor old Georgie. He was just a bit unconventional. But we did have some fun, eh?" Bea threw me a sly grin.

I looked at my friend, a vision of demure innocence in her silky black *abaya* and matching veil. It was quite a contrast after the pink frilly dress, not to mention the wig. A more sublime change of scene was definitely in order.

Wisam was waiting for us near the brick wall leading to his house.

"Mashallah!" He praised our new look.

"Yallah, Wisam!"

I started to run, holding up the edges of my ankle-length coat to avoid tripping over the ends. All the color and noise had been sucked out of the *souq* on the Friday Sabbath. Reams of Quranic verses dribbled over the loudspeaker like falling water, increasing in pitch and intensity as we slid into the immense courtyard of the mosque, framed on two sides by a rhythmic arrangement of arched columns and pillars. I was stung to tears and could not move at first, overwhelmed with its beauty.

Built in the early part of the 8th century on the former site of a pagan temple, then a Christian basilica, the Ummayad Mosque is an architectural triumph of lightness, solidity, and the purity of space. Vaults soar toward heaven. Turquoise, lapis lazuli, and mustard yellow transform the mosaic and ceramic tiles into tender harmonies. They appear to move and at the same time remain absolutely still. Bea and I walked around the courtyard arm and arm, slowly, deliberately, panning our eyes in slow motion to take in all the subtle details. Regarded as one of the wonders of the world in its time, the mosque had miraculously survived six earthquakes and seven fires. Its imaginative use of gold-cut mosaics interlaced with vibrant emerald greens conjure Tolkien forests and fairytale castles, a child's fantasy world where dreaming takes place alongside living.

A group of women in huge black cloaks were scattering seeds for visiting pigeons. One of them came up to me and offered fresh dates. I followed her into the main prayer hall, a vast chamber of plush red carpets and marble columns, and the resting place of the head of St. John the Baptist. Bea instinctively settled herself in an inconspicuous corner. The black-cloaked visitors took some time for a quick photo shoot, standing next to the pulpit with grave expressions. When they saw me sitting by myself, fingers curled to motion me forward to sit next to my adopted kin. We listened to the *khutbah,* or sermon, delivered in a deep baritone; it was something about charity, as I caught the word *zakah,* meaning alms. A rustle of fabric rippled across the room as the imam started the prayer. Women and men stood on opposite sides of the immense interior, all of us equal in the eyes of God.

Act Three, Final Scene

Ahmed's face collapsed when Bea told him that we would be leaving Damascus in two days. "Too soon, it is too soon," his eyes said.

"When is it ever not?" I replied with mine.

We left on the holiday of Eid al-Adha, a day commemorating Abraham's willingness to sacrifice Ishmael as requested by God, only to have a slaughtered ram substituted at the last minute for his son. A literal rendition of this story takes place every year across the Muslim world.

Ahmed accompanied us to the *servees* stand, where we had to endure a three-hour delay, as the driver had disappeared in search of a butcher and his choice cuts of lamb or goat's meat. It turned out that he had delivered the package at the mosque to feed the poor. The line of grumbling waiting passengers, including Bea and me, swallowed our complaints in chagrin when the driver returned and passed around some Damascene sweets.

Ahmed's charcoal eyebrows seemed to have deepened in shade. Perhaps the water swirling in his dark eyes made them blacker. As I handed over my pack to be stowed in the luggage compartment, it felt ten pounds heavier with memories. The van was overcrowded with passengers, and we were assigned seats in the stuffy back end, next to a hefty Arab woman and her wailing babies. The driver unleashed a volley of horns and slowly reversed.

Syria
(Aleppo)

In My Own Skin

The way is full of perils and the goal far out of sight
There is no road to which there is no end, do not despair

HAFEZ

At eight in the morning, the bus station in Beirut slowly stirred to life. Two coaches pulled in with bumper-sticker-size cards inside the driver's-side window indicating their destinations. They were both heading to Tripoli. I watched a group of rowdy boys and girls in starched school uniforms climb on board and fill all the empty seats. Some of them poked their heads out the window and made funny faces at me as the buses rolled on their way.

I wriggled out of my pack and used it as a waiting bench. The day was still young and there was no rush to move about and do things. The tip of my journal peeked through my shoulder bag, inviting me to flip through its pages to relive the recent past.

After leaving Damascus, Bea and I had lived in a Beirut apartment for one month. It came with Noha, our Singing Architect college roommate. She used to study all night long, poring over textbooks and blueprints, her room a mess of compasses, straightedges, and empty coffee cups. Whenever Noha was frustrated or stuck in the middle of some problem, she would belt out Fairuz classics in a voice as sweet as honey. Our four-story complex was nestled in Tarik el Jedideh, an old Arab neighborhood crammed with little shops selling fresh *labneh, kibbe,* and falafel. In the mornings, the three of us woke up to delicious smells wafting from the bakery just across the street and a virtual extension of our living room balcony. I would lean over its waist-high iron grille and call out to the baker's little boy to bring us some croissants for breakfast. When he was too lazy to come up the two flights of stairs, the boy would just throw the package up to the open balcony. His aim never failed.

On weekends, Bea and I would shop for farm-fresh vegetables near the Sabra and Shatila refugee camps. At the time, I was completely ignorant about the scores of Palestinians killed there, some say massacred, in 1982. The darker passages of those places were obscured by the present moment as the vendor filled my string shopping bag with cloves of garlic, tomatoes, and eggplants while admiring Bea's ponytailed profile. All over Beirut, our footprints treaded on cinder cones of history that we could not relate to or understand, but only experience as one who trespasses in somebody else's dream.

Time was a slick operator, fusing a can-do capitalist spirit with remnants from the city's fifteen-year-old civil war past, regardless of the strange juxtapositions it produced. A Swatch store shared the same block as a wounded building with collapsed ceilings and floors. Construction zones with cranes and concrete emerged kitty-corner from war-ravaged walls pockmarked with bullet holes. Some days, Bea and I would come home to see DEATH TO ISRAEL graffitied on the building next to the bakery. On the way over, we had sipped lattes at Starbucks and window-shopped the Versace store. Beirut's visual contrasts cajoled the senses like a magician's sleight of hand.

Then Bea had started running seriously low on money. She had figured back in Damascus that her dwindling bank account would allow her to get as far as Lebanon, and maybe a bit farther if we were frugal. But frugality was nowhere in the picture once we decided to take the apartment. It was hardly expensive, about US$50 a week, but it meant that Beirut would be the last station of our journey together. Bea found a cheap flight to London, where she planned to do some temp work. We parted ways at the airport amid tearful good-byes and hoped to meet again in Turkey or the shores of a Greek island.

I moped around the apartment for days, listening to Fairuz (the actual diva plus my roommate) and eating sinful amounts of baklava and chocolate cake. Bea's absence seemed to have drained all the juices and flavors of our adventures together, leaving me with empty canisters labeled Dahab, Amman, Beirut, and Damascus. I missed Bea's voice with the charming Aussie lilt, her cool, calm demeanor that often tempered my impulsive swings, her unhurried lushness.

It was a mixed blessing to find myself suddenly alone. To be free to do anything I wanted or didn't want to do. I had lingered in Beirut for a week, going on day trips around Lebanon. Despite warnings of land mines, hostile territory, and Hezbollah militants, I went south to Tyre and Sidon. In the old *souqs,* I encountered the usual friendliness and curiosity. A teenage boy with a cowlick hairdo asked me to take his picture for good luck in an upcoming soccer match. I did a double take when the boy told me that the team he was representing, al-Ahd, was loyal to Hezbollah. Soccer players? Hezbollah?

In the minds of most Americans, the name Hezbollah conjures images of burly Islamic thugs conducting guerrilla warfare. But I learned that Hezbollah's militant reputation was tempered by another side, one that combined political action with social welfare programs. The boy on the soccer team mentioned that Hezbollah was also responsible for building many schools, hospitals, and clinics neglected by the Lebanese government. He eagerly anticipated the day he would grow up and join Hezbollah as a full-fledged party member. I hoped only that my young acquaintance would make peaceful choices that wouldn't hurt others.

When I returned to the apartment, my landlady was looking for long-term tenants. Noha had graduated and moved back with her family. She had left me a note with a hand sketch of the Temple of Jupiter, the one with the enormous long columns that I had seen in the ancient Roman city of Baalbeck. My time was up in Lebanon. I decided to return to Syria, this time farther north to Aleppo. But Aleppo did not appear on the horizon when the buses started rolling in again. More signs for Tripoli. In desperation, I turned to the local version of the public information booth—a boy selling hot tea and roasted sunflower seeds.

"Aleppo?"

"Mafi mushkil." No problem.

We approached a rusty beige Chevy. A man was leaning against the hood, sticking his pinky in his right ear to scoop out some wax on an extraordinarily long nail and wiping it off with the hem of his shirt. I learned he was the taxi driver.

"Aleppo?" I inquired again.

He grunted a yes and went back to cleaning his ears. When I started walking away, the driver let out a piercing whistle to make me retract my steps. The trunk was open and a stiff outstretched arm gestured toward my pack. I handed it over, trying not to be too concerned about the contents of unmarked cartons forming a small fortress around an exclusive piece of luggage. A little wrestling match with the back door followed before I made contact with the wafer-thin floorboards. Then the driver took out a fresh pack of al-Hamra cigarettes from the glove box. I wondered what else he concealed in there, imagining his real occupation as some sort of smuggler rather than a reputable chauffeur with a reliable set of wheels. A cobweb of loose black wires dangling below the dashboard did not inspire confidence. We waited two hours for more passengers, but no one showed up. Prepared to spend another night in Beirut, I thought of canceling the whole expedition when a plump, well-dressed man approached the Chevy.

Something about him instantly reminded me of Saleh, a musician Bea and I had befriended at a UNESCO concert in Beirut. It played on the theme of cultural bridges, mingling classical Arabic songs by Wadi al Safi with the Spanish ballads of a husky crooner named José Fernandez. After the performance, we had strayed into the parking lot for some reason. A man was loading a *qanun*, or zither, in the back seat of a white Peugeot, and Bea asked him for a light. He had bright, clear eyes and a smile that made him appear slightly startled. The face looked trustworthy. So when he offered us a lift, Bea and I accepted without hesitation. Instead of going back to our apartment, we accompanied Saleh to another gig at a hotel in Jouneih, a trendy beachfront neighborhood north of Beirut showcasing casinos and fancy living.

Everyone had stared when Bea and I walked inside that glam palace in our crumpled cotton dresses, carrying audio speakers and microphones like two starstruck groupies. But Saleh had shown not a trace of embarrassment. He winked and pointed out a corner table in the front. The place was packed at two in the morning. I stared with dismayed fascination at the high-society Lebanese women in their low-cut dresses and their cheap sultry dancing. Bea had appeared more interested in Saleh. Apparently, he had his gaze on her the entire time he played his instrument on stage, plucking its strings with those long steel-tipped fingers. By dawn, we ventured along the Corniche, the Mediterranean promenade of Beirut and a place to see and be seen. Saleh insisted on buying us *manakeesh*, a rolled-up crepe soaked with thyme and olive oil, at a twenty-four-hour café that played Elvis Presley songs. Then Bea had taken over the wheel of Saleh's car and driven us back to the apartment without needing directions. I was so proud of her.

"Fifty-fifty?"

The well-dressed man who rekindled my memory of Saleh turned to me and explained that we could leave Beirut right away if I agreed to split the entire cost of the taxi (about $60), a ransom price compared to the public bus fare. Deciding not to waste any more time, I forked over the cash. The driver squatted on his haunches and drank tea in a shot glass before hitting the road.

He had to be on something. Or maybe it was the giddy rush of some narcotic buried in the tea. I was glad I hadn't touched the stuff, but now I prayed we would make it to Aleppo with our limbs intact. The old Chevy ricocheted like a stray bullet, overtaking every single vehicle that dared to block its way. A madman sat in the driver's seat, apparently practicing for the Indy 500. He floored the gas pedal, straining the engine to the maximum 120 kilometers of his flying mobile. Any minute, I expected to see him push a button on the dashboard for liftoff. My fellow passenger, who called himself Dr. Malik, flashed me a reassuring smile as he chain-smoked and crossed one leg over the other. I liked the pinstriped pattern of his socks and the way his overcoat draped across his shoulders. But it was hard to concentrate on Dr. Malik's debonair style when my mind was besieged with visions of red blinking lights and state troopers who got off on flagging speed demons.

Tires screeched to a halt at the Syrian border checkpoint. The race ended with smashing success, not to mention a half-broken tailpipe sizzling with exhaust fumes. Having arrived this far in one piece, I willed my luck to hold out on the prospect of reentering Syria with an expired visa on an American passport and not being able to explain myself in my kindergarten Arabic. The friendly doc intervened as my spokesperson to facilitate the formalities.

After five harrowing hours, we cruised into Aleppo, the cityscape speckled with the onion-shaped bulbs of mosque domes and Lego-like stacks of sand-colored buildings. Dr. Malik disembarked near a busy traffic circle, wishing me good luck and issuing some stern warnings to the taxi driver to deposit me at a proper hotel.

The poor man had the look of a decompressed hot-air balloon. Despite the wild ride, I started feeling sorry for him. Is this what his whole life amounted to, driving back and forth between two countries like a maniac? Maybe it was a coping mechanism of some sort.

"*Wayn fondouk?*"

The driver asked the whereabouts of my hotel. I gave him the address that I had picked up from the Camp Mermaid gang in Aqaba more than four months ago. He had never heard of it, but we managed to find the place after squeezing into some narrow lanes lined with tire and auto-parts shops. The driver opened the trunk and retrieved my pack. His pursed lips indicated that the race ended right here, right now.

"*Shukrun.*"

I thanked him and stumbled out of the battered Chevy straight into the clutches of an inebriated old man. He mumbled Arabic drivel under his stale beer breath. A steady stream of pale-yellow mucus dripped from the man's rather bulbous red nose. Neighboring Syrian mechanics stepped outside their shops, looking me over as if a traveling circus clown had just come to town. Perhaps they had never seen a short girl in maroon glasses, harem pants, a gauzy peasant blouse, and a crumpled brown head scarf, hunched underneath a backpack. It no longer weighed as much as fifty pounds, thanks to my numerous visits to the local postal services en route to ship things home.

The male stares followed me like a shaft of spotlight as I inched toward the hotel sign with my escort staggering by my side. We paused between two tire shops. A five-foot-tall metal door wedged into a stone wall served as the hotel entrance. The drunkard began pulling at the straps of my pack to steady his constant wobbling. At one point, he laid his right hand at the top of my head and then moved the hand to the door frame to indicate that we matched in height.

One of the mechanics approached us and looked me in the eye. His gray overalls were smeared with greasy stains. He said something to the drunkard in a sharp tone and glanced my way again. The drunkard started laughing. I pried his fingers loose from my shoulder straps with some help from the mechanic and quickly darted inside the tiny doorway, making sure to bolt the lock. A steep flight of stairs led to the reception desk, where a fair-skinned young man with cool gray eyes greeted me in French.

"*Complet*," he told me they were full.

"Can I sleep on the rooftop?"

"*C'est pas possible.*"

Dismissing the roof idea, he rose from his chair and walked out of the little office, which was no bigger than the size of a two- by four-foot storage unit. A girl in a sarong and tight T-shirt skimming her midriff came down the stairs, shouting in a high-pitched British accent to some invisible companion.

"I'm just popping out for some fags."

I lobbed a friendly "Hey."

A pair of pale blue eyes appraised me from head to toe.

"Where are *you* from?"

"The States."

"That's funny. Don't see too many Americans with one of those." She pointed to my covered head.

I made no comment and turned my attention to the nickel-size Celtic tattoo perched on her right shoulder. It looked rather like a dead fly.

"Where did he go?" I asked about the abrupt disappearance of the man at the reception desk.

"Oh, he's probably watching TV upstairs with Claudia." Her lips twitched into a mischievous curve. "You new here?"

"Yeah."

"Better bolt your door at night. This place is known for its intruders." She gestured a pair of mock quotes around the last word, making it sound more like an invitation than a threat.

"I don't have a door to bolt. They have no rooms. I'm homeless at the moment."

"Poor you. Well, I'm sure Osama will think of something."

I could have sworn she winked.

The man with the cool gray eyes bounded down the stairs, his face and clothes newly moistened with perspiration.

"Still here?" he grumbled. "I told you we are full."

I gave him my best Ingrid Bergman wide-eyed stare.

"The roof?"

Osama shrugged okay with some mutterings of *quelle horreur*.

"*Merci!*"

The smirking Brit waved me cheerio.

The rooftop was a rectangular slab of concrete bordered by thick stone walls about six feet tall. Only the occasional cries of street vendors and the metallic hammerings of the mechanics indicated any signs of life. The late-afternoon heat lulled me to sleep on a thin foam mattress pad already in place. I dreamed of Beirut. . . .

The ATMs had provided the option of cash withdrawals in U.S. dollars or Lebanese lira. I was enamored with Rue Hamra, Beirut's answer to Manhattan's 5th Avenue, with glitzy designer shops next door to snack bars with American soda fountains and a Wimpy's burger joint. The platform-heeled hipsters dressed in flared jeans made me feel like a dowdy peasant. But Bea and I got our share of attention when a handsome duo on motorcycles followed us around Ras al Beirut all the way to the American University. They thought we wanted a ride.

I had looked the other way, but not before the Antonio Banderas lookalike in the back ripped an empty cigarette box and wrote a phone number on the clear white inside. The motorcyclists zipped off, their shaggy black hair whipping in the sea breeze. We ran into them at a nightclub where half the crowd was high on Ecstasy. Girls in leather miniskirts and thigh-high boots danced on tabletops or wriggled in cages suspended from the ceiling. We heard about a funky new place in

Ashrafiyeh. And Bea had the nerve to thumb for a ride at three in the morning. When we got into the back seat of a car, the driver had made the sign of the cross.

"Take some tea?" a man's voice chanted from somewhere above.

"Whaaat??"

"Tea, *shai!*"

A head lowered to meet my drowsy gaze. "Did you just arrive from Beirut?"

I mumbled a yes while untangling the head scarf jumbled around my neck. As the resident gofer at the hotel, Khalil was the all-in-one cook/cleaner/concierge/tea maker. He told me to watch out for Osama, the hotel manager, who appeared to favor certain guests and disregard things such as room reservations. But if I paid him in advance, I was more likely to hold on to my room as long as one became available. I drank hot sweet tea with Khalil and recreated the thrilling Indy 500 race in the old Chevy. He threw his head back and laughed, causing me to double over with laughter too. We slapped a couple of high fives.

The following morning, the rooftop radiated the cool and serene atmosphere of a Japanese tea garden. I huddled on a low stool with a stack of three-month-old issues of *Le Figaro* magazines, courtesy of a departed guest. Breakfast was *labneh* and *khubz*, ordered from a little stall just outside the hotel. I smeared the thick yogurt on a pita disk and wolfed it down. Khalil stopped by and handed me a cup of tea and a plate of hard-boiled eggs dipped in olive oil. We pooled our food and ate together in a civilized silence.

A slim, hollow-cheeked man dressed in a black jogging suit poked his head out of the stairwell and stepped up to join us. Throwing a cursory nod at Khalil, he plopped down on the floor, wiping the sweat from his brow with a large white handkerchief neatly folded like a triangle. He asked me my name and upon hearing my response, the stranger in black started reciting reams of Arabic poetry with theatrical exaggeration. I guessed his age in the midforties. After running out of verses, the hollow-faced man/bard stared at me like a hypnotist. Khalil referred to him as Sharif, a name that means "respect." I heard the two men exchange a few words. Sharif spoke in soft, modulated tones that gave his voice the feel of a soothing balm. Then he slipped back down the stairs.

I spent the rest of the day on the rooftop reading, feeling the need to catch my breath after the marathon of the preceding three months. Lebanon had been a blast and Damascus had been an even bigger blast. But with Bea gone, I had to find a new rhythm. In a way, I was glad to be alone again and sink into my own company. Aloneness was no longer a bad thing. It was necessary for self-awakening. And now in Aleppo, my aloneness felt very different from what I had first experienced upon arriving in Cairo. Then, it was mostly all nerves and tension because I was alone *and* lonely. Now, it was calm and peaceful, because I was alone but far from lonely. I was looking forward to my solo transition.

Caravan City

When the Andalusian traveler Ibn Jubayr visited Aleppo in 1184, he wrote, "The city is as old as eternity, but still young, and it has never ceased to exist." Legend has it that Abraham passed through Aleppo on his way to the Holy Land, and that he even milked his cows on the grassy mound now crowned by the citadel. The Arabic name of the city is Halab, commonly interpreted as a derivative of the word *halib*, meaning milk.

I had spent all morning settling in my new room, which opened up four days later. It had a nice cozy feel to it, but the lack of windows was a little suffocating. Almost a week had passed since my arrival in

Aleppo, and I hadn't stepped out of the hotel all this time. The front door was already wide open, as someone was moving in with an enormous amount of luggage. I held my head high and marched past the slew of auto-mechanic shops with rubber tires dangling on rusty old nails. All of a sudden, I became aware of my right arm. It was used to nestling in the inner hollow of Bea's left elbow whenever we walked together in the streets. Her absence from my side triggered the phantom-limb effect of a recent amputee and pangs of nostalgia for our adventures in Lebanon.

We had wanted to see Beitiddine, the early-19th-century palace in the southern Lebanese mountains. Having just missed our bus and not being inclined to wait for the next one, which could have arrived in the next fifteen minutes to two hours later (printed schedules and posted timings being an unnecessary nuisance in the Middle East), we had opted for a taxi. The driver demanded extra money because Beitiddine was out of his way. Grumbling like an old radiator, he had dropped us off at the base of a windy, hilly road. Bea did not intend to walk the three miles up to Beitiddine, so she stood in the middle of the road with an upturned thumb. Her waist-length tresses were a cape around her back (the *hijab* had converted into a fashionable headband), black-framed glasses skidded midway down that chiseled Roman nose, and a cigarette dangled from the corner of her mouth. We were picked up by the first car that came along, and spent the entire afternoon walking around the palace, absorbing its silent beauty.

"Khamsa, khamsa, khamsa!"

A brood of young children with the large innocent eyes of animals surrounded me like a mob, asking five piastres for little cartons of juice. I strolled past a colorful outdoor fruit and vegetable market. Men in floor-length tunics known as *jelbab* and turbans made out of the kaffiyeh jostled for space in the crowded market. Sturdy-looking, face-tattooed women shouted and bargained for the best produce at rock-bottom prices. With no sidewalk, everyone walked on the road, side by side with the snarling traffic of minivans, donkey carts, and taxis.

I stopped a man with Bedouin features to confirm my sense of direction.

"Bab Antakiya?"

"Awal shimael." First left. He pointed out the way.

A curving lane off the main road revealed a huge wooden door, one of the eight ancient gateways enclosing the old city of Aleppo. It was undergoing a massive face-lift. Men drilled into an open ditch with a deafening machine. A rickety wooden plank bridged this gaping hole and a steady trickle of human traffic stepped across it with stolid, purposeful faces that knew where they were going. Making my own little crossing, I imagined Alice falling down the rabbit hole.

"Merhaba!" A man selling *fuul* sandwiches from a little cart just inside the congested entrance exuded a familiar friendliness. A teenage boy with startling green eyes and chipped front teeth approached with a basket of fresh ripe strawberries. I took their photo and they smiled shyly and asked me to return *"bukra,"* or tomorrow. An ancient mosque with a tightly shuttered door loomed behind the cart. The *fuul* seller wanted to send a friend to find its guardian, but I waved him aside and penetrated deeper into the *souq.*

Rows of shops emerged on both sides of a covered arcade displaying silk scarves in shades of burgundy, turquoise, vermilion, and ochre, embroidered shawls with tasseled fringes, and thick cotton tapestries stacked from floor to ceiling. Farther along, more shops no bigger than office cubicles sold cheap cotton T-shirts proudly made in Syria, with slogans such as BEACH BOYS or UNIVERSITY OF CANADA. Slipping into a side street, I felt a soft and furry brush against my bare forearms and glimpsed the back of a donkey loaded with jute sacks as its bare-backed owner guided the animal with clucks of his tongue. A heady draft of sweet cardamom mingled with something unidentifiable but equally enticing—perhaps the crushed orange threads of saffron—penetrated my nostrils. I went from shop to shop asking for *kahve*. Finally, a businessman carrying a briefcase heard my pleas, led me down a dark passageway, and pointed to a decrepit little stall that produced not only traditional Arabic coffee brewed in long-stemmed copper pots but also the finest cappuccino I had tasted this far east of Italy.

One morning, as I made my way outside the ramparts of the old citadel of Aleppo, I noticed a string of sidewalk cafés. Glossy youth lounged in clusters of gender cliques, boys sneaking long looks from behind potted palms at girls. Biceps and tight jeans vied with veils paired with flared trousers and platform boots. A rusting tail-finned Buick cruised by, its occupants a boisterous quartet of high-school-aged hipsters with gelled spiky hair. The car dodged a tangle of three-wheeled scooters. It was a scene from 1950s Americana transplanted to a conservative Arab society developed far from mainstream capitalism and MTV. Yet watching those Aleppian teens, I couldn't help but think of their similarities to boys and girls anywhere in the world, where secret crushes and hushed whispers in best friends' ears toyed with hormones and heartstrings.

When I got back to my hotel room and lay down in bed, images of all the teenagers I had seen in the Middle East—from the café congregation this morning to the doe-eyed *hijabi* coeds in Cairo to the savvy globalized citizens of Amman, to Ahmed and his hardships in Damascus—flitted across my mind. I couldn't help but compare them to myself and wonder how my life would have turned out if I had spent my teenage years in a Muslim country. If I had remained in Pakistan until my early twenties, in what way would I be different?

For one thing, I would have been far more pampered in Pakistan, where my clothes were always washed and ironed, where I never had to do the dishes or take out the garbage. I learned these chores in America, where my mom was no longer a housewife but a working woman who was on her feet for ten hours a day at a retail shop. I used to think that she had it so much easier back in Karachi, but she told me it was better in the States because she was learning how to be independent and self-sufficient. It meant a lot of hard work, and I sort of saw my mom's point when I got my first part-time job as a fourteen-year-old.

I was a cashier and kitchen helper in a Mexican eatery. My mom had helped me get the position, and I remembered the day she had come to see me and how mortified I was to be mopping the floors, wearing a silly paper hat, and having customers shouting at me for their orders. It was the same thing when I later became a bag girl at the local Safeway. I spotted Mr. Ramsey, my high school chemistry teacher, in line and I fled my post, not being able to stand the humiliation of watching him watch me bag his groceries.

It was hard to take pride in my humble work situations because a part of me was still wedded to that life I had left behind in Pakistan, where the concept of an after-school part-time job simply did not exist. I received from my dad a weekly allowance that he referred to as pocket money. Only after we came to America did I have the option of going out and earning my own wages for the things I wanted. But these options came with the price of being inundated with choices, and when I didn't know what to choose, it was easy to get hurt, angry, and disillusioned. That was why I dithered around during junior high and high school, shutting out my family and blaming the world for all my woes.

Had I been in Karachi during those years, my problems would have been less about *me* and more about my environment that didn't allow the indulgence of wallowing in daily existential crisis. There, I would have had to worry about teachers who couldn't care less whether I passed or failed, about elements on the streets that made the commute from home to school a daily lesson in survival, about the government and its policies interfering with the things or the clothes I could and could not do or wear.

It was in Aleppo that night on my twin hotel bed with the lumpy mattress that I finally understood my dad's appreciation of the freedoms we enjoyed in America. That was why we had come. And by coming to America and leaving Pakistan, I had transformed my identity for good by becoming Seattle Maliha. I would never fully know the shape of Karachi Maliha because she had been only partially formed. My goal was to reconcile the two Malihas, and since I wasn't able to do that in my own back yard, I had taken to the road to be transformed by the journey itself.

Hostage to Hospitality

In contrast to the heart-stopping beauty of the Ummayad Mosque in Damascus, the Great Mosque, or Jama al Kebir, of Aleppo was less extravagant. Built in the early 8th century, its central feature is a six-story square minaret with each story displaying a distinct architectural style. I found myself in front of the *mawdah*, where Muslims perform their ablutions by cleansing with water before praying. A group of women sprawled in front of its rusting pillars, cracking shell-roasted pumpkin seeds between their teeth and smoking clove-scented cigarettes. I circled them, deliberating on a resting spot. Fingers curled and mouths twitched in laughter at my continuing circumambulations. One of the women tugged at the hem of my pants, causing me to trip forward and land on the dusty floor in the middle of the brood.

All eyes appraised me as if I were some strange new bird fallen from the sky that nobody quite knew what to do with. I learned the five women were part of a family. The mother, a large Bedouin woman with several bluish lines tattooed at the bottom of her chin, was joined by two restless daughters around my age and their two equally restless younger teenage cousins. It was a rare treat to be up close with women in the public sphere. The two younger girls wore floor-length dresses in fuchsia and parrot green, newly starched in the manner of clothes reserved for excursions from home. Their head scarves were worn bandanna-style. The mother continued to chain-smoke, her legs spread open to reveal a tattered pink petticoat. Tiny shreds of dead skin flaked off the soles of her feet like sawdust on a carpenter's workbench. She maintained a steady gaze on my face as her girls bombarded me with questions.

What was I doing in Aleppo? How long would I be staying? Where was I staying? Did I know anyone here? Why was I all by myself? Was I married? Did I have any children?

We conversed in Arabic. My staccato sentences lacked conjugated verbs. I improvised by stringing bits of relevant vocabulary, heavily relying on *mussafira, taliba, katiba* (traveler, student, writer) to sketch out my identity. In response, they would fling their hands in the air, slap their hands on foreheads, and burst out in florid impromptu speeches bemoaning my strange and tragic circumstances that had me traveling alone in an unknown country without any friends or relatives.

I accepted the family's invitation to go home with them, even though I hadn't a clue where they lived, how I would be getting back to the hotel that night, or what would happen to me from this point forward. When it came to adventure, I often heard two voices at once, the nagging worrywart and the romantic impulsive. The voices represented twin halves—my Western mind, trained to think too much and analyze its way through life, and my Eastern heart, wanting to experience a moment for what it is instead of formulating it in terms of something else.

In the next instant, we all crammed into a taxi. The squealing cousins talked in one breath to the driver. His head swung back and forth between the front windshield and the rearview mirror, where it lingered at times, until the sound of screeching tires and angry horns forced his attention up front. Fatima and Zoya, the two sisters whose house we were heading to, pinched me on the cheeks and winked. Their mother rolled down the window and blew out cigarette smoke like a practiced Hollywood diva.

We drove for nearly an hour, well outside the city, finally reaching a small settlement of mud-brick homes laid out like uniform matchboxes. The taxi inched farther into the narrow lanes of what seemed to be a secluded, conservative, less well-to-do community. Even with the visible form of five women from the neighborhood, people on the streets sensed the presence of a stranger among them and peered intently inside the passing car. Children chased us, laughing merrily in their dusty clothes, old men slowed their walking, their unblinking gazes riveted in our direction, and young mothers poked their heads from doorways to stare in suspicion or just plain curiosity. The two young cousins got out along the way, their squeals of laughter louder in pitch. By the time the taxi halted in front of a squat mud-brick house, identical to all the others, news of a foreigner had spread among the neighbors like ripples in a dark pond.

Shoes removed, we entered a room stripped of all furniture except a few bedrolls and pillows neatly stacked against the wall. The two sisters immediately flung off their scarves, shaking loose wavy rivulets of waist-length black hair that they piled up in messy but fashionable buns. The colorful dresses disappeared into a tin trunk and were replaced with worn cotton nighties. Their mother brought us sweet mint tea and a packet of more pumpkin seeds. I called her Um Jasim, which means Mother of Jasim, her eldest son. She kept asking why I was not yet married and even tapped her plastic wristwatch to drop a few subtle hints.

I shrugged and feigned indifference, choosing to concentrate on her two daughters. Fatima, the older one, smoldered with the mischief of a rebel at heart. Her sister Zoya had a petulant mouth, drooping at the edges like a closed flower bud. She played with me as if I were her own life-size doll. Kneeling behind my back, Zoya removed my head scarf and began combing her fingers through a tangle of knots, tacking a handful of colorful metallic hair ornaments with little springs in the middle in my hair until I looked like a jazzed-up Christmas tree.

A gruff old man (Father) shuffled in and collapsed on the floor. Fatima whispered to me that his chief occupation consisted of smoking cigarettes and drinking coffee with his friends at the local café while she, her sister, and the mother worked at odd jobs around the community, from sewing to baking bricks, to provide food and shelter for the whole family. I learned they were Bedouins from Palmyra, forced to abandon their nomadic lifestyle for economic mobility in the city. But something in Fatima's eyes told me the move had resulted in unprofitable trade-offs.

A neighboring couple came over unannounced to visit. The man tumbled out a string of prefabricated English sentences at me. "What is your good name? Such a pleasure to meet you. Do pay us the honor of visiting our humble home." This caused a momentary lull in my first-grade Arabic one-liners with Um Jasim and her daughters that probably sounded to their ears just as silly as the man's textbook English did to mine. A simple dinner of rice and lentils followed. Zoya said something about a *hammam*. I leaned back in the cushions and played cards with Zoya, fully aware that it was approaching 11:00 PM but with no clue of an exit strategy. A massive protest broke out among the family upon my desire to depart. They expected me to spend the night.

To someone growing up in the West, the Arab code of hospitality may seem overly effusive. Its Bedouin/nomadic roots dictated that if a stranger dropped by a tent in the desert, he or she would receive food and shelter for up to three days, no questions asked. I often used to overhear my fellow backpackers at the hotel raving, "Arabs are just so amazingly generous; they wouldn't let us pay for anything," as if their expectations were to the contrary. Had they acknowledged the perspective of their hosts, they would have understood that in the Middle East, as in many Asian cultures, hospitality and charity are benefits to the giver and a means of practicing what is good for his or her own self. It would go against the deepest instinct not to offer the best to anyone who steps across the doorstep.

Um Jasim and her daughters were itching to keep me near them as a source of amusement in their humdrum lives. Fatima dragged a double-size bedroll to the middle of the living/dining room, patting the left side to indicate my sleeping quarters. Zoya glowed with the excitement of a teenager at her first slumber party, though my less-than-enthusiastic reception must have appeared confusing. After dinner, I wrapped my scarf tightly around my head and shoulder and performed the nightly *isha* prayers. None of the family members joined me. Then I got out my journal and tried to write for a bit under the full scrutiny of three pairs of female eyes, occasionally peering at close range at the backward-moving script flowing from my pen.

I wanted to escape their clutches and find a nice quiet place to write or just be alone with my thoughts. Seven months ago, as a new-comer to Cairo, I was hankering for the very opposite, to be invited into people's homes, maybe even get adopted by a local family, to always have company and never be on my own. But the journey's evolution had trimmed the novelty factor of being a hostage to hospitality. While I appreciated Um Jasim's generosity and personal attention, I was also tired of being on display like some windup toy forced to sing and dance on cue.

Father, who had earlier passed out in the corner of the room, shuffled to his feet in search of a taxi when I insisted more loudly on making an exit. The girls decided to escort me back to the hotel, and I squeezed in the middle again with a more subdued Fatima and Zoya. Um Jasim remained at home. She looked me squarely in the eyes and said, *"Bukra al beit."* I was supposed to return to their house tomorrow. It seemed more of an order than an invitation. But I never saw them again.

A Man Named Sharif

He seemed at once ancient and modern, as if embodying two periods of history meeting inside him. A daily uniform of sky-blue button-down shirt, polyester gray herringbone-patterned jacket, black wool trousers much too long, and gleaming black patent pointy-toed oxfords clothed his gymnast's nimble frame. He was darkish in complexion, like the color of fine espresso. I noticed right away his sensitive hands, fine and slender instruments made to carry nerves and tendons and the fragile thoughts that moved them.

He was the man I had met on the hotel rooftop at breakfast shortly after arriving in Aleppo. He liked to recite Arabic poetry, and I wasn't quite sure what to make of him. We had barely spoken at that point. Then he turned up again a few days later, when I was installed in my room. I heard a light rap at the door at seven in the morning, and I opened it to find him in a tracksuit, asking me to go for a run in a nearby park. I threw some cold water on my face and brushed my teeth while Sharif waited outside my room, doing sit-ups and jumping jacks to warm up.

The streets were calm at that early hour. We both ran at the same pace and maintained an easy rhythm as we headed toward the park. It was a delightful little place, an oasis of greenery and peace, scattered with white marble statues of poets and statesmen and trellised pathways ringed around fountains. To my surprise, the lilting voice of Fairuz, an aural morning ritual piped through some ingenious sound system, flowed over us as we ran around the park's woodsy perimeter.

Some old men in fraying wool suits shuffled by with newspapers; a few young mothers with baby strollers walked along briskly; a girl in a velour pink tracksuit clutching a Walkman passed us on the left, her buttocks jiggling up and down like a seesaw. My modest jogging attire was a baggy long T-shirt with the word GRANADA stenciled in the upper left-hand corner and loose drawstring pants. A spandex headband replaced the head scarf to keep my hair pulled back. Sharif picked up his speed and called for two more rounds. It felt exhilarating to be running again, to concentrate on my feet pounding the earth and my quickening breath, to rediscover a long-forgotten ritual and break out in a good clean sweat.

"You are always a sport?" Sharif inquired as we started walking to cool off. He meant to ask if I was athletic, but I rather liked the way it came out with his inventive English.

"Yes," I answered truthfully to both meanings.

"I enjoyed that," I added as we started doing leg lunges inside a gazebo. A small crowd had gathered to watch our stretching session.

"Same time tomorrow?" he asked.

"Okay."

We had breakfast together in a dark little café, mopping up fried runny eggs with pieces of flat bread. Afterward, Sharif went about his business and I wandered back to the *souq*. The sun climbed higher in the mid-June sky, reminding me for some reason of a huge lemon drop.

I thought about Sharif as I poked around the shops. He had struck me as different right away. A brooding intensity was in his gaze, and his face had aged beyond his twenty-six years, making him look closer to forty. I wondered if was just the harshness of the desert sun that had taken a toll on his leathery skin, or whether some other sort of harsh living had robbed him of a youthful appearance.

Harem Girl

"Are you sure you will be all right?"

"Yes, yes, I'll be fine."

"Do you know where the ladies' entrance is?"

"Yes, I see someone going there now. I'll just follow her."

"I will wait for you by the graveyard. The *khutba* should be finished by one thirty."

"Okay."

"No okay."

"Mashi!"

"Tamam!"

Sharif and I were standing near Jama Firdaws, a historic mosque and religious school founded by the wife of Aleppo's ruler back in the 13th century. He had come by the hotel earlier in the day for our second morning run, but it started to rain, and by the time the skies cleared up, it was almost noon and I had lost my energy. I decided instead on a small excursion for Friday prayers and was just heading out the door when I saw Sharif coming up the alley. I told him my plans and he said we could go together. It was his day off and he hadn't yet been to Jama Firdaws, despite living in Aleppo all these years.

We took a taxi and got off near a dusty compound well outside the old city walls. The Jama was a stark solid mass of stone capped with eleven domes. Sharif hung a left to another part of the mosque where the men sat while I veered right toward my own section. Two hours later, when I came out, it was pouring again, the sky swirled with angry gray clouds, and I couldn't find Sharif anywhere. I thought he had ditched me and taken off for the day. Then I saw him squatting on his haunches just where he had told me to meet him. He motioned me to take shelter under his shawl, which he was holding with both hands. It felt like a little burrow.

"All finished?"

"Yes, it was nice."

"You like to pray in mosque?"

"It's a good feeling. It makes me calm down."

"What is this calm?"

"Peace. *Salaam.*"

"You are not in peace?"

"Not always. But I'm trying to be. It's not easy, you know."

"Maybe you try too hard."

I didn't know how to respond, so I just stared ahead. There was nothing to look at but muddy puddles. Sharif had closed his eyes and was rocking back and forth on his heels. It seemed to be some sort of practiced ritual, and again I wondered about his lapses into silence. We remained quiet and listened to the raindrops. My breaths grew deeper and I became aware of feeling nothing, thinking nothing, as if I had turned off a switch somewhere inside me. I couldn't tell how long that moment lasted, but it was disrupted rudely by an insistent car horn. The driver of a minivan taxi was looking for more passengers, and Sharif and I climbed in with the reluctant air of schoolchildren leaving the play-ground after recess.

The driver let me off near Bab Antakiya. Sharif asked if I wanted him to accompany me, but as it was a Friday, when the *souq* would be closed for business, I wanted to spend a quiet afternoon on my own, tak-ing photographs. Sharif nodded and waved to me from the moving cab.

A tomblike stillness permeated the empty cobblestoned passage-ways, amplifying the *click-clack* of my heels, which were attached to a pair of Italian leather boots that I had bought in Florence nine months earlier. I sometimes wore them as a concrete reminder of having been there because it was so hard to believe sometimes that I had a life out-side the Middle East. And home was a distant world whose shape I had forgotten. I had all sorts of important things to decide about home, when I would return, where I would live, what I would do, but some-how those decisions didn't seem to matter so much. They hovered just beyond the horizon that I still couldn't see, but I knew it was getting closer. Rustling leaves chased after my footsteps as they slipped into the labyrinth of the old city. Slender cones of sunlight dodged in and out of curving alleyways, and as I walked, I had the odd sensation of traveling through tunnels, alternating between lightness and darkness, leaping huge distances in a single step.

Halfway down a lane, a bronzed stone archway intricately carved with Quranic verses in elegant Kufi script caught my eye. The verses unfolded like a scroll across the top part of the wall, which I tried to photograph in segments. A small group of men had assembled to watch my performance with obvious amusement.

"Subhanallah." Someone tapped me on the shoulder to express praise for God and concur in my appreciation of the fabulous carving.

An old man with the face of an ancient Assyrian smiled at me and remarked on our similar navy embroidered jackets. Billowy trousers hung like a great big sheet at his inseam, tightening snugly below the knees. His head was wrapped in a snow-white turban with fringy ends dangling loosely on one shoulder. The other members of the crowd, teenage boys in T-shirts with Nike and Adidas logos and young men in cargo pants, hailed from the more modern era. They peered at me inquiringly. I knew right away that my next move would set the stage for the following sequence of events. The original desire for spending time alone and exploring the old city in my own private reverie suddenly sounded quite boring.

A tall young Syrian with a bushy mustache and eyes that drooped at the edges separated from the crowd and approached me.

"If you like, I can show you my house. It is very old and beautiful. You take many pictures there!" he said in nearly flawless English.

I hesitated, but only for a split second. It seemed a harmless offer.

"What is your name?" I asked.

"Bashir."

Two young boys clung to his side, reminding me of the way I used to clutch my mother's sari as a kid.

"My sons," he responded to my unspoken question. I decided to explore this unexpected twist to my course and walked with them to their home. The old Assyrian was sad to see me leave.

We slipped into a narrow alley with whitewashed walls painted with the black cubed images of the Holy Kaaba in Mecca and Arabic notations of God and the Prophet.

"All the families who live here are *hajjis*," said Bashir, referring to Muslims who have performed the pilgrimage to Mecca. We stopped by an enormous green metallic door that he struggled to unlock.

"Are you *hajji* too?" I asked.

"No, but my father yes."

I noticed the traditional door knocker, a solid chunk of iron shaped into the slender hand of Fatima, the Prophet's daughter, a symbol of protection from the evil eye. All the old houses in Aleppo seemed to have one. We entered a large open courtyard with a fountain dancing in the middle and rooms on the periphery like spokes jutting from a wheel.

Bashir unlocked one of the rooms, dark and musty with age. As my eyes became accustomed to the dimness, I began to make out wall panels embellished with arabesque stencils and delicate flourishes of Arabic script. Another wall was decorated with beautifully carved wooden *mashrabiya* window screens punctured with tiny holes to allow the women of the house to see outside without being seen inside. Now those holes housed spiderwebs. I clicked some photographs. Bashir waited outside, presumably not interested in the frozen past.

An elderly man looking remarkably like George Burns met my gaze in the courtyard. He was sitting on a chair holding on to a walking cane. A woman squatted next to his feet, massaging them with olive oil. Bashir introduced his father and his wife. Bashir's wife looked up at me with a friendly smile and resumed her attention to the massage. The old man greeted me in the traditional style, by placing his right hand above his heart and slightly bowing his head. He had a pensive expression, as if he wanted to say something profound, but he asked only, *"Enti Muslima?"* I showed him the gold Allah pendant that I still wore around my neck testifying to my Muslimness. A slow smile spread across his wrinkled face as he reached into his front coat pocket and handed me a small strand of hematite rosary beads.

"Shukrun." I voiced my thanks as Bashir ushered me to follow him.

We climbed a long flight of stone stairs leading to the rooftop, which offered a view of minarets and domes mingling with squat stone buildings spiked with satellite dishes. A chorus of muezzins chanted the *adhan,* the harmony of notes ascending and descending in the pink and gold twilight. Two of Bashir's male cousins joined us with a platter of black tea and olives. We sat atop a low wall on soft sheep's wool rugs and spoke in simple Arabic about simple things, such as family and home. I took some more snapshots. The cousins refilled our empty tea glasses. Meanwhile, someone handed me a black *abaya* for warmth that I slipped over my clothes.

"Now you look like Arab woman." Bashir gazed at me thoughtfully.

He asked to look at my journal and proceeded to draw pictures in it. One of them showed a girl's face, crying, next to a lit candle.

"Thank you for showing me your house," I said. "I'd better be leaving now."

"No, you stay here." Bashir's tone sounded sharp.

"I'm sorry, but I really must go," I repeated.

"You cannot go. You stay here."

"I really would like to go back."

I stood up, only to face Bashir staring down at me with flashing eyes.

"I want you to stay."

"Why?"

"I like you for my second wife."

He announced it in a matter-of-fact tone with the look of someone whose mind was made up.

A bomb exploded in my head. "But, but I don't want to marry you!"

So that was the plan all along. The house, the fancy room, it had all been a ruse to snare me in his net. He hadn't appeared the polygamous type; the cargo pants and polished English marked him as a hipper creature moving with the times. It appeared doubtful that I could reason my way out of this debacle through an intellectual discourse addressing the widely perceived assumption that Islam condones polygamy. The oft-quoted Quranic verse sanctioning marriage with two, three, up to four wives is taken out of context, dismissing its crucial clause of conditionality that requires a man to treat multiple wives equally. Since this onerous burden for fair and equal treatment defies the fallibility of human nature, one and only one wife is the default in Islam. But all this would fly over Bashir's head. I resorted to straight logic, setting myself up for instant failure.

"You, you don't understand," I stammered. "I have no interest in marrying you or anyone else. Besides, you are married already! What will your wife say?"

"Oh, she does not mind! She has seen you and likes you. Look, she is saying hello!"

I peered down from the roof to a balcony below, where the woman who was giving the foot massage waved to me with another friendly smile. So the wife was an obliging partner! Who else knew about his scheme? The father? Certainly. Why else had he asked me if I was Muslim? The cousins were in on it as well, having plied me with all that tea to buy time.

Bashir looked at me like a triumphant hunter picking up his fallen prize. My earlier satisfaction in giving in to spontaneous encounters morphed into a claustrophobic dread. It reminded me of the ten worst minutes of my life, when once I was stuck in an office elevator with a pasty-faced accountant with the eyes of a beetle. At least Bashir scored higher in the looks department, but that still implied no reason to marry the man. Panic-stricken, I raced down the long stairwell only to face a bolted door. I banged on the rusty iron frame with all my force and shouted for someone to open it. No one came to my rescue.

Dragging my feet back up the stairs, I returned to the rooftop, thinking I could just bide my time until help arrived. But help wasn't likely to arrive when no one would be missing me. Sharif had seen me earlier in the day and he knew I was roaming about the old city, but he couldn't have guessed my whereabouts or predicted my little crisis. I had no way of getting hold of him without a phone number or phone in sight. The budget hotel where I was staying certainly did not keep strict tabs on the comings and goings of its guests. There was nothing to do but wait and try to think of an exit strategy.

A full moon slipped in and out of the clouds as if mocking the cliché that had sprung to life. Bashir suddenly mentioned that he was getting cold and headed toward the stairwell. I tore after him, but he wrestled me down to the floor, pinning my arms and twisting them behind my back until I cried aloud in protest. When he raised his hand in the air, I instinctively closed my eyes and ducked my head. Then I heard his footsteps clambering downstairs. A door swung open and slammed shut. I imagined Bashir returning with a blanket, preparing to cozy up for the night. I had no time to think. Unzipping my leather boots and clutching them in one hand, I braced myself on the rooftop's wall, bent my knees like a diver, and jumped about fifteen feet down to the concrete ground.

It could have been a worse fall. I landed flat on my stockinged feet, badly bruising my left ankle. Sharp stabs of pain crept up as I limped forward on the good leg, turning my head back every other minute to make sure Bashir wasn't trailing behind. The darkness offered a welcome shroud of invisibility enhanced by the black *abaya* I was still wearing. I couldn't see a thing at first, and my hands kept flying to adjust my glasses as if to ensure they had remained miraculously intact. *Move! Just keep moving*, I told myself. Some boys wearing skullcaps passed by, giggling hysterically at some private joke.

A minaret that I remembered passing on the way to Bashir's house came into view, for a minute appearing as a dingy old rocket booster. I breathed a sigh of relief and hobbled past the thick stone walls of the old city, vowing never to go back again. It seemed as if hours had passed before the bright headlights of oncoming cars signaled my freedom. I hailed a taxi back to the hotel, rolling down its window and gulping gobs of smog-infested air. The cabbie offered me a fresh cigarette. His hand was glued to the horn like every other car-and-driver combo on the road. This time the racket sounded like a symphony.

Food for the Soul

Caveats notwithstanding, one of the most gratifying aspects of my travels in the Middle East was the way chance encounters in public settings developed into instant connections. Of course, these connections had the potential of turning into disasters, as evidenced by my narrow escape from Bashir's house and the doping tea party with Mahmoud back in Damascus. But for the most part, the random ways in which I met people also led to friendships. The frequency was now a recognizable pattern, like a melody from a favorite song. Yasser and Mohammad in Cairo, Asma at the Amr Ibn al As Mosque during Ramadan, Waheed in Dahab, the trio of cousins at the Dead Sea, Ahmed at al-Rabie hotel. They were all vital connections that taught me people were always around to lend you a hand, reveal a story or an adventure, and offer all kinds of insights and lessons.

I wasn't sure what the connection was with Sharif in the beginning, apart from the fact that we both liked to jog. After that soggy Friday at Jama Firdaws and our meditative reprieve in the rain, I sensed there was something to explore with him. Compared to all my other friends, Sharif was more reserved and contemplative, and though we were nearly the same age, he looked and acted so much older and wiser. In those initial moments of meeting, Sharif took on the lure of a puzzle I wanted to crack, and I was drawn to him for many of the same reasons I had gravitated toward Bea, for the way they both exuded serenity and self-composure that was in direct opposition to my fiery restless energy. Bea had taught me the value of slowing down and not forcing things to happen, and now I wished she were hovering about like an invisible genie to see me put her advice into practice.

Rooftops were turning out to be some kind of theme in Aleppo. From escaping the confines of one, I was now tied up on a more familiar and welcoming turf back at the hotel. My ankle was swollen, but I was thankful it was not sprained. I doted on it with an ice pack and a roll of Ace bandage that I had been carrying around in my first aid kit since my hiking days in the Pyrenees. This was how Sharif found me the following morning when he came around in a new tracksuit with bold red piping down the pant legs. I wrapped some more layers of putty-colored bandage and sadly informed Sharif that our running days were over, at least for a while, and then I gave him the full hostage report. He whistled back surprise. I acknowledged being a dimwit. He said it could have happened to anybody. I emphasized it could have happened only to me because I was just plain stupid. He told me not to be so hard on myself.

"It is okay. Most important thing is that you are okay."

"Alhamdulillah," I murmured my thanks to God.

"Alhamdulillah."

"Well, I don't want to keep you from running."

"Today, no run. Today only talk. With you."

Sharif settled down on a stool near where I was sitting leaning against a wall.

"But aren't you going to be late for work?"

"I work when I choose."

"What do you do?"

"I sell watches."

"That's nice. Do you have a shop?"

"Here is my shop!" Sharif stretched out his forearm and thumped it a few times. "It is hard work but some days I make good sale. Maybe ten, fifteen U.S. dollar. Then I say *Alhamdulillah* many times!"

"Say it again. Slowly."

"Al-ham-du-lil-lah."

"It sounds like a song!"

"Al-hammm-du-lil-lah. Al-hammm-du-lil-lah. Al-ham-du-lillahhhh."

Sharif sang the words and urged me to do the same. I started humming in tune. We kept repeating it over and over like a mantra. Then Sharif burst into some impromptu songs that sounded more like wails in an altogether different language. Not Arabic. Something else that I hadn't heard until now.

"It is Kurdi," he said. "I am Kurd."

"So you are not native to Syria?"

Sharif laughed. "I have lived in Soorya all my life. First place I live was al-Sham, you know, Damascus. Then I come to Aleppo ten years ago for university. I study Arabic literature and history. My dream was to be teacher. But it is difficult to find teaching job. Especially for Kurdi people."

"You must keep trying."

"It is what I do."

"How do you say *try* in Arabic?"

"Hawala."

"And in Kurdi?"

"Hewlldan."

"In Urdu, we say *koshish*."

"Ko-shish," Sharif repeated slowly. "It is good word."

"If you teach me more Arabic, I'll teach you some Urdu," I volunteered.

Sharif looked at me with a bemused smile.

"You stay in Aleppo long?"

"I'm not sure yet."

"I think you will like it here. But you must stop all this moving around by yourself. It is not safe for woman to be too much alone."

"But I want to explore places!"

"Then I take you. Wherever you want to go. We see places together."

"If you don't mind."

"It is no problem."

"That's very kind of you."

"It is my duty."

"Shukrun."

"Afwan."

We were silent for a while. The cushion I was sitting on was damp with sweat. It was turning out to be a hot and muggy day, and for a brief moment, I thought of the approaching summer and where I would be by July, in a month's time. Sharif was picking up some clothes hanging on a taut wire extending from a utility pole on the street to the hotel's plastered outer wall. I hadn't realized he had left his laundry here. He folded the T-shirts in a neat pile and left them on a bench. Then he turned to me and asked if I was hungry. I was indeed feeling famished. Sharif and I stepped outside in the blazing heat.

It was an unassuming little place tucked inside a narrow indoor passage and seemingly deserted, as if boycotted by a silent conspiracy. But Sharif insisted the restaurant served simple, tasty dishes such as *fricki,* a type of wheat *bulgar,* and *fasoli,* or hearty bean stew, all for less than $1. We dubbed the place Simple Restaurant. Its owner/waiter/cashier/ dishwasher beckoned us inside, where we chose a corner back table next to a hot-water heater. Two warm cups of black tea instantly appeared. Sharif insisted they would alleviate my thirst better than ice-cold water. I remembered the same principle being at work in my visits to India during the hot summer. While waiting for the food, I wanted something to write on, and when I started scribbling on a paper napkin, the restaurant owner provided me some stationery paper decorated with red balloons and yellow flowers.

Innocents on the Move

On a dreary overcast day, Sharif proposed an excursion to Qalat Samman, or the basilica of San Simeon. According to my trusty guidebook, it has ranked as a popular tourist magnet since medieval times and is one of several hundreds of Christian remnants littered across Syria. We hailed a minibus that drove through abandoned villages with broken chunks of Roman ruins and rings of limestone hills. At Dar al Aaz, the closest town to the basilica, we got off the bus and made our way there on foot. Giant boulders of stone greeted us everywhere. The most famous of these was a ten-foot-tall egg-shaped pillar, where the hermit Simeon had lived without once climbing down for longer than a quarter of a century. Apparently, resident monks fed him small portions of food with the aid of a ladder. I wondered how the poor fellow had managed never to fall down, contrasting such self-inflicted austerity in early Christianity with the Islamic seamlessness between flesh and spirit.

I voiced my thoughts to Sharif, and he agreed that in Islam, spiritual devotion did not imply a strictly monastic existence. It was actually more difficult to attain while renouncing worldly comforts.

"But don't you think it should be the other way around?" I asked. "I mean, if you wanted to devote your life to serving God, then why must you still live in a material world? You should withdraw completely like this guy Simeon did. Like the Hindu *sanyasins*. Isn't that better?"

"That is too simple," Sharif replied.

"What do you mean?"

"It is not mark of holy person to give up everything and hide from the world."

"But they're not hiding! They're purifying themselves without any distractions. What's wrong with that?"

"It is too simple," Sharif repeated.

I knew he didn't like to waste words, but I couldn't understand his reasoning. He couldn't possibly be looking down on spiritual ascetics when his own life relied on faith for spirituality and sustenance.

We sat down on a grassy bluff looking out toward a jade-green valley. I peeled some apples with my Swiss army knife and handed Sharif some slices on a cloth plate. In the late afternoon's hush, the air seemed weighted with a stillness that our human voices could not banish with words alone.

We sang some songs. He taught me an old Kurdish folk song, and I recognized some of the words as similar to Urdu, so perhaps we were distant cousins somewhere back on the same linguistic branch. Succumbing to the languid air, we dozed off in the sun, stretching out our limbs on two long stone pillars that Simeon might have tried out before reaching his chosen abode on the way to sainthood.

Then they came. It was like finding yourself inside a strange dream when three men leap from behind and shake you like a fragile leaf, shouting unintelligibly in a foreign tongue, and wagging accusing fingers for reasons not obvious to anyone but them. This dream happened to be real.

One of the men, a ticket collector at the basilica, had spotted our little picnic, which was hardly out of bounds, but the sight of a local man clearly not an official tour guide, with a foreign-looking girl (for some reason, I failed the usual blending-in test, which may or may not have had something to do with my head scarf's being worn like a turban) produced the same effect as a firecracker exploding in his brain. In no time he alerted his cohorts, a local gendarme and his sidekick, that this odd couple were engaging in an illicit affair right under their noses and that he had caught them red-handed. They sneaked up on us and shattered our peace when we were sitting on the pillars, gazing at the valley beyond, smoking cigarettes, and apparently looking very suspicious.

I couldn't understand much of what the men were raving about in Arabic, but given their accusing tones and smug looks, it wasn't hard to figure out the scenario brewing in their pea-size brains. Poor Sharif was dragged by the arm like a convicted felon as our innocent outing contorted into some sort of a scandal right before my incredulous eyes. All three men looked at us and smirked knowingly. One of them even winked at me and slapped Sharif playfully on the back.

"What is going on here?" I shouted angrily. "We haven't done anything wrong!"

The ticket collector understood some English and spelled out our crime. "You and you, sex together!" he sputtered.

"Laa, laa!" I protested at the top of my voice. I rifled through my memory bank for the crucial words. *"Nahnoo sadiq."* I tried to say we were just friends.

The situation might have defused had I been able to hold a proper conversation in Arabic and tell these men off. But when they demanded to see my passport and realized my nationality, I had no chance, even if I could speak classical *fushah*. According to the prevailing logic, there was no way Sharif and I could simply be friends; a local man hanging around a foreigner, especially a girl from America, could be after only one thing, and it was their job to punish him for stepping over the line and to ensure my safety.

Sharif's arms were pinned tightly behind his back, and he pleaded with the men to let him go, but they wouldn't listen to a word. It sickened me to hear his profuse apologies for some imaginary crime concocted by the village idiots. Upon learning that Sharif was Kurdish, they, who were all Arab, badgered him even more. The ticket collector, the leading madman of the bunch, was now yelling angrily and threatening physical violence. I began to fear the consequences.

The gendarme, revealing a trace of sanity, smiled at me and said, "You no worry. You okay."

There was no point in reasoning with the men. We would have to play out the farce. The shouting subsided and our captors escorted us outside the basilica toward a waiting jeep. We climbed into the open back and five minutes later jolted to a halt at the village square. The gendarme tried to help me out, but I ignored him and jumped off on my own. Sharif was taken to the police station. I waited underneath a tree, wondering what forms of torture they were inflicting on him. I did not intend to return to Aleppo alone, even if I were forced to spend the night here. If they were going to detain Sharif, they would have to keep me as well.

After an agonizing two hours, he finally came out looking exhausted and embarrassed. The farce ended on a dubious note. It had accomplished nothing beyond treating us like outcasts, disturbing our sanctity, and extorting a humble man's meager reserves, not to mention his pride.

They told us a minibus was leaving for Aleppo from the next village in half an hour. One of the local boys offered to give us a ride to the bus stop on his twin motorcycle. Sharif straddled the back of the bike while I sat quite comfortably in the adjoining passenger compartment, bouncing up and down in my low seat during the potholed ride. It was a relief to head back to the city. There we could walk (or run) freely, even if watched by idle park-goers or curious auto mechanics. At least there we could eat or smoke or even snooze in the sun without the hassles of nosy ticket collectors with peepholed mentalities. Or maybe I was just fooling myself.

On the way back, I tried to figure out whether hanging out with Sharif was not such a good idea after all. On one hand, he was showing me around Aleppo of his own volition, and it really made things easier to travel with someone who knew his way about, and if he happened to be male, then I didn't get so many strange looks as my solo amblings would have warranted. But I didn't think of Sharif as simply my tour guide taking me sightseeing. I was really beginning to enjoy spending time with him, singing, laughing, talking. We were building a good rapport and getting to be friends, and this friendship felt deeper than all others in the past. And this was precisely why I was also worried that we would have to put up with more complications, not just from people on the streets and their lust-driven trashy conclusions, but more likely from the ongoing duel between our own hearts and minds.

Sacred Spaces

Instead of breaking our resolve, the basilica farce emboldened our spirits toward more action. The following weekend, Sharif and I escaped Aleppo to see more sights of spiritual significance.

"I know you don't like tombs, but you must visit Sayyida Zeinab if you are in Soorya," was the way he put it.

Despite having stayed in Damascus for longer than two months, I had never stepped foot inside the venerated Shiite shrine/mosque just outside the city, built in honor of the Prophet's granddaughter. We worked out a simple plan to leave Aleppo undetected by prying eyes. I slipped out of my hotel room at two in the morning, covered in a maroon shawl worn over my head and the black *abaya*, courtesy of Bashir and company. Sharif was waiting near a corner store of used appliances.

"Mashallah!" he whispered to compliment my disguise. We caught a taxi to the bus station and the first bus to Damascus. I fell asleep on the way, resting my head on his shoulder, secure enough that with my local dress and familiar looks, I would be taken by others as a slumbering cousin, sister, or possibly even wife.

A glorious sunrise welcomed us into the city center I had known so well with Bea as my companion in the not-so-distant past. Sharif and I walked through the stirring Slaughter Street, mercifully clean of animal debris as merchants were just setting out the day's new collection of choice innards and entrails. We breakfasted in a spacious restaurant adjacent to a hotel mostly full of businessmen and a few large families with piles of suitcases near their tables. He paid the bill that I knew exceeded the limits of his modest budget. The minibus for Sayyida Zeinab was packed even at nine in the morning. I had to sit on the knee of a hefty mother built like a sumo wrestler surrounded by her clan of five small children, all with runny noses. Sharif shot me a sympathetic look from his perch near the driver's glove box. My human chair pinched my cheeks and smiled with approval, apparently pleased with my choice of husband.

A blinding dome of solid gold brick blazed against the clear blue sky with an unearthly brilliance. Quranic verses ran along the top perimeter of the mosque in a dark blue frieze with tightly woven script. Sharif recognized it as the "Surah Yassin" and began reciting it by memory as we circumambulated arm in arm around the Sayyida Zeinab mausoleum. The grounds teemed with picnicking families, sitting on straw mats unfurling cloth bundles of food, and groups of Iranian pilgrims moaning in prayer. We took photographs around sunken fountains, arched doorways, and walls decorated with tile work in shades of turquoise and teal framing sacred words.

The call for Friday-afternoon prayers triggered a human stampede to scuttle for places inside. I found myself stepping around worshippers in mid-prostration and had to squeeze between some women reciting the Quran, rocking back and forth. Above us, a showy canopy of chandeliers and mirror mosaics glittered in a visual assault of crystal, glass, and aquamarine jewel tones. Sideways to the prayer hall, a cage of solid silver protected the tomb. Pilgrims feverishly kissed its threshold. An elderly matron dropped a gold chain into the slot of a large mailbox contraption. I didn't particularly care for all this ostentatious display, and the veneration of tombs and saints was not, in my mind, strictly in line with Islam, in which Allah and the disciple engage in direct communication without intermediaries.

By midafternoon, we collected our shoes and headed back to Damascus. If I were still traveling with Bea or with a male friend who was either a) foreign (therefore immune from rules) or b) local and upper class (and therefore beyond rules), the idea of checking into a hotel and taking some rest would have been perfectly feasible. With Sharif by my side, it was not so simple, given society's unwritten but strictly observed taboos against our unlikely pairing. It had nothing to do with the fact that he was local and I was foreign or even the hint that we were a potential couple.

The problem arose in the fact that Sharif was not a well-off man. I was never sure how much money he did or did not have, but some days it alarmed me to hear him say, "I have no money in pocket." Sharif didn't sound too worried. His faith in Allah was rock-solid, and he reinforced his faith every time he made a good sale just when he most needed to. I couldn't help but wonder if the customers who bought watches from Sharif were maybe angels in disguise sent by God to provide for his believer. Sharif wouldn't deny that he lived a life of dignified poverty, but he refused to give into helplessness.

It wasn't entirely obvious from his appearance, which he preserved with an innate sense of dignity in the way he dressed. Even if he did wear the same herringbone-patterned jacket and black trousers day after day, at least they were clean and presentable. But those clothes and his haggard face would have turned heads in posh hotels, where people such as Sharif would have clashed with smooth-shaven three-piece-suited businessmen and perfumed sheikhs in flowing white robes. I didn't want to add further insult by offering to pay for things. I had made that mistake once by taking Sharif to a fancy eatery in al-Jadid, the old Armenian quarter in Aleppo. The waiter had asked us to wait until he secured permission from the restaurant manager to seat us inside in the same room as foreigners and rich Arab hipsters. Of course, their smirks and sneers didn't help ease Sharif's sense of discomfort at being in the wrong crowd. I had longed to leave and take refuge in the Simple Restaurant.

So back in Damascus, we skipped the afternoon nap in favor of continuing to our next destination, Deir Mar Mousa, a historic monastery tucked into the walls of a cliff near the surrounding desert. My guidebook warned that Mar Mousa was not an easy place to reach by public transport, but Sharif planned on improvising. We hailed a bus to Nabak and got off at a dusty, desolate town square with no discernable traces of the monastery. I consulted the guidebook again and pointed to a high ridge just off the road. Sharif and I started climbing single file a gully cut into the steep limbs of the ridge. He turned around and gave me the thumbs-up sign when Mar Mousa appeared as a bas-relief carved into the brown hillside.

We followed the well-cut pathway to an arched doorway flung open toward an outdoor terrace. A smiling priest wearing a medi-eval-looking robe with a rope belt and drooping hood welcomed us for evening supper. We ate boiled potatoes and brown rice served from massive aluminum tureens that reminded me of the hippie commune I had visited in Amsterdam. The priest, who turned out to be an Ital-ian Jesuit, told us in fluent English that the fourteen-hundred-year-old monastery housed a cadre of monks, nuns, and hermits, some of them of European origin, stationed for years and subsisting on a spiritual diet of daily meditations at dawn and group prayer sessions. Sharif raised his eyebrows in awe. We stayed until sunset, wandering through cliff-side rooms and rocky esplanades, the isolation of the place at once lib-erating and claustrophobic.

"How do we get back?" I asked.

Night had fallen by the time we made our descent into town. An ominous blackness shrouded Nabak and its invisible inhabitants. It was kind of creepy.

Sharif remained optimistic. "Don't worry. We will find something."

He walked around some piles of sand, searching for signs of life. Not a soul was around. I sunk to the ground, cradling my head against my knees, shivering in the nightly chill with the thin *abaya* as my only outer layer.

"Well?"

He shook his head in resignation.

"We will just have to wait for the bus," he said matter-of-factly.

"Bus, what bus? There is no bus. We are in the middle of nowhere, in case you hadn't noticed!"

He ignored my outburst and walked over to the side of a two-lane highway, raising his hand to flag two oncoming buses. They flew by like comets. Sharif continued this charade for half an hour, at one point inching toward the middle of the road to make himself more visible. A sea of headlights flowed amid a spray of blaring horns.

"This is crazy. You are going to get yourself killed. No one is going to stop for us. They probably think you are some kind of nutcase."

For an instant, my mind recalled the suspended judgment of desperation that had once caused me to spend the night at the house of a complete stranger when the youth hostel in San Sebastián, Spain, had been full. Sharif was acting within reasonable bounds.

Finally, a full hour later, a bus slowed down. *"Yallah!"* We sprinted on board like a pair of refugees, braving the shell-shocked looks from fellow passengers. Sharif paid our fare for Damascus. I leaned back into the vinyl seat and, once again, laid my head on his shoulder. We found a connecting bus to Aleppo at midnight, lurching back into familiar environs around sunrise.

It was a beautiful morning. The sky wore a coat in soft pinks monogrammed with a small sliver of a rising moon. As Sharif secured me in a taxi toward my hotel and went off to work, I was beginning to realize that places mattered less than the spirit and connections forged along the way. And I was getting so used to having Sharif beside me, not just to talk to or go on excursions with, but simply as a presence that was being recognized as someone I seemed to have known all my life.

Of Human Bondage

Four days passed and there was no sign of Sharif. He seemed to have fallen off the face of the earth, but then I corrected myself and realized he had only vanished from my little world and that I had started to presume Sharif would become a daily fixture in it. It was a silly presumption. After our recent outings together, Sharif probably had to settle back down and get busy with his work. And I had no right to monopolize his undivided time and attention.

So I just hung around the hotel, mingling with the other guests and backpackers I had barely spoken to beyond cursory greetings. Our interactions were awkward, mostly because my mind was somewhere else, which made it a monumental challenge to engage in small talk. Even when I met a twenty-two-year-old college boy from my home state of Washington, I found myself groping for sentences as if I had forgotten the fundamentals of conversing. He probably thought I was stuck-up because I turned down his invitation to grab some dinner together, despite having dined quite often with my hostel bunkmates back in Europe. But now it seemed a rather dull prospect. I decided to clear my head by walking to the old city just before sunset.

I hadn't been back there ever since the night I was momentarily held captive on the rooftop I had jumped from. Part of me dreaded the thought of running into Bashir again, so I avoided the alleys around his house and explored a newer section running parallel to thick stone walls. A few yards ahead, there was a shallow opening in the walls and a short staircase leading to an open archway. A golden plaque on the walls spelled out in Arabic JAMA ADELIYE. I entered the mosque's courtyard. No one was around so I just sat on a raised concrete platform leading to the prayer hall's entrance. On my right rose yet another rooftop that seemed to be an extension of the mosque with four cylindrical domes nestled next to each other in a straight row.

A hushed stillness settled over me, and I could hear my mind rumbling with thoughts. *Was I still traveling?* Invariably I was, but the rhythm of my voyage had changed, making me realize that being a traveler was not just an escape from home. It was also being entirely in my own skin because there were fewer masks behind which to hide. My journey was getting rid of these exterior shells that I had relied upon at home to make an impression or to put on a show for others, whether by choice or necessity. But now I didn't need to. Traveling had stripped my borders, making me nothing other than purely myself. It was this level of purity that haunted me, and I wanted to cling to it forever. Knowing that this pure self wouldn't last, that someday the travels had to come to a logical end, made me mourn for the part of myself that I would have let go of.

And then there was Sharif. He was a big part of my newfound self-honesty, this peeling away of all my excess pretensions. When I was with him, I felt more real, more alive, more awake than ever before. And I could tell he too was revived in my presence, as if I had something to offer besides just the zany enthusiasm of a traveler. Why then had he disappeared? Was he in some kind of trouble? Maybe he would come around to the hotel tomorrow, asking me to go on a run. Or maybe he wouldn't. There was still so much to understand, so many questions to ask, so much to discuss. I had to go find him, and I could think of only one place where he might possibly be.

It turned out I was wrong. He hadn't shown up at the Simple Restaurant, not for many days, according to the owner. No one had seen him around the premises. Maybe he was out of town. I refused to believe Sharif wouldn't show up any minute. Surely, he had to eat, and he was the one who had raved about the food and the low prices. He was bound to turn up tonight. Any minute, actually. I waited there for three hours skimming through a dog-eared copy of Dostoevsky's *Crime and Punishment* that had somehow fallen into my possession. The restaurant had run out of bean stew as I gradually finished the whole pot. It was nearly 11:00 PM and the owner wanted to close up. I willed him to stay open just a bit longer. He agreed and smiled good-naturedly. The clock hit midnight and Sharif was still missing. I apologized for my intrusion and went back to the hotel.

Low murmuring voices came from the small kitchen on the rooftop. I thought it was Khalil brewing a late pot of tea for some guests. Instead, I saw Sharif making an omelet. No one else was around, so I figured he was singing or maybe just talking to himself, as he seemed to have lost his mind anyway by abandoning me as a friend. I was tremendously relieved. Happy too, but I wasn't going to let him see that.

"Where have you been? I've been worried sick about you."

"I was busy."

"Doing what?"

"I was helping friend with move."

"I see."

"You are okay?"

"Okay."

"Come, let us sit and talk. Are you hungry?"

He cracked some more eggs. We sat on a bench on the rooftop, eating and talking halfway through the night. He told me things I didn't know before. His parents had died when he was fifteen. Sharif's elder sister had raised him. And he had been married once, to a woman much older than him. They got divorced within a year when she couldn't have any children. It was assumed to be his fault. Sharif laughed to cover up an old wound. He told me we would go jogging again in the morning if it wasn't too hot. I told him about the mosque I had just discovered. He looked at me without saying anything, and when I pressed him to speak, he just recited some Quranic verses in Arabic. I said some in Urdu. Then we sang songs again.

He was beginning to know the lyrics to a *ghazal* I was teaching him. It was about desires and dreams. Surely, he felt these things just like anyone else with a heart. And when the heart speaks, why is it sometimes so difficult to listen? I wasn't falling in love with him, yet our bond was deepening, and I couldn't exactly express it in words. So I simply squeezed Sharif's hands. The skin was rough and dry. He leaned closer.

I threw my arms around his neck, and he rocked me back and forth like a baby. I looked up at the sky where the stars had now faded into dawn. The muezzin announced the first call to prayer as Sharif held me in a tight grip. He didn't speak, he barely even breathed. He only hummed in tune to the *adhan*. When it was finished, Sharif released me from his embrace. Then without saying anything, he pulled out his running shoes from a small duffel bag that was underneath the bench we had been sitting on. I splashed my face with cold water, feeling strangely energized after a sleepless night. It was quiet on the streets, and our pounding footsteps matched the echoes of my beating heart.

Later that day, we went to the Jama al-Adeliye for *maghrib* prayers at dusk. It was still early, so we sat in the mosque's courtyard near a dried-up fountain to rest. I took out my old *tazbi*, or rosary beads, and fingered them slowly. Sharif looked at me with a serious face.

"What will you do when you go back to America?"

"I don't know. Find another job. Get my own apartment."

"And will you be happy with that?"

"Probably not."

"So why go back?"

"Well, I can't stay here forever, you know. I must have plans."

He unleashed a wry laugh. "If you go back to your country, you will become like machine. You will forget how to live again."

Before I could think of a reply, a squad of pigeons fluttered off the ground as the call to prayer began. It triggered a second call, and a third, and so on, until a train of wavering notes stretched across the darkening sky in an aural concoction of devotion and longing that was not so much a cry as a joyful deliverance.

No other women were present. Sharif went inside the mosque to pray, and when I tried to follow him, someone admonished me to remain outside as there was apparently no space (or more likely, no division of space) for women to join in. I didn't let it bother me too much and improvised by praying on a stone walkway near the mosque's entrance. Hearing the imam's baritone voice leading the prayers, I mouthed in silence the Quranic verses that we each knew by heart. The movements the men made in worship—bowing from the waist, hands on knees, standing upright, diving down, forehead on the floor, then sitting and repeating the prostration—were the same as mine. In those movements, I felt peacefulness, but even as I concentrated, I knew that I hadn't yet learned how to sustain the feeling beyond this moment. It frustrated me, and when the prayers ended, I grew more frustrated thinking about Sharif.

I had been trying to figure him out, but it was like asking why the sky is blue. I couldn't understand his serenity given so much uncertainty in the life he led, and why, when he held me last night, he was so composed and contained. I remembered reading somewhere that peace did not mean to be in a place where there is no noise, trouble, or hard work. It was about being in the midst of those things and still being calm in your heart. Maybe there was some sort of secret that Sharif ought to share. I was certain that we had made some kind of a breakthrough that paved the path we were charting toward a smoother grade. Yet just when I thought we were speaking the same language, he said things that puzzled me. Become like a machine again. Forgetting how to live back home. Home was all I had in the end.

The mosque door flung open and men filtered outside, scattering in different directions, like mice darting into their respective burrows. I remained seated and waited for Sharif. He walked toward me in the dark. I told him I admired his sense of inner peace. He said it was easy. All you had to do was surrender. My mind reeled and screeched to a halt. Surrender? It was my journey's motto. Why, then, was it taking me so long to get to where he was?

Rites of Passage

I started meeting Sharif in the mornings at a tiny juice stand near the hotel. He had given up his work peddling watches on his arm so that we could spend more time together. His selflessness doused me in shame. When I voiced concern about his earning money, Sharif tossed the matter aside and said he could manage. Acceptance of insecurity is a way of life for some people in the East, an abstract foundation to life that somehow renders it in sharper light and a deeper significance. Sharif knew no other form of existence.

One morning, I noticed a postcard taped to the wall behind the juice counter. It curled up around the edges, but I could still make out remnants of an old stone footbridge framed by lush golden fields and a ridge of sawtoothed mountains. Sharif followed my gaze toward the postcard and smiled knowingly.

"That is Kurdish land just north of Aleppo."

"I wish we could see it." I continued staring at the image until it burrowed into my mind and refused to leave.

"Let us try." Sharif gulped down the fruit cocktail, his prominent Adam's apple jogging up and down his throat in a frenzied race.

We hailed a minibus and got off at a busy intersection with more minibuses.

"Wait here." Sharif motioned for me to huddle next to a dusty wall with a group of village women with enormous cloth bundles mounted on their backs like primitive rucksacks. I imagined them as a forgotten tribe of 16th-century female nomad warriors crusading through rugged hinterlands and urban jungles to spread the ideals of personal wayfaring as a way to reach inner peace. One of the women, perhaps the self-appointed leader, smiled at me and instructed the others to make some room in their tight little circle so I too could squat on my haunches and wait in weary resignation for the next leg of the journey. They were a tough-looking lot with the strong silent features of mountains.

I watched Sharif haggle with a taxi driver. He kept waving his hands like a conductor without a baton and shaking his head with the same tempo. At one point, Sharif bunched up the fingers of his right hand and brought them close to his mouth as if he wanted some food. Maybe it was a new bargaining tactic to sweeten the deal. But the taxi driver was not buying. He just threw his head back and laughed like the devil. Sharif lowered his head and slouched back.

"What happened?" I asked.

"He is very greedy man. He wants a thousand pounds each to take us as far as Cyrrhus."

It amounted to $20 apiece, reasonable back home, but near extortion in Syria.

"That's *haram*. Absolutely wrong. I'll go tell him to get his head screwed back on."

"No. Don't do that." Sharif grabbed me by the arm. "Leave it alone. We will find another way."

It was classic Sharif behavior—to accept unfairness instead of trying to fight it every step of the way as I did in waging battles. At first, it struck me as a defeatist attitude to give in so easily to the driver's heavy-handedness, but what I called "giving in" required more self-control, which he seemed to have mastered to an art form.

Eyes downcast, we shuffled past children playing football in side streets and tiny stalls selling fresh falafels—bubbling golden-brown golf balls in a cauldron of hot oil. All of a sudden, the sound of screeching brakes and squealing tires jolted us awake. A van swung around in an elaborate arc and froze a few inches away from my feet.

In the next instant, Sharif burst out in wild laughter, his shoulders shaking like unsettled Jell-O.

"What is so funny?" I wondered, still trembling from the shock of our near disaster.

The driver of the van stepped out, also hooting like a hyena. I stared in disbelief as the two crazed men threw their arms around each other in a rib-shattering hug.

Sharif approached me with his new friend.

"Look who we've run into! This is my dearest friend, Sharki. He says he will take us to Cyrrhus."

I stared at a very tall man built like a sturdy oak tree.

"Let us go to my house and have lunch," he announced.

A little girl of five with a messy ponytail opened the door. Her father scooped her up in his arms and threw her into the air like a rubber ball. She laughed excitedly. Laughing apparently ran strong in this family. Another little girl, a carbon copy of her sister, came along and wrapped herself around one of her father's massive legs.

"Come in, come in!" Sharki ushered us into the living room, where we sat on a brightly colored kilim draped on the floor.

The twin girls climbed into my lap and flapped tiny fingers at my earrings and rings. Both had sandy-brown hair, soft as silk, with long bangs falling into honey-colored eyes. We were playing with my jewelry when their mother joined us. She wore an emerald-green scarf, the exact shade of her eyes, tied behind her neck like a bandanna. Ridges and valleys fanned across her face, seemingly sculpted out of rough-hewn mountains. Her name was Jiyan, translating as "life" in Kurdish. She spoke only her native tongue and Arabic, but our communication relied on the far more fluent prose of eye talk. My presence intrigued her, and she wanted to know why I was traveling alone and what I hoped to find. Her grave beauty and sad eyes drew me into a well of silence.

Sharki handed his wife some olives and cheese in clear plastic bags that he had bought on the way home. She dutifully disappeared into the tiny kitchen to prepare our lunch. Their two older boys came home from school and solemnly shook hands with me.

"Sharki is engineer in Aleppo," Sharif informed me. "He knows a lot about Kurdish culture and history so you can ask him all the questions you want."

I wondered why he was acting as translator when his friend spoke good English. Perhaps it was just habit.

My cursory knowledge about the Kurds did not allow for a rousing debate. I knew only that as an ethnic minority in the Middle East, they were up against systematic political and cultural repression. So I asked Sharki why.

"Because they are afraid," he responded.

"Afraid of what? Who is afraid?"

"The government is afraid of our Kurdish freedom. They don't want to give us a home of our own. So they keep us chained like prisoners."

"Or they kill," I said in reference to Saddam Hussein's gassing of the Kurds in Halabja.

We had more to talk about, but I hesitated as our lunch arrived on a gleaming silver platter, big as a cart wheel. The boys draped a plastic tablecloth on the carpet. We all gathered in a circle, holding oblong slabs of hot flat bread for dipping in and out of little earthenware bowls of vegetable *shorba,* or broth and green lentils, that Jiyan had speedily prepared. It was decided that we would go to Cyrrhus tomorrow. Sharki said something to Sharif in Kurdish, and he translated that I was welcome to stay overnight. Jiyan looked at me encouragingly. I murmured thanks, but as I was without my camera and a proper change of clothes, I wanted to get back to the hotel to be more prepared for our excursion.

A Picnic in Cyrrhus

The following morning, Sharif and I went back to the family's house. The twin girls were smartly dressed in black velvet frocks, white stockings, and polished buckled shoes. Their older brother, in the guise of self-appointed personal assistant, proudly carried my portable cassette player, delighting his siblings with the sound of their recorded voices bouncing back from the machine. They shrieked in surprise and clapped their little hands in vigorous applause. Sharki loaded the van with supplies: food, water, the essential water pipe, or *nargileh,* musical instruments, and enough blankets and carpets to stock a small warehouse. It looked as if we were going away for a month.

Jiyan's eyes gleamed like those of an excited schoolgirl. For a minute, she held my gaze and smiled broadly. I noticed a tiny bundle snuggling in her arms and wondered why I hadn't noticed the infant the day before.

"Are we ready?" Sharif asked playfully.

"Ready, ready!" the children sang back.

The van slowly careened down the road, blowing up plumes of dust and joy.

Just two hours outside of Aleppo emerged one of the most stunning landscapes I have ever laid eyes on. Fields of wheat in rust, gold, and ochre crisscrossed like giant chessboards, clusters of olive trees vied for attention with wild mountain flowers, and jagged walls of mountains hemmed the border with Turkey, as if they had all conspired to safeguard this lush enclave from meddlesome intruders.

"Welcome to Kurdistan!" Sharki swept his arm around the tableau vivant.

We picked a dirt track and drove deeper into the rainbow fields. The scenery reminded me a little of Tuscany with its gentle rolling hills of muted browns and greens, but the Italian sense of formality and orderliness was different from the rugged beauty of this Kurdish landscape. It shouted freedom and something wild and mysterious at the same time.

Sharki spotted an ideal picnic spot next to a shady tree ringed by stone boulders to serve as handy tables and chairs. The children eagerly helped to lug out our supplies. Their father had thought of everything, right down to ropes and pillows that were soon fashioned into swings for the girls. They perched on their seats like two pretty butterflies, squealing with laughter as I pushed from behind. The wind whipped their little ponytails.

Sharif busied himself with the task of firing up the *nargileh*. The men and I shared it, each taking a turn at inhaling the sweet flavored mixture of apple, cinnamon, molasses, tobacco, and water and blowing out elaborate curlicues of smoke—a ritual so satisfying that it eclipsed expression in words. We were sitting between clumps of tall wild grass in fields smelling of freshly minted earth.

Jiyan was breastfeeding her baby. She did not attempt to cover her exposed breast when the men were not present. Her sensuality was as lush as the countryside around us. In slow measured Arabic, she conveyed that we were not too far away from her ancestral village. Then she closed her eyes briefly. I noticed limpid eyelids moving back and forth as if rewinding and playing back the nostalgic reel of childhood.

After lunch, the boys and I scrambled up a hill and found the ruins of a Roman fortress where the outer walls had crumbled like half-eaten biscuits. In front of us, the landscape rippled its curves as far as the eye could see. We sat on the broken edges of the fort, watching little cotton-wool clouds scudding above the sun-baked earth. There was a sense of precarious peace, like the waiting stillness before a summer thunderstorm.

The sound of a stringlike instrument drifted toward us. I could almost picture the musical notes dancing up the steep ridge, urging us to join the party below.

"What's that?" I asked.

"It is Father playing the *settar,*" the eldest son replied.

The soft tones reminded me of the sound of water trickling over rocks. We raced down to the concert.

Sharki played intuitively, with eyes closed and head swaying ever so slightly from side to side. I watched him strike the four strings with the nail of his right index finger, which he had let grow long. Sharif made a *darbouka* from the backside of a crate and drummed a steady rhythm, while Sharki extracted more and more complex notes from his *settar.* After some encouragement, I joined in and began to sing half-remembered snatches of Urdu *ghazals.* Our multicultural concert was a big hit with some visiting herdsmen, who dropped by and clapped in time to the music. We lost track of time. Time seemed to have lost all significance that day. And in a strange but profound way, so did words. It was the silent, wordless communication, stripped of Kurdish, Arabic, or English belongings, that bound us together.

Hearts and Minds

"We are invited to a wedding," Sharif told me three days later when he came to wake me up for our morning run in the park, which we had neglected in the recent flurry of activities. I had been resting in my hotel room ever since the night of the family picnic and feeling lazy and out of sorts in the silence of my own company. I thought I needed to be alone for a while after spending so much time with such kind and gracious hosts. I hoped I hadn't imposed myself too much on their time, but I also felt that time was a sacred gift, and when someone gives it to you wholeheartedly, it is meant to be enjoyed and appreciated. So I eagerly accepted the invitation for Sharki's cousin's betrothal. Sharif told me he would pick me up at the hotel in the evening by seven. I spent the rest of the day falling in and out of sleep.

The wedding did not take place at a hotel, as I had expected, but in some kind of a theater. Loud echoes of an electric synthesizer rippled through the commotion of Aleppo's nightly throngs as Sharif and I inched our way to the festivities. We were greeted at the door by a man on whose back was strapped an enormous brass samovar from which he poured us two tiny cups of bitter coffee, the traditional welcome ceremony. I noticed that he was using the same two cups for all the guests. Inside, a few people were lounging in their seats, as if waiting for a movie.

"Are you sure this is the right place?" I asked.

"Yes, yes, we are just early," Sharif responded. *"Sabar, sabar!"* He urged me to be patient.

I noticed he was wearing a new jacket and his shoes were freshly polished. The synthesizer droned with modern Kurdish rhythms, sounding remarkably like 1970s disco music. Sharki finally arrived, towing a herd of giggling females. One of them was dressed to impress in a sleeveless scarlet sequined dress and a beehive hairdo. The room was filling rapidly as more and more people streamed in. I wondered if we would be able to see the ceremony.

"They already performed the marriage ceremony in their village," Sharif informed me. "This is reception for people in Aleppo."

We found some empty seats. A deafening pounding of drums signaled the arrival of the bride and groom. I watched the couple stride in, arm in arm. The bride, with her face unveiled, wore a white Western-style gown with a beaded bodice. Someone whispered that the groom was a lawyer and had freshly returned from Italy. They climbed a little stage and sat stiffly upon their thrones, surveying the audience with somber expressions. Suddenly the music picked up and people began to fill the floor in front of the stage for traditional Kurdish dancing.

Men and women formed two separate rows and faced each other. I found myself joining hands with the women, who graciously welcomed a stranger in their midst. It was a simple four-step dance. We stayed in place and shuffled our feet back and forth, the line ebbing and flowing like the tide. Someone at the end of the line waved a white handkerchief like a flag. I felt harmony in that movement, as if I had danced like this before. The bride and groom joined in with an elaborate jig. Everyone smiled and laughed. We continued dancing in that line, now moving counterclockwise. At one point, I was squarely facing Sharki. He lowered his gaze to meet mine and then he gave me a friendly wink, as if to say, "Welcome to the club."

In the days following the wedding, I spent many evenings in Aleppo with my adopted Kurdish family. Sharif would come along, and I realized if it hadn't been for him, I would never have met them. Sometimes Sharif would take off with Sharki to visit other friends in the neighborhood. They seemed to be a tight-knit community, just like most minorities who band together to fortify themselves. I elected to stay at the house and play with the children. So much innocence was in their eyes, and I wondered if it would stay that way when they grew older. As for their mother, she seemed to live on her memories. One evening, she showed me a box full of black-and-white family photos. The Kurdish women in those pictures looked feisty and beautiful. Jiyan gave me an eight- by ten-inch black-and-white picture of herself as a sixteen-year-old. She had ribbons in her plaits and the same broad forehead that reminded me of a wild mountain plateau.

"So you got my message."

Sharif was sitting inside the gazebo. I hadn't seen him in the two days after the Kurdish wedding. He had left a note for me at the juice stand requesting a meeting in our jogging park.

"What's wrong, why the long face?" I teased him.

"It is all you. Now you are so deep inside my heart, but I know you will soon go away and leave me alone in this crazy place. You have no heart."

When he met my gaze, his pupils were blazing like liquid magma.

A gust of wind blew some pieces of paper from the folds of his book. I recognized the red balloons and yellow flowers from the stationery pad courtesy of Simple Restaurant. Sharif's neat textbook-style handwriting was scribbled all over the pages. I picked one up and started to read. It was a poem in Arabic titled "Dream." I couldn't understand very much, but I knew the words bristled with emotions. To give them some personality, the accent marks that add vowels to Arabic were colored in red and green ink. On the back of the page, he had written in English, perhaps a crude translation of the original. This one I had no trouble comprehending.

She taught me eagerness under her shadow's voices. A test of her mind, she pushed me to madness. When she is thirsty, I will give her my tears to drink.

My ears burned as I read and reread his wounded sentiments.

Sharif was watching me closely. He wanted me to respond to what I had just discovered, what I hadn't even suspected, because I thought we were above and beyond all that, as if life were ever so simple. I had no words at my disposal, at least not the ones that he wanted to hear. Instead, I folded the paper and inserted it back inside his book. It was a copy of Charles Dickens's *Tale of Two Cities*.

"Where did you get that?" I asked. It was a most unusual book. Pages on the right-hand side had printed the text in Arabic, on the left in English.

"At the book fair in central square," he mumbled and buried his face in the book.

"Come on, let's read together out loud. You read the English and I read the Arabic and we can correct each other's mistakes."

My words sounded disingenuous and hollow. A total copout. I handed him a damp cigarette.

"It was the best of times, it was the worst of times," Sharif began in audiobook fashion.

He was wearing his thin, woolen black turtleneck and faded black pants, reminding me of an avant-garde beatnik with a touch of a pilgrim's restlessness.

It seemed as if Dickens were speaking to our dilemma with that first sentence. It was a fine old mess, and I didn't know how to get out of it without being an absolute brute. Why did he have to do this? Why couldn't he have spared his feelings and mine? But then again, he was human after all, though I had propelled him to the status of a saint because of that serenity he radiated, as if he didn't know the meaning of worry or pain. And the last thing I wanted was to cause pain to such a supremely decent man, who had shown me such generosity, kindness, and humility. I couldn't give him an answer just yet. Not until I had figured out whether I was ready to fall off my journey's map, whether the war in my head was over or not.

Sharif had been reading like an automaton. I took a turn until darkness erased the words from the book. Then we plunged back into our old comfortable silence. He seemed to have read my mind because he didn't raise the subject again, the one that we were avoiding with the help of Charles Dickens. I was grateful for his stories, but now I had to deal with the real-life story that had snagged me with such unfathomable stealth and grace. Sharif was staring at the floor. I was afraid to ask him what he was thinking. Maybe he had already guessed my unspoken response and didn't want to hear me voice it. If only I knew what I wanted to say.

Rapture

The following morning, I insisted on tagging along with Sharif to the town of Afrin, where he had some "business matters" to take care of.

"But you will get bored," he said. "There is nothing to do there."

I wanted to have nothing to do and procrastinate. It was the perfect remedy.

"Oh, but how silly of me to forget!" Sharif slapped his forehead as if he had just remembered something. "You can go to Ain Dara. It is nice place to relax. You stay all day and write there."

He put me on a minivan heading in its direction, telling the driver to deposit me at the foot of a hill. We agreed to meet up there by 6:00 PM.

The bus drove through a swath of rich black earth cultivated with fields of vegetables. A grassy knoll emerged in the near distance with a neat row of evenly spaced trees ceremoniously decorating its summit. "Ain Dara." The driver pointed beyond the mound as I disembarked and walked closer to its base, near which sat a small tourist office. The boy inside handed me a couple of brochures. I learned that Ain Dara ranks as one of the ancient Hittite remnants in Syria dating to the first millennium BC. Paying for my entrance ticket, I started to climb the hill, spiraling around lush olive groves.

The ruins consisted of broken rocks and pillars scattered like the pillows and mattresses in Bedouin tents. Intricate carvings of lions and pagan deities decorated shiny black stones. I walked around the crest of the hill, inventing songs in Urdu that I sang at the top of my voice to an invisible audience. It began to rain lightly, and I made a shelter with my shawl and crouched in a field of stones, grass, and red poppies, my singing unabated. Solitude floated from the massive slabs placed thousands of years ago. The intimacy of the open air united me with myself.

I recalled one of my mother's sayings—that we tend to look outside for answers that are inside of us. My journey was precisely such a case. I had thought that the stimulation of foreign places would disentangle me from a life at home that I had found boring and joyless. There had been so much hunger inside me to escape, to give myself room to breathe fresh air. And now that I had done that for nearly a year and a half, I was coming right back to where I started, to little old me. So my mom was right, of course. But if she were here now, I would tell her that tapping into these internal answers requires external knowledge. If I had not taken the trouble to travel to far-flung corners of the world and meet such strange and wonderful people, I wouldn't have had the perspective and distance to see inside myself. Perhaps that's why a journey can be so transformative, because it gives you a type of self-monitored x-ray vision and the rate at which you mature and grow during fifteen months on the road is much faster than fifteen months at home.

I started to think of a departure date from Aleppo. My visa was valid for only a month, and I would be nearing the end of it in a few days. Of course I knew that leaving Aleppo would imply leaving Sharif. I didn't think I had any other choice. Maybe I did, but I wasn't allowing myself an alternate route. It was enough just to have reached a pivot point in my journey and in my life, which was perhaps what I was searching for all this time. I had wanted to be transformed, and here was my chance.

Sharif showed up promptly at six in the evening just as he had promised. At my urging, he climbed a tall statue in the shape of a lion. He sat cross-legged on top of it with my shawl wrapped around his head like a turban. I zoomed in with my camera for a great shot. The rain had stopped, and the setting sun poured a liquid flame, turning the stones to gold. Then it vanished over the lip of some distant hills.

Back down the mound, we met a man at the ticket booth. He was an old friend of Sharif's named Abu Salah. Even in the receding twilight, I noticed right away his twinkling blue eyes. As the local magistrate, one of Abu Salah's duties was to oversee Ain Dara and handle all related management matters. He was also a successful businessman with considerable clout in his village. I immediately warmed to Abu Salah's easygoing manner. Apparently, he was used to dealing with foreigners and could speak bits of French and German. It amused me to hear him call me "Madame." As nightfall descended, we moved to the little caretaker's cottage behind the booth to drink lukewarm tea under a burned-out lightbulb. Sharif and I were invited to spend the night at Abu Salah's house.

We got there nearly three hours late, after getting lost in muddy farm fields during a sudden downpour. Abu Salah lived in a large stone bungalow overlooking acres of land. He was waiting for us at the front porch veranda, and after taking in our rain-drenched clothes caked with mud, he immediately sent us inside to freshen up. I followed a woman to a bedroom, where I stripped off my wet rags in exchange for clean dry ones. She was energetic and petite with a trim figure and a marvelous face of ivory smooth skin, high cheekbones, and dark smoky eyes. I could scarcely believe her to be Abu Salah's wife, aged fifty-five and who had borne seven grown children. They were all absorbed in watching the video of a cousin's recent wedding on a large-screen television flanked by two upright speakers. Apparently, Abu Salah was a well-off man and determined to move with the times.

Dinner was served in large silver platters. If I could eat the same meal day after day for the rest of my life, it would be this—salty black olives, hard-boiled eggs, sheep's-milk cheese, juicy tomatoes, cucumbers, hummus, and flat bread. And if I ever had the choice of waking up to the same view over and over, it would be the one I saw the following morning from Abu Salah's front yard. The muddy fields through which we had tramped in the rain last night had transformed into a velvety green softness. Some were densely planted with fava beans and eggplants. Groves of olive trees rustled in the distance, where there seemed to be no discernible roads.

Abu Salah asked me if I wanted to buy a house in his village. It would cost roughly $5,000–15,000. And if I really wanted to live out here, Abu Salah would clear all bureaucratic hurdles and provide me all the comfort I needed. Then I could live with the Kurds, learn Kurdish, maybe even teach in the village school, and have a nice little life in this idyllic part of earth. I mumbled something about thinking it over, and

Abu Salah laughed merrily. He towered over me at more than six feet tall. His closely cropped salt-and-pepper hair had the texture of jute.

As I tagged along with Abu Salah during his morning rounds, he told me about two Western women, one from Germany, the other from France, who were living in a neighboring village, having married into local families. I wondered what it was that compelled them to change their lives, and why I couldn't be more like them, why I could go only halfway on the wheel of change. It gave me the feeling of being partially dressed, as if by discarding my old skin, I had not fully embraced the new one but was only trying it on for size to see if I liked the way it fit.

A Blip in the Night

Back in Aleppo, I spent the next three days in a bureaucratic quagmire. The authorities refused to renew my visa, which left me precisely forty-eight hours within which to leave the country. I was both relieved and saddened. At least I had an official reason for my departure. And had I wanted to sidestep the rules and overstay illegally, I knew that I would have had to go beyond sightseeing and other frivolities. Someone wanted to spend his life with me, and it was too big a question to ignore. I hadn't ignored it in my head, but to tell him outright what I was thinking or feeling required more courage. I was trying to summon it by taking long walks around the old city, but then I would think of Sharif all by himself, and I would go back to wherever he was, which in most cases was at the park, where he seemed to be running around the clock. I no longer had the urge to run alongside him, so I would just sit and wait until he finished his laps. Then we would linger for a bit, sip some tea, and end up at the hotel or the Simple Restaurant. It was comforting to be carrying on with all our old routines as if nothing had changed, but deep down I suspected it was a coping strategy for us both.

On my last evening in Aleppo, Sharif announced that he would take me to a Sufi *dhikir*. In Arabic, *dhikir* means remembrance. It is often a public ceremony to recollect the attributes of God through music and dance. I was curious about Sufism, which is also known by the Arabic word *tasawwuf*, referring to the process of self-improvement and purification as a means to know God. Sufi philosophy emphasizes the interior over the external manifestations of religion. It embraces the Islamic concept of *tawhhid*, an uncompromising unity and oneness of divinity. God is both transcendent from creation as well as immanent in creation. And Sufis believe that nothing is apart from God, as asserted in the Quranic verse, "We are closer to you than your jugular vein."

I kept pestering Sharif about what to expect. "You will see," was his evasive response. We headed to the *souq*, entering it from Bab Antakiya, where I had first tumbled into the old city almost a month ago.

"Wait outside," Sharif said. We stopped near a small green door that I had never noticed before, although I had passed by it a dozen times. Sharif removed his shoes and disappeared inside a small, poorly lit room with an open, iron-grilled window. Minutes later, he returned with a rotund, well-built man dressed in a white cotton gown and a long cone-shaped hat.

"This is my friend Murad. He is Sufi dervish," Sharif said.

The face of the dervish reminded me of gazing into a serene lake. We smiled and shook hands.

"My friend says he is sorry, but because you are woman, you are not permitted to enter the room. It is for men only. But you can sit outside and listen." Sharif translated the Sufi's Arabic.

I was disappointed that gender alone barred me from the audience, even though women in Islam have been known to participate in and even lead a *dhikir*. In 8th-century Iraq, Rabia al-Adawiya was revered for her all-night vigils to convene with God. She was also known for her insistence that love of God ought to be selfless rather than motivated by fear or the prospect of reward.

A man stepped outside and handed me a plate of digestive biscuits and a cup of lukewarm tea. After I finished eating, he gave me a large black cloak. I covered myself in its voluminous folds and perched on the stool strategically positioned next to the window. The *dhikir* began with the rhythmic praising of Allah's virtues. *"Subhannallah, Subhannallah."*

I made a slit in my black tent and peeked into the room, where men were sitting in a circle, slowly rocking back and forth, some swaying their heads from side to side. The chanting increased in pitch and fervor, *"La ilaha il-Allah,"* they repeated over and over. There is no God but God, negation and affirmation in a single breath. All is one. One is all.

I closed my eyes, enraptured by the rhythm of those familiar words, a tiny gateway opening in my mind, triggering spasms of nostalgia for a nameless entity. People were coming and going from the busy portal and I was sure that every head and eye as turning toward me with gleeful astonishment as they witnessed one of the oddest sights in recent memory of the ancient *souq*. I must have cut a dashing figure, huddled in black, covered from head to toe, swaying to my own inner beat as the Sufis whirled in ecstasy inside.

The piercing wail of the *ney,* an open-mouthed reed instrument symbolizing a yearning to return to unity and wholeness, held me captive. Through the window, I glimpsed a swooshing figure in white, twirling in the middle of the circle. It was Murad, our dervish friend. His eyes were closed and his face arched toward the unseen sky. Arms crossed over his chest, he was spinning counterclockwise, in the same direction as the rotation of the earth. Faster and faster, he continued to turn. I thought of my little Sufi in the blood-red appliquéd gown, the tapestry hanging above my bed since Cairo that I gazed at night after night before drifting off to sleep. I never understood what he was trying to tell me all these months. But as I watched Murad, my Sufi came to life.

Murad was a human satellite in total submission to his Maker. His submission was the source of his happiness. And submission was the source of Sharif's serenity. It was written all over his face, and I had seen him exercise it countless times and even heard it in his words. He had called it surrender. His surrender was not a fatalistic attitude toward life. It was an active choice in letting go of the self and its demands, a daily test in trusting God's will.

I thought I knew surrender well. It was about having faith in the unseen, and I had put this faith into practice the day I left home on that one-way flight, embracing uncertainty and swallowing my fears. But surrender was not applicable to just my journey. That was what the dervish was conveying in his dance and what Sharif had expressed in his words and his actions. Surrender was also a part of everyday life, the biggest journey of all. I hadn't done this yet. I had chosen instead to run away from my life, from all the things I didn't like, things I was fed up with. But now I realized that running away was not so brave; it was surrender that was the braver thing to do, and the hardest.

Suddenly it was all over. The music, the chanting, the dancing evaporated into the dark night as suddenly as it had started. Murad came out, followed by Sharif and the other men. They all smiled at me. I was still shrouded in my black cloak. It was a soft, protective shelter, and I didn't want to give it back. Someone lit a cigarette. I was offered another cup of tea. I appreciated their hospitality. It did not really bother me that I hadn't been permitted inside to sit with the Sufis. I had performed the *dhikir* in my heart as a welcomed observer.

Murad smiled again with that same serene expression and asked me if I had enjoyed the *dhikir*.

I nodded mutely, wishing my knowledge of Arabic stretched to the capacity of forming full-fledged sentences of meaning and worth. Instead, I nudged Sharif's elbow.

"Ask him what it means to be a Sufi."

The answer came back in a single breath.

"He says it means trying to carry out efforts," Sharif translated.

"Yes, but what does it mean in practical terms?" I persisted.

"You must follow the path of a desert highway."

"But that's impossible!" I blurted out. "There is no highway in the desert. Where is the path?"

Murad fixed his luminous eyes on me and said something softly.

"He says you must learn to see with your heart to find the path," Sharif responded.

We asked Murad to join us for tea, but he declined because he had to catch a late-night bus back to his village. He had changed from his long white frock to jeans and a thick sweater. It was strange to see him looking so ordinary with none of the pretensions or self-consciousness of his dervishness. This was one of the most endearing aspects of the Sufi. He did not withdraw from the world for a hallowed existence. He thoroughly engaged with living life, being and doing at the same time.

Sharif and I walked back to the hotel.

"Aren't you happy here?" he asked.

I remained silent.

"Why don't you stay then? You can go to university in Aleppo or Damascus. Learn more Arabic. Maybe I get job in Lebanon and we go to live in Beirut."

He was concocting dreams. I played along. It was good to dream from time to time.

"Beirut! What would I do there? Dance in some nightclub?"

"Fine. Fine. We stay in Soorya. Here we talk, we meet, we pray, we live. You will not like it if you go back to USA. You will feel like *ajnabee*, a stranger in your own country."

If only I could do it. Surrender to myself. Surrender to life. Surrender to love.

"It's still my home."

"And you will go back?"

"I have to."

"But why?"

"You won't understand."

He became quiet, lost in his own thoughts. The night was dark, and I willed it to seize my fraying mind.

Out of Bounds

I am used to leading a double life and not even being aware of it. I dream in Urdu and speak in English. I wear saris or Levi's. I pray and I dance. The selves that reside inside me switch sides as appropriate. I feel them inside myself, like two different seas jostling liquid against each other. It's a nice feeling. I like the interchanging rhythms and currents of my two seas. They lend me a passport to connect with multiple shores. But in this connection, there is also a certain unfurling detachment, not like a holding back of something, but more a matter of complete openness that allows me to experience intimately people and places that are considered by some as bizarre or dangerous.

I recognize the foreign as a flimsy veil that separates the nearness of friends, maybe even soul mates, who are initially masquerading as strangers. At some point, we are all strangers to each other. Apart from our families, every relation we forge in life begins at first with a total stranger, transcending into a vortex of emotions, call it friendship, love, or something else. I often wonder what happens during the process of two souls meeting, strangers one moment, and in the next, they know what makes the other tick without even realizing how their familiarity was born.

There is no easy way to leave a place or person that you have deeply connected to. I didn't want to leave, but I wasn't brave enough to stay. So I bypassed the turn to a whole other journey that I would never come to know, not because I didn't care for him, but because I was afraid of letting go of my heart, of holding my hands in the air and falling backward to be caught and held. I didn't have the capacity to do that just yet, not with Sharif, nor with anyone else, so I didn't even try. I had given him the classic speech, "It's all about me, not you," which he really couldn't have bought. But I think he knew, as I knew, that the time we spent together was a blessing. The important and perhaps most difficult thing was to get our cumbersome egos out of the way, to let go and simply surrender.

I still had a lot to learn about this surrender business. I needed to factor it into my entire existence, and only then would I become true to myself, true to God, and true to the practice and meaning of Islam. As a parting gift, I bought a round pendant in silver and black inscribed with the indelible words of our religion—*La ilaha il-Allah, Muhamad-ur-Rasool Allah*—there is no God but God and Muhammad is His last Prophet. The pendant was perforated in the middle, and I split it apart, gave one slice to Sharif, and kept the other. Wearing it would remind me of his claim to the past we had shared. And if I listened hard, his voice would still echo loud and clear, reminding me of one of my favorite lines from Rumi.

> *And I am the flame dancing in love's fire,*
> *that flickering light in the depths of desire.*
> *Wouldst thou know the pain that severance breeds,*
> *listen then to the strain of the reed.*

Looking at Sharif, I often had the strange but not unpleasant sensation of going *into* his dark espresso eyes, seeing far deeper into his being than possible with the more closed and flat irises of lighter-colored eyes. He had taught me to see by polishing the mirror of my heart.

Restless and edgy, Sharif stayed up all night on the hotel rooftop, as I finished packing. My bus for Antakya near the Turkish border was scheduled to leave at 6:00 AM. Before I knew it, faint lyrics of the dawn *adhan* slowly soared into flight. I stood on the rooftop and listened one last time. It was time to go. We slipped out of the small metal door through which I had first arrived, escorted by the drunken old man, four weeks ago. So much to have happened in such little time. Four weeks as densely packed as a lifetime with feelings too nebulous to decipher.

The bus depot was only five minutes away. Since I already had my ticket in hand, there was nothing to do but wait. We were an hour early and planned to settle down with a hot cup of tea and some last-minute words. Instead, a bus pulled in and the conductor announced my destination. It was leaving right away. There would be no morning tea, no languorous parting. We didn't even shake hands. I desperately wanted to give him a quick hug to express my frozen feelings. But all eyes were on us, and the public scrutiny made me lose my nerve. I got on the bus. Sharif stood rooted to the ground as if zapped by lightning. A look of utter dismay mingling with a sweet sorrow washed across his unshaven face.

Turkey

Bends in the River

*Be in this world as if you are a traveler, a passerby,
with your clothes and shoes full of dust.*
A SAYING OF THE PROPHET MUHAMMAD

At first impression, Cappadocia appeared as a real-life cartoon drawing of bizarre rock formations sprouting from the earth, lopsided triangles and phallic-shaped freaks of nature. The Turkish minibus known as the *dolmuş* lurched to a stop in the town of Göreme. Two young men disembarked at a deserted ring road that functioned as the bus station. Ignoring my stiff limbs, I stepped out and watched the men disappear into a side alley. My back hunched under the weight of my pack, the same cobalt-blue cylinder that accompanied me to Cairo. But this time, there was no Auntie Nadia at the airport to drive me to an apartment in her red Mazda, no Ghuma at the gate to carry luggage up six flights of stairs. It was midnight, and I was alone in central Turkey after traveling twenty hours, having completely forgotten why I came and where I intended to go.

The road seemed to sigh with me as I traced its curve up a steep hill, my footsteps crunching on gravel. A slew of pensions advertised their names in large bold English letters. I picked the pension with the nicest name (Paradise) and walked through a little metal gate to a dimly lit office. The manager on call had startling green eyes and a halo of frizzy curls standing on end that made him look like the survivor of a recent electrocution. He introduced himself as Bŭlent.

"We are full," Bŭlent announced. "But you can sleep in the fairy chimney if you like."

I was too tired and disoriented to contemplate what a fairy chimney implied. But I found myself agreeing to the offer, paying a room deposit, and following Bŭlent to an open-air terrace, where piles of wet laundry hung out to dry on two ropes fastened between utility poles.

"Come!" Bŭlent beckoned me to hurry.

He climbed a short staircase with an iron railing leading to a triangle-shaped hunk of rock with a rounded base caulked with cement. A wooden plank serving as a makeshift door leaned against a three-foot hole. Bŭlent moved the plank aside and ducked his head through the small opening. I followed suit to enter a cozy chamber with coarse, grainy walls with built-in rocky ledges. It really was a cave.

"You like?" Bŭlent grinned, exposing a row of brown-stained teeth.

"It's fine. I've never stayed in a cave before."

"Not cave, fairy chimney," he solemnly corrected me.

A thin, twin-size mattress sprawled on the floor, coated with a fine layer of dust and tiny nuggets of crumbling rock. The low ceiling brushed against my head.

"I'll get you new mattress." Bŭlent bent his tall frame and slipped back out the hole.

The next few days were a blur. I slept ten, twelve hours straight, venturing out on the terrace only for meals, served by a sullen teenage girl wearing headphones and a Mickey Mouse T-shirt. She showed no interest in why I chose to remain confined in a room no bigger than a one-person spaceship. Bŭlent visited from time to time just to make sure I had plenty of warm covers and to check if the roof had caved in. He told me about a guest who had stayed in the fairy chimney for three months and never once stepped into town. It didn't seem such a bad idea.

My abrupt departure from Aleppo—and Sharif—to this strange Turkish town of cave dwellers made me want to curl into a fetal position and burrow under the itchy woolen blanket. Sharif's shell-shocked face haunted me night and day. I had no desire to talk to people unless I was forced to. And I couldn't have cared less about exploring my new sur- roundings. I simply wanted to hide out from the world.

It was awful, the way I had left, ejecting myself out of a friend's life with the speed of a ready cannonball. Time had morphed from a languorous flowing river to zealous rapids, pushing me onto a bus that had arrived much too early. I shouldn't have gotten on board; I should have waved at the driver to go on without me and waited for the next bus, so that we would have had some time to talk and safeguard memories. They seemed to be in tatters now, like the broken fragments of a half- remembered dream. The more I stayed asleep, the more it seemed as if I had dreamed that whole experience. And as the days slipped by, Aleppo and Sharif quietly scuttled to the back recesses of my mind, a place I dared not visit for a while, save in my dreams.

It was early evening of day number 7 when I began thinking of venturing beyond the confines of my cave. I was beginning to suffocate in there, and even when I breathed fresh air out on the terrace, the drip- ping laundry and the sulky looks of that girl bringing forth my requested honey yogurt and toast were not helping to lighten my mood. I took a shower in the communal coed bathroom downstairs, making sure to change into my clothes inside the stall in case of any wandering eyes. It was the usual ensemble of floral-printed harem pants and peasant blouse but I chucked my head scarf. It no longer seemed necessary now that I was in a far more touristy kind of town.

At first, it thrilled me to find Clairol shampoos and Kleenex boxes at every corner store, and a dizzying array of Internet cafés with unre- stricted access to Hotmail. Having arrived on Turkish soil from the Syr- ian hinterland, I had the impression of traveling from the third world to the first. Göreme could have passed for a rugged version of Granada in southern Spain. I walked along its main drag, a dusty dirt road lined with carpet shops, souvenir stands, artsy boutiques, and cafés catering to an international set of chilled-out backpackers. Everyone spoke English. I chatted with a friendly waiter watering some plants in tin cans. He welcomed me inside the Local Café. I sat among a boisterous group of foreigners bragging about their latest Turkish finds. We all exchanged hellos. Then I buried my face in a bowl of hot lentil soup.

A thin, rakish man wearing a baseball hat with an Adidas logo and fraying blue jeans caught my eye and tried to hold it. He crossed his legs and hunched over a tall glass of chalky-white liquid, his chin cradled with the left hand as if it were in danger of slumping into his half-finished drink. Every time I looked up from my soup, his gaze wandered in my direction, occasionally accompanied by a wry, close-lipped smile. The other foreigners clambered to their feet and left the restaurant, laughing and talking loudly. I ordered more soup and read parts of my guidebook, flipping through the pages and taking notes. It was a radical change from my behavior in Middle Eastern restaurants, where I wouldn't even have peered into a map while eating, let alone my guidebook, in an effort to remain inconspicuous and blend in as much as possible. But in small-town Göreme, all nonlocals were evidently tourists. The inability to hide this label left me with a strange sense of untrammeled freedom. I was not used to such comforts.

The waiter who had been watering plants approached with a bottle of clear liquid with its label peeled off. In the next instant, a series of small dishes began to arrive in waves. First some salad, followed by slabs of white cheese, green olives, sliced tomatoes, and sausage-thick dolmas, then a platter of pureed dips and a basket of bread. Mr. Adidas raised his glass and winked from across the room. Apparently, he had decided to host a party, and I was the guest of honor.

"Merhaba!"

A pair of gray eyes smiled shyly as my host pulled up a nearby chair and straddled it backward.

"Hello." I pretended to act blasé, as if used to strangers ordering food for my table.

He uncapped the bottle and poured its contents into two glasses, filling them halfway, and then adding water, instantly causing the mixture to turn cloudy.

"What is it?" I asked.

"Try some. You will like it." He raised his glass again and made a little toast. *"Sheray fay."*

I sipped the beverage, feeling rather nervous given my luck with mixed drinks. It tasted strongly of aniseed and licorice.

"You must eat," the man moved dishes toward me. "Raki is not good on empty stomach."

"Raki?"

"Raki," he repeated. "Strong Turkish liquor. The world's finest."

"Sorry. I'm not much of a drinker." I shoved the glass aside.

He laughed and grabbed a few olives. "My name is Mehmet."

Rifling in his small pack, Mehmet produced a colorful brochure advertising guided hikes around Cappadocia. It featured hot-air balloons flying over what looked like a moonscape.

"Great! I love hiking."

"Why don't you come along tomorrow? We meet here tomorrow morning at nine."

"Perfect."

"Or I can come to Paradise. You're lucky to get into the fairy chimney. It's a very popular place to stay."

I nearly choked on my dolma. "How do you know that?"

"I know everything that goes on in Göreme."

"What are you, the secret police?"

"Listen, I've lived here all my life. Don't trust anyone in this town. Except me, of course."

"Uh-huh."

I didn't give much weight to what Mehmet was saying, mostly because I seemed to have lost the will to study and contemplate random conversations with people I had just met with the same intensity as before. It was beginning to wear me down, and I felt relieved and uplifted to have absolved myself of this responsibility that I had considered mandatory for much of my travels in the Middle East, certainly since Damascus, when the alienation from home had made me hyperanalyze my surroundings to stay sane. Now I couldn't have cared less for analysis, not because I wanted to go stark raving mad, but because I sensed the gap diminishing, the horizon moving closer, promising an eventual return to old comforts.

The following morning, I met Mehmet outside the café. He was poring over some maps with two young German girls with painful sunburns.

"Merhaba! Merhaba!" Mehmet raised the visor of his baseball cap to wish me good morning.

"Merhaba!" I replied and handed him some bills for the guided walk.

The German girls rubbed more lotion on their charred skin. I put on a red cloth hat with an enormous brim that appeared to swallow my face. Bea had lent it to me back in Beirut and somehow never managed to get it back.

"Let's go!" Mehmet called. The Germans hoisted their packs. I had nothing on me save for a camera slung around my shoulder and a liter of water, which is how I preferred to go hiking. For an instant, I recalled my urban treks around Rome and Paris and a silly mishap in the Dolomites; I had veered off-trail and was scrambling up a moraine field when a friendly group of Austrian hikers adopted me into their party. Those days seemed a lifetime away, but I was glad to have lived them. And now I was even more glad to be back in my long-neglected outdoorsiness that was put on hold for a whole different set of adventures in Cairo, Amman, Damascus, Beirut, and Aleppo, where I had scaled the slopes of hearts and minds. I hadn't realized what an exhausting effort it was, and as Mehmet signaled for us to follow him, my feet seemed attached to a trampoline. I literally skipped my way into Göreme's amphitheater of molten-honeycombed cliff sides.

Our guide lectured on Cappadocia's history. Its original name of Kapatukya derived from Persian, meaning "country of beautiful horses." Two major volcanic eruptions millions of years ago had given birth to the landscape before our eyes. The exposed lava debris stiffened into tufa and basalt that rain and wind erosion sculpted into surrealist rock shapes. As we walked deeper into the valley, Mehmet pointed out a grassy plateau littered with the famous fairy chimneys, similar to the one I was staying in. These fairy chimneys were slender, tubular towers with a curious dark stone perched on their tops like a cap. Mehmet also mentioned that Cappadocia was an area of early Christian settlements going as far back as the 4th century and that Göreme was the site of hundreds of rock-cut churches and monasteries. We found some by climbing ladders and squeezing through narrow tunnels that led to secret worlds of columned arches and frescoes with vivid red and green dyes that reminded me of frosted Christmas cookies.

By late afternoon, Mehmet decided on a lunch stop in the nearby village of Zelve. We ate at a simple outdoor café facing a mural of caves gouged with tiny holes that served as windows and doors. According to Mehmet, these caves were inhabited by people as recently as 1950, until they had to be evacuated for safety reasons. He also talked about the underground cities of Kaymakli and Derinkuyu. It was hard to say who built them and when, but they were presumably used as temporary troglodytic shelters by Christians escaping the Arab invasions during the 7th and 8th centuries.

Mehmet explained the intricacy of the subterranean complex, where a total of eighteen levels (of which ten were accessible) were interconnected by a network of tunnels to form some of the grandest catacombs in the world. In addition to living and sleeping quarters, amenities included kitchens, cisterns, wine cellars, chapels, and stables. It was beyond my understanding how anyone could have spent an entire lifetime in the cloistered dankness of a windowless space, even if it were equipped with chimneys and air shafts.

We returned to Göreme by sundown. The Germans headed straight to the bus station for the evening connection to Istanbul. Mehmet and I hung out at the Local Café playing cards. Instead of seeing diamonds and spades, my eyes conjured more caves and rocky esplanades.

"That was incredible," I said. "We must go back."

"You haven't seen anything yet. Tomorrow we will go to Pigeon Valley."

"To see pigeons?"

"Pigeon lofts. Inside caves."

"You have customers?"

"I will find some."

I admired his confidence. Mehmet treated his guided excursions with professional pride, and every morning I found him at the café, ready to head to the surrounding "office" with a cluster of tourists, including me. On days business was slow, Mehmet and I would pack a lunch and head to Rose Valley, named for the soft pink tinge of its rockscape. It was Mehmet's favorite place in Göreme, and when we got there, I instantly saw why. The ancient layers of molten rock bunched like wrinkled sheets beneath our feet. Rugged hillsides carved a frieze of pointy pinnacles with serrated edges.

"Wow! This is just wild. What a landscape!" I kept on wowing as we trudged deeper into the valley, my hiking fervor at a strong pitch.

"Slow down. You're making me tired!" Mehmet called out as I raced ahead.

"It's amazing out here. I don't think I could ever get enough of this place!"

I felt kilowatts of energy burning in my legs. Maybe they were compensating for the mental and emotional energy I seemed to have drained. It wasn't so bad; it was actually quite a relief, in that way you feel after finishing a grueling school term or a taxing project at work.

We crossed ravine after ravine exposing hidden tunnels, caves, and archways. The local stone was soft and crumbly like pieces of feta cheese. After a picnic lunch, Mehmet and I would lie on our backs in the sun and pick out animals hidden in the white clouds that swirled above our heads. It was nearly three weeks since I had arrived in Göreme, not counting the first week of hibernation and abject despair. I still thought about Sharif, and the time we had shared had begun to take on the quality of a cherished dream that was indeed for real. Maybe it was a moment when dreaming was required to be absolutely awake in life. I had serious doubts that I would ever experience such a moment again.

Mehmet was a taciturn man, similar to Sharif in the way he preserved his words, as if keeping them in a verbal storage tank to be sparingly used. But quite unlike Sharif, Mehmet was fond of teasing me. He characterized my recent nine-month sojourn in the Middle East as an exercise in self-inflicted torture. Whenever I raved about the wonders of the Western Desert or Ramadan in Cairo, Mehmet screwed his eyes shut and started singing Billy Joel songs at the top of his voice. It was pointless to tell him about the crazy fun that Bea and I had shared in Damascus and my soulful adventures in Aleppo. Mehmet disdained the Arab world as a vulgar, backward place, a stark contrast to Turkey's progressive path of "secular democracy" championed by his hero, Mustafa Kemal Atatürk. He often talked about the charismatic leader, hailed as the father of the modern Turkish Republic, and now proceeded to give me a crash course in Atatürk's modernizing legacy.

From the abolishment of Islamic courts, to the banning of the traditional crimson tasseled hat known as the fez, to speaking out against the barbarity of veiling women, Atatürk was determined to transition Turkey's ancient cultural heritage toward a more "civilized" world grounded in Western values. One of his most significant measures had changed the written form of the Turkish language from Arabic script into Latinized letters.

"He shouldn't have done that," I said defiantly. "At least in the Arab world I could read and write the language, if not speak the lingo. Here I am totally illiterate!"

Mehmet offered to teach me some Turkish. But I turned down his offer, feeling a dismal lack of enthusiasm to learn a whole new set of prepositions, tenses, and irregular verbs. I had stretched my linguistic prowess enough with Arabic and ran out of fuel to stretch some more. Maybe I was getting lazy. Or maybe I was just tired.

"Here, I forgot to give you this earlier." I handed Mehmet some money. He refused to take it.

"You are not my customer today. Now you are *arkadaş!* Friend! Understand?"

He closed my fist around the wad of bills. I understood. A friend implied honor and respect. It was a priceless privilege.

Then Mehmet suggested going to the local mosque for Friday prayers.

"I didn't know you prayed!"

He laughed. "I am still Muslim. Why shouldn't I pray if I feel like it?"

"What about the raki?" Now it was my turn to tease.

"What about it? Nothing wrong with a little raki. It strengthens the spirit."

"The spirit to pray?"

"The spirit to be alive," he countered.

"By the way," Mehmet stood up from the rock we were resting on and extended his hand toward me. "According to Turkish law, a person can go to jail for saying bad things about Atatürk. So be careful what you say in public."

"You mean I can't speak my mind freely in the great democracy of Turkey?" I feigned mock horror.

He shook his head and smiled. "You are impossible. Come. Let's go eat. I'm starving."

We turned our backs on Rose Valley and walked back into town.

The Wild, Wild East

Living in my very own fairy chimney had its charms. For one thing, I developed a new reverence for Fred Flintstone and all former cave dwellers, real or otherwise. But after a month of sleeping on a mattress dusted with rock shavings, going to and from my rooftop shelter to the communal bathroom near the pension's reception hall, and spending long days trekking through fantastical moonscapes from nine in the morning till six or seven in the evening, I contracted a severe case of cabin fever. The small-town atmosphere was getting claustrophobic, but I wasn't inclined to move on right away to the next bigger city. Mulling over an exit strategy, I ran into sallow-faced Ali puffing on damp cigarettes outside my favorite carpet shop. We didn't know each other well, but I had seen him around Göreme, usually hobnobbing with tourists in some trendy café.

That evening Ali was squatting on his haunches in a light drizzle and moodily staring off into space with heavy-lidded eyes. When I complained about my boredom, he suggested an excursion to Nemrut Mountain in eastern Turkey. I had seen postcards of Nemrut. They showed colossal stone heads of pagan gods burnished golden under the rising sun. I wanted to take advantage of being smack in the middle of Turkey, from which I had closer access to the eastern part of the country, than I would have had if I were already in Istanbul way over on its westernmost edge. My guidebook mentioned that eastern Turkey was the Kurdish heartland, where insurgents frequently skirmished with government forces and much of the area was heavily patrolled by the *jandarma,* a Turkish military unit functioning as the rural police force. But the idea of exploring the eastern front, which was also crammed with history and far less touristy, sounded appealing. Without a second thought, I accepted Ali's offer.

The next morning, I approached a silver-gray Land Rover with a small duffel bag in hand. My pack remained in the laundry room of Paradise pension, where I relinquished my fairy chimney to be let out to future guests, preferably not as hapless but just as impressed with the burrowing potential on offer. The Rover was parked outside the Local Café, where Mehmet lingered over an early-morning breakfast waiting for his tour group to gather. I marched over to him and announced my plans, bragging shamelessly of the adventure that loomed ahead. Mehmet raised his faint eyebrows and mashed his thin lips in a tight smile.

"Be careful. I don't like that Ali. He is nothing but trouble."

I rolled my eyes. "You are so paranoid. We are just going to climb the mountain and see a nice little sunrise. What can possibly go wrong?"

Mehmet turned a deaf ear and kept smiling with a know-it-all air.

"I'll be back in a few days. And then we'll go on more treks. We'll go back to Rose Valley and camp out under the full moon."

He remained silent.

"I'll see you when I get back. It's a promise."

Mehmet raised his right hand in a mock salute and stared into an empty plate. I ran toward the Land Rover as somebody blasted its horn. Ali slid open the back door and took my bag.

"Ready to go?"

"Ready, set, go!" I beamed at him. The relief of escaping the monotony of Göreme and the fairy chimney for a road trip with people I hardly knew filled my veins with adrenaline.

Our driver, Hikmet, owned a horse ranch in the nearby town of Avanos. He wore a stone-colored L. L. Bean jacket and grinned at me like a schoolboy. I noticed two of his upper front teeth were missing. A young French couple sat with Hikmet in the front row, clearly the guests of honor. They mumbled the requisite *bonjours* and resumed their discussion of horse breeding with their host. Hikmet's English hinted at a slight Texan twang. He had some business to attend to in the east and decided to make an excursion out of it, swinging by Nemrut on the way. The trip was free, minus our accommodations. There was plenty of room in the vehicle and nobody seemed to mind my unexpected company. We set off in a southeastwardly direction toward the town of Kahta, about three hundred miles away.

Ali turned out to be a gifted musician. He strummed his *saz,* a long-necked mandolinlike instrument, and sang folk tunes with a husky voice, breaking at the end of the chorus line. His plaintive melodies suited the passing mountain scenery, stoic and brooding in its grandeur on a misty overcast day. With every hundred miles, the Land Rover sped farther east along the rugged central Asian plateau of old Anatolia, deeper into the "real" Turkey that remains unknown to the majority of foreign tourists and even to most Turks.

By nightfall, we pulled into the driveway of a lakeside lodge, our base for Nemrut. The plan was to leave by 2:00 AM for the drive up the mountain with a knowledgeable chauffeur provided by the lodge. That would provide ample time to reach the summit by five to catch the sun's first rays. Hikmet had been to Nemrut several times and preferred to snuggle in bed rather than join in on our ambitious agenda. He advised me to dress warmly, given the freezing temperatures at the mountain in the early morning. To compensate for my lack of cold-weather gear, I wore five layers of every available item of clothing in the duffel bag and waddled into the lobby like an overstuffed duck. The French couple sat on a sofa, dressed to impress in snazzy, high-tech jackets and warm woolens. Ali still looked half-asleep. We could hear the pounding rain but went ahead with our plans anyway as soon as the driver showed up.

He drove as far as the road allowed, and we walked up to the guest-house at the summit. A lone American couple sat by a crackling fire, cooking their oatmeal and writing in their journals. They were obviously well prepared and rather too sure of themselves. It made me a tad envious. We waited for the rain to stop. It was exactly 5:00 AM. Our group wallowed in fatigue and the sort of crankiness that can lead even a sane person to strangle someone simply for asking the time of day. Words were scarce to conserve energy.

The rain continued. According to the old caretaker, it was turning into a hailstorm. The clock struck six. We had to make a decision. It was now or never. Ali zipped up his jacket until the upturned collar hit his drooping earlobes. I borrowed the caretaker's fur hat. The wind blew like a hurricane when the door swung open. Hailstones pummeled my face like ice-cold bullets. Our brave troop trudged up the rocky incline leading to the summit, cameras bulging in pockets, ready for those glossy shots we had all anticipated. After an hour of heaving our soaking bodies through the raging storm, we glimpsed some of the famous sculptures as if peering at them through blurred lenses.

I bumped into an eagle's head and another massive head that resembled the Buddha. The stone figures didn't look too happy sitting in this soggy wasteland, where they must have witnessed thousands of similar storms through the years. But storms matter more to human beings than to stone statues. Make that some very stupid human beings fighting a losing battle against Mother Nature. The hailstones turned to small hand grenades, doubling the damage they inflicted on our bodies. I had seen enough of this wretched place. The rest of the group had already vanished, and I searched in vain for Ali's fire-engine-red jacket. Giving up and staggering back to the guesthouse, I discovered the others waiting for me with glum faces.

"Where have you been?" Ali asked demurely.

I shouted the obvious. "To hell and back, that's where I've been!"

The storm had abated to a light drizzle on the way down the mountain. Our driver, too busy rhapsodizing over the wondrous beauty of the alpine landscape, failed to notice the oncoming car. He swerved just in time to avoid a head-on collision. A few miles farther down the road, the *jandarma* ordered us to stop. An officer issued a heated statement in Turkish to our driver. He drove to what looked like a police station and was immediately summoned inside. The French couple, Ali, and I waited inside the Land Rover without receiving a word of explanation.

"What's going on?" I asked Ali.

His head was swinging from side to side with metronomic regularity.

"I don't believe it. I don't believe it," Ali kept repeating.

"Do you mind explaining?"

According to Ali, the car we had nearly hit contained a political dignitary. The dignitary was angered by the driver's carelessness and had radioed ahead to the *jandarma* to deal with him as appropriate. It was just bad luck, plain and simple.

An hour passed. Then another and another until time lost all relevance. We sat in the Land Rover while the chief inspector told us it was for our "security" and "protection" to be in their charge. Ali stepped outside for a smoke. Someone from the station brought a tray of tea and biscuits. I refused to eat from the hands of our jailers despite my hunger pangs. The French couple helped themselves to the food and talked softly between themselves. None of us intended to argue for our release with men in uniform.

A surly-faced officer kept a watchful eye on us. I noticed that he fixed his eyes on me from time to time. Then I noticed this happening more frequently. I shifted in my seat and averted my gaze. This only caused him to stare harder. His eyes narrowed in suspicion, and he started shooting daggers from black olive-pit pupils. Even the French couple looked alarmed.

"You!" He pointed straight at me.

"Me?" I pointed back a finger at myself.

He said something in Turkish to a younger officer standing beside him, presumably an apprentice in training, who immediately translated in English.

"Please step out of the car."

I told myself to remain calm as I unlocked the door and passed a man with an automatic rifle. He stared through me with eyes frozen like a lake in winter. The commanding officer with the surly face motioned for me to follow him. His translator trailed behind us. Visions of humid underground cells infested with rats flashed across my mind. Instead, we stopped near a thick clump of trees in clear view of the detained car and surrounding gendarmes. The rain had cleared by now. Small patches of blue peeked through the cloud layer.

"Your identification papers?" the young apprentice translated.

I pulled out the black, sweat-stained travel pouch worn underneath my shirt, fastened with a nylon cord around my neck. The passport was buried deep inside, and I handed it over with some satisfaction.

The officer grunted in surprise. He had not expected me to be an American. I fondly recalled the incident in Cairo's subway over my wrong ticket stub, but this situation appeared more mysterious and scarier. The officer barked another command, followed with a curt angling of the head.

"We would like to search your bag."

This I did not expect, but there was nothing to hide. I shrugged and loosened the nylon cord, causing the pouch to slump down to my waist.

"Here you go."

The officer opened the Velcro flap and fished out a few thousand-lire notes. Then his fingers pried deeper inside the bag and unearthed an old silver ring and some recent photographs.

"Who is he?" the apprentice demanded.

I stared at a pensive profile of Sharif at Ain Dara.

"Oh, that's my friend from Aleppo."

The officer grunted again. I was getting to understand his grunts. This one alerted his translator to probe deeper.

"He looks Kurdi."

"Why, yes, I suppose that's because he is Kurdi."

Sarcasm made no dent on them. Because of the language barrier, I communicated directly with the English-speaking apprentice, who also possessed the uncanny ability to read his commanding officer's thoughts and ask all the right questions. Some more pictures emerged of Sharki and his kids playing in the fields on that day we had our picnic.

"These people are your friends as well?"

I nodded, slightly perplexed at what they were trying to say. A thought occurred to me, but I dismissed it as being too absurd.

"They also look Kurdi. You have many Kurdi friends?"

"A few."

"Where were you living before coming to Turkey?"

"Syria."

"Which city?"

"Aleppo."

"Many Kurdi people in Aleppo. You stay how long there?"

"Four weeks."

"And before that?"

"Lebanon."

"Very bad people there. Hezbollah and Islamic jihad."

The apprentice stared at me hard, suddenly not looking so young anymore.

"You are Muslim?"

I nodded and swallowed some gulps.

"Your country of birth?"

"Pakistan."

"Pakistan very dangerous. But Musharraf good man. He love Turkey too much."

"Me, too," I said. "I love Turkey too. *"Çok guzel."* I added the only Turkish phrase in my vocabulary, meaning "very nice."

They weren't put off so easily. More questions followed. Why was I going to Nemrut in this horrible weather? Surely I couldn't be a tourist if the rain wasn't enough to deter me. Where was I really going to? Who were my local contacts?

The race was on to pin me down. My efforts to pass for a tourist faltered horribly on account of my recent residencies in Syria and Lebanon. When they scrutinized my passport in more detail and found entry stamps for Jordan and Egypt, going further back to Italy, Spain, Portugal, France, Netherlands, and the Czech Republic, they were positive I couldn't possibly be a tourist. No tourist remained on the road through so many countries for such a long time. How long was it? Almost one and a half years? Impossible for a tourist. Highly out of order. I toyed with the idea of explaining the concept of travel as a means of self-discovery, a challenging quest for personal growth, but I had serious doubts they would have understood.

Surly-faced officer issued a stern statement in Turkish and folded his arms with authority. The translation floored me.

"We believe you are a spy for the PKK."

My emotions roller-coastered from frustration to anger to confusion to panic-stricken fear.

"But that's just crazy. You can't possibly be serious." I started to laugh.

They didn't respond well to the laughter. But I was just covering up my anxiety at the significance of their dreadful assertion. The conflict between Turkish and Kurdish nationalism has remained a festering national wound. The PKK, or Kurdistan Workers Party, emerged as a political party demanding basic political, cultural, and linguistic rights for Turkey's ethnic Kurds. By the early 1990s, the PKK began seizing control of eastern territory, inciting resentment against Turkish institutions and launching attacks by insurgent forces. Its campaign was brutally squashed by the Turkish army and police. In the eyes of the national government, the PKK embodies a ruthless terrorist organization threatening to dismember the Turkish motherland. Collaborating with Kurdish nationalists was equivalent to state conspiracy.

"If you are not working as undercover agent for PKK, then how do you explain your photos of Kurdi friends in Syria? You lived in Damascus and Aleppo. What were you doing there?" my interrogator demanded.

"Nothing!" I blurted. "I was just traveling around. Besides, I don't even speak Kurdish!"

"That does not matter. You look Kurdi and your French is good. I heard you speaking with the people in the car."

"But you still have no evidence that I'm a spy."

"We have enough to start with."

I couldn't possibly figure out what to do to prove my innocence. The question-and-answer session lasted a good hour or two. Dusk had settled by now. Our 2:00 AM rising and the failed sunrise at the mountain summit were hazy delusions. I wondered what Ali and the French couple were up to. Our driver was still missing. And here I was, under suspicion for working with Kurdish insurgents, the worst possible offense that can occur in Turkey.

A senior-looking official, his uniform dotted with medals, called my interrogators to attention. They escorted me back inside the empty Land Rover, where I was told to wait as they went inside the police station. A crew of gendarmes with machine guns kept a strict watch. I waited and watched the sky darken with more clouds. My watch indicated it was nearly two in the afternoon, exactly twelve hours since this whole Nemrut ordeal had swung into action. The gendarmes stood still as statues. Finally, I heard the sound of a familiar laugh and saw Hikmet's grinning face with the missing front teeth as he walked out of the station. He was arm in arm with some other officer I had not seen before. The French couple and Ali followed, looking well rested. The driver had a sheepish look. They all approached the car, where I was shivering in the back seat, my clothes still damp from the rain.

I stared at Hikmet as if he were a ghost. "Where did you come from?" I asked. "I thought you were asleep at the lodge!"

"Well, I got a call from Ali and came to see what the trouble was all about. You don't look so good."

"Oh, don't you know? They think I'm spying for the PKK. Imagine such rubbish."

Hikmet gave me a warning look to calm down. "Don't worry. It's all taken care of," he replied. "I explained everything."

"But what did you say? You hardly know me!"

"Well, you are my guest, aren't you? And I brought you here from Avanos, where you stayed at my ranch? You are helping me with my English so I can speak with big American accent!" he said, winking hard.

"Yes, yes, of course." I caught his drift. "So I'm really off the hook?" I whispered to him.

"Clean as a whistle!"

"Hey! Where did you learn that expression?"

"I watch satellite TV. *Cosby Show* is my favorite."

The surly-faced officer and his apprentice did not show up to bid us farewell. Gallant waves all around and encouragements to visit their paradise at a future occasion trailed the Land Rover as it started moving again.

"That was really, really strange," I murmured over and over.

"*Très bizarre,*" the French couple concurred.

Ali looked impressed. He hadn't expected a diminutive shrimp of a girl would be taken so seriously by the Turkish military. The Egyptian stationmaster revisited my mind. I couldn't possibly be an American new-comer, he had assumed. My face and name robbed me of the foreigner label, at least in appearance. It was getting to be tiresome, this chame-leonesque quality that kept misconstruing my identity in the Middle East and now in Turkey. Why did I have to look so damn familiar to these people? I was beginning to despise my genes. Now I would give anything to be back in the States, sipping a double-tall, extra-hot, no-foam, nonfat latte at the local Starbucks, reading the op-ed pages in the Sunday *New York Times,* maybe going to the gym later to work out on the elliptical climber and do some circuit training, just getting back to my old routine without having to worry about this blending-in business that would get me into trouble with the local authorities.

"You are lucky," Hikmet proclaimed. "It could have been much worse."

It was a sobering thought. Then we all burst into gales of laughter, clutching our aching stomachs. I felt strangely elated for having scored a twisted, backhanded compliment, for not standing out as a stranger in strange lands, but the novelty of it had long faded.

Stolen Dreams

Without movement, life as we know it would cease to exist. There would be no change of seasons, no births or deaths, no disasters or creations. We move by habit and routine, and then there are times when our move-ments are more orchestrated and deliberate, as in the case of travel. To travel in Turkey is to move across vast distances and cultures, given the sheer size and diversity of the country. After the caves of Cappadocia and adventures in the east, I said my farewells to Mehmet, Ali, Bülent, and the Paradise fairy chimney and headed to the *otogar,* or bus station, for a westbound connection.

First, I stopped in Konya to pay my respects to Rumi at his

mausoleum. It was packed with tourists, and the ebb and flow of human activity distracted me from feeling the spiritual connection I was counting on. So I left the teal-colored, pointy-domed building and wandered around the quiet back streets, trying to imagine the footsteps of Rumi, more than six hundred years ago, in these very same grooves in the asphalt touching my shoes. I recalled reading about Rumi's seminal meeting with the wandering dervish, Shams of Tabriz, who had been traveling throughout the Middle East searching and praying for someone who would tolerate his company. He was told to find a certain learned sheikh by the name of Jelaluddin living in Konya. When the two finally met, they became inseparable as friends.

Months passed and Shams and Rumi were immersed in each other's presence, transported by their conversation. On the night of December 5, 1248, as they were talking, Shams was called to the door. He went out and was never seen again. The mystery of his friend's absence compelled Rumi to go on a search. He traveled to Damascus, where he came to the realization, *Why should I seek? I am the same as he. His essence speaks through me. I have been looking for myself!*

I kept thinking about those words as I continued moving through Turkey. I trekked through forests and meadows in the idyllic Lake District and small towns with idyllic names, such as Ladik, Egirdir, and Beyshehir. Then I made my way down to the southern coastline. A travel tip led me to Kaş, a laid-back coastal town on the Mediterranean shoreline. I checked in to a small family-run pension and had my own room with a small balcony looking out over the sea. It would have made for a cozy retreat, but I seemed to have forgotten how to rest—not because I didn't want to; God knows I needed rest after nearly a year and a half of travel, but at that point, I felt like a marathoner sprinting toward the finish line. It wasn't quite visible, but there was something in my bones that knew the end was near.

One morning, I hailed a *dolmuş* and headed to Patara beach, about ten miles away from Kaş. A shimmering sandy white affair with a turquoise sea greeted my eyes. Not being much of a beach aficionado, I managed to sit in the sun for a few hours, caught up in some reveries of coming home soon and seeing my family and friends again. What I really hankered for at this moment was the feather-soft coziness of my own bed—not all those different beds I had lain in across two dozen countries—but the twin bunk bed with the forest-green flannel sheets and goose-down comforter covered with an Indian block-print tapestry that waited in my parents' basement in Seattle.

That bed had served as an extension of my body, a place that provided refuge as well as some regret. According to my father, I had spent more than half my life in bed. He was exaggerating, but I remembered the way he used to tell me, after I spent days in bed depressed, that I was wasting my potential by sleeping life away. I hadn't known what my potential was as I slumbered underneath the covers, hiding out from a world that I wanted so badly but didn't know how to reach. Now I wondered what Dad would say to the daughter reborn on the road.

That was how it felt, rebirth, renewal, resurgence by virtue of a necessary pilgrimage. I had crossed a threshold of my old self, and though it was hard to know where this new self had arrived, whether I could now call it happiness or peace, I was sure that it was not the same place as before. Even though I would be returning to the exact same home that I had left seventeen months ago, to the same faces and landmarks and geography I had known for the greater part of my life, I knew they wouldn't be seen in the same light now that I had grown in perspective. It revealed to me that home wasn't meant to be fled, that the desperate attempt to get away from it all for a tryst with the world was really just another way to come back to home. On that note, perhaps much of human yearning has to do with finding a way home, whether home is a physical entity or a mental, spiritual, emotional construct that provides a newfound self-awareness, an inner axis of gravity.

As I lay on my back to soak in the Turkish sunshine, I sensed lightness inside, not a floating kind of sensation but as if something had been extracted from me, a certain itch or restlessness alleviated. I lingered at the beach until sunset, nearly missing the last *dolmuş* back into town. It was already on its way and I started to run, waving my hat at the driver until he braked to a halt.

When I returned to my room, I noticed the top drawer of the nightstand was wide open and empty. I had left my black travel pouch in it, the one fingered and searched by the surly-faced *jandarma* officer in the Nemrut ordeal. But the pouch was no longer there. Even as I ravaged the room searching for it, a sinking feeling told me that my passport and money had been stolen.

Tense with panic, I tracked down Hashim, the pension owner, smoking a water pipe on the terrace with his Californian girlfriend. He gave me a ride on his motorcycle to the Kaş police station. A group of fresh-faced officers watched a soccer game on TV.

I marched up to a green-eyed officer with his legs propped up on an exquisitely carved wooden table.

"I want to report a theft."

He lit up another cigarette and kept his eyes peeled on the flickering screen.

"I said I want to report a theft."

Another officer turned toward me with half his attention still on the game.

"Yes?"

I repeated my request.

He offered me some apple tea. I gulped it down and tried again. The officer inserted a form into an ancient typewriter, the paper fluttering at its edges in the breeze from his sighs.

"Your name?"

My answer surprised him, and he did a double take. "My sister is Melihé!" he said, pronouncing the Turkish version.

This was no time to find a long-lost cousin.

"So what did you lose?"

"What do you mean, lose? I didn't lose anything. I was robbed of my passport, my money, my credit card, everything!"

Hashim cleared his throat and translated on my behalf for the police officer typing up the report. The two men engaged in a long discussion, heads occasionally bobbing up and down in consensus.

The officer clacked away at the typewriter keys and then rolled out the paper with a flourish.

"Sign here," he commanded.

My father's voice sounded stern on the phone. "Enough of your gallivanting around the world. It's time to come home!" He was no longer encouraging me to eat mackerel sandwiches on the docks of the Bosporus and buy prayer rugs in the *souqs*.

I assured Dad that I was planning on heading back, and as soon as I reached the Turkish capital, I would buy a ticket homebound. But I couldn't very well get out of the country without my passport. Plus I was all out of money, with not even a spare traveler's check to tide me over.

Both my parents were relieved that I was resuming some semblance of sanity. They weren't exactly thrilled about the senseless loss I had just suffered, but they helped me out just so I could move and come back where I belonged. The first hurdle was to pick up an international wire transfer sent from home, a generous sum that ought to fetch me a one-way return ticket. Kaş had no major banks, so I had to head to a specified branch in Antalya, a bigger city about five hours away by bus. Some fellow backpackers chipped in for the bus fare and Hashim lent me some cash for food and pension fees. *It's all right now. It's all right,* I told myself three days later, boarding the early-morning connection to Antalya.

Walking toward the bank on a sweltering afternoon, my stomach churned at the improbability of receiving $1,000 without a trace of ID save the incomprehensible police report. But the young female teller understood the gray shades of life and handed me a thick cash bundle secured with rubber bands. I headed back to Kaş and settled my accounts. Of course, I still lacked my passport, without which I had no chance of boarding a jet. But I considered it a trifling matter that would soon be ironed out at the consulate in Istanbul. In the meantime, I had one more stop to make.

Anyone in his or her right mind would have rushed straight home after the shock of stolen valuables. But I still had to see Bursa, the old Ottoman capital of Turkey. It was a lovely city, a fusion of water, silk, and mosques. My neighborhood *lokanta*, or Turkish-style bistro, served simple, hearty meals of sun-ripened tomatoes; steaming green lentils, tangy yogurt with diced cucumbers, known as *cacik*; and freshly baked bread locally known as *ekmek*. I feasted on Bursa's offerings, from live puppet shows to the local cottage industry of silk weaving.

My cultural immersion wouldn't have been complete without Dogan, a school principal in his midforties I had met at Ulu Jami, or the Great Mosque of Bursa. I used to pray there in the late afternoons and when I finished, I would simply continue sitting, allowing the feeling to stay with me just a little bit longer. And now, the peaceful afterglow of prayers that I had wanted to fuse into my everyday life was indeed lingering, catching in my spirit and holding it aloft like a taut, wind-filled sail.

Dogan adopted me as an honored guest and restored my faith in the kindness of strangers, opening an appealing world of Turkish living that could have sustained its momentum had I chosen to change the journey's script. He even offered me a job teaching English at his school and knew of a vacant apartment. Just like that, Dogan was handing me the very basics I would have to look for when I got home—find a job, get a place of my own if I didn't want to continue living with my parents. But I wasn't really tempted to stay on in Bursa and build a life.

It certainly had a romantic appeal—to live and work abroad, in a historic Turkish city, with open-air cafés next to gurgling fountains in cobblestoned courtyards, a place where you could buy dirt-cheap fresh produce that would be called organic back home, and pray in 14th-century Ottoman mosques instead of apartment buildings converted into makeshift mosques in American suburbs.

All that I would miss, just as I would miss a dozen other habits and rituals gathered from my travels in the Middle East and that would be impossible to replicate in Seattle, such as smoking a *nargileh* under clear desert skies with a group of boisterous Bedouin men, dancing to Amr Diab in the middle of the road on a snowy winter night in Amman, jogging in a Syrian park while listening to Fairuz without the need of a Walkman. None of it would ever be relived, but it was enough at this stage to have lived it for once and to hold on to it forever.

In the balmy evenings, Dogan and some colleagues of his from school took me to a local *saz* café, where men who were bank clerks and accountants by day turned into soulful folk musicians by night. They welcomed me to practice with them. I learned how to press the frets and pick the strings of the *saz* I had just bought, a long-necked beauty handcrafted in mulberry wood, the color of fine chocolate, with my name inscribed in bold black letters at its base.

One evening, I met one of Dogan's most interesting friends, a beggar named Ragib. He was crippled from the waist down, causing him to squat on his haunches. To provide the momentum to drag his useless limbs, Ragib walked with his hands as his front legs. Ragib's mind was sharp, alert, and not at all crippled, and his handsome features and lively, intelligent eyes gave him a certain stature. In fact, his whole being radiated light, energy, and warmth. He was the classiest beggar I had ever known.

When I expressed interest in going to one of Bursa's famous thermal spas, Ragib decided to escort me there. We strode through the streets together, Ragib darting through traffic like a nimble spider, using his left foot and his right hand to propel his body forward. People looked at us with interest but not an ounce of pity, for Ragib's innate sense of dignity commanded respect. We found a taxi, and he hopped in the front seat. I sat directly behind him and admired his bright, inquisitive face in the side-view mirror, reflecting the allure of someone important.

Upon reaching the bathhouse, I soaked for an hour in a tepid pool of water rich in minerals. Ragib waited courteously all this time, a small figure huddling next to a wall on a moonlit night. For an instant, I pictured him as an illustrious professor, lecturing on the Ottoman history that he knew so well. He also spoke excellent English and had taught himself Arabic and French. We headed back to town to meet our friends.

This time in the taxi, Ragib sat next to me with his hazel eyes glued to my profile. He gave me his cell phone number and said we should meet up in Istanbul. I puzzled over his freshness, having assumed that disabled beggars were humble and downcast. But this one behaved with confidence and pride, even a bit of arrogance. He was living proof of the triumph of human will over physical limitations. Despite the constraints of his body, Ragib refused to become a prisoner of his mind. He knew the importance of pushing personal limits, but he also seemed to know when to accept them.

I recalled an old saying of my father's to "work within my limits." I seemed to have done just that. Like Ragib, I had wanted to test my limits, to know what I was and wasn't capable of. So I had banished fear from my vocabulary and charted a journey without a return ticket, without a coherent plan, without any solid purpose or reason other than a desire to prove myself to no one other than myself, and now that I had, I could pat myself on the back and know, as Ragib seemed to know, that once the limits have been stretched as far as their elasticity allows, then perhaps it's time to stretch no further and simply acknowledge the terms of the accomplishment.

Back at the *otogar* a week later, I called out the Turkish good-bye to my friends.

"Allahaismarladik." I am putting myself in God's hands.

They responded. *"Güle, güle."* Go happily, go happily.

What fun words. They danced on my tongue.

Home Run

The sandy-haired, blue-eyed official at the American consulate in Istanbul scrutinized the police report I had handed over, a slight frown creasing his forehead.

"There is no mention of a theft here. It only says that you lost your passport and money at the beach."

"That's not entirely correct, officer. I can assure you that my passport was not just lost, it was in fact stolen."

"Then why doesn't it say so on the police report you filed in Kaş?"

I shrugged my shoulders, too shaken up and furious over the blatant lie to breathe aloud the real reasons why the truth behind my case had been concealed. It all made sense now. I recalled Hashim's intervening as my spokesperson, his long monologue in Turkish to the police officer, heads nodding between the two men, apparently in agreement to avoid publicizing a theft at the pension and chalking up the incident instead as a scatterbrained tourist's "loss" at the beach. And I had signed the document to legitimize their doctored-up story. If only I could mentally strangle the cowards.

"I don't know why the theft is not recorded on the form, officer. I am illiterate in Turkish. But I would like my passport replaced." My voice strained with fatigue and the stress of a temporarily blocked exit strategy.

The consul glanced at me out of the corner of his eye while stamping some forms.

"Been on the road a while, haven't you?"

I managed a faint smile as he instructed me to return later that day with the completed application and two photographs with a white—not colored—background.

Before coming to Istanbul, I had met a young Turkish journalist on a tour boat in Fethiye, a seafaring town just west of Kaş. The two-hour excursion in a Turkish *gulet* along the southern coastline had struck me as a pleasant way to while away the afternoon before I caught the connecting bus to Bursa, where I had managed to recover from the awful theft/loss.

Ferhat had peered over my notebook and extended his hand in a friendly shake.

"You can stay with me and my sister in Istanbul," he said in a thick accent and proceeded to scribble a phone number on the inside cover of my grimy Lonely Planet guide as we hung out on deck. Ferhat's greasy, shoulder-length black hair was pulled back in a ponytail with a few stray pieces sticking out on the sides like the purls of an old sweater. He wore a pair of faded jeans with holes at the knees. I had instantly pictured him as a grunge rocker. It was an unexpected offer of hospitality from a complete stranger that I trusted simply because I was exhausted. Istanbul hovered on the horizon as the journey's final leg.

It was 7:00 AM when I arrived at the bus station on the "Asian side" of the city, as specified by Ferhat. Then I called him from the public pay phone, guessing two of the last digits smeared by some water I had spilled. The phone rang ten times before he answered.

"Wait for me," Ferhat commanded and hung up. I sat on my backpack and waited for more than two hours. Just ahead, I could make out the glimmering Bosporus and ferryboats chugging passengers on their early-morning commute. Ferhat kept his word and showed up with his black hair slightly longer than before—and just as greasy—flying in the sea breeze. A little circle of concerned onlookers had congregated around me while I waited for Ferhat. They all smiled with relief when he showed up and I thrust myself in his care. We hopped into a taxi and crossed the long bridge that spans the Bosporus and links Europe and Asia. It was a magnificent setting for a city.

Ferhat lived in a modern residential area quite isolated from the Istanbul of guidebooks. We walked up seven flights of stairs to reach a spacious apartment that he shared with his sister, who had just gone off to work. From the whiff of perfume lingering in the air, I knew that he had not lied about the sister part. Even if she weren't a blood relative, traces of a woman's presence in the apartment were evident from bottles of nail polish lying on the coffee table and a pale pink shawl that probably did not jibe with Ferhat's taste.

His English was not very good. Ferhat struggled to remember words as if they were locked in a dusty attic of his mind for which he kept losing the key. Sometimes it would take as long as five minutes for Ferhat to finish one simple sentence. But I could hardly complain, given my total deficiency in Turkish. With his long-drawn-out phrases in English, Ferhat managed to communicate that I would be on my own in Istanbul. He was just providing me a place to stay, with no obligation to show me around. The apartment lacked a spare key, but I was free to come and go as I pleased so long as I headed out with Ferhat in the mornings on his way to work. The arrangement suited me just fine.

On my first day in the city, I bypassed must-see sights—the Byzantine church turned mosque known as Aya Sofia, the Topkapi palace, and the historic, touristy quarter of Sultanahmet—and instead took a boat to Uşkudar, back on the Asian side. There I hired a taxi and asked the driver to take me to the highest point in Istanbul. He drove toward a grassy knoll converted into a sort of amusement park with stunning views of the Bosporus stretching out like a blue serpent. The first speckles of summer heat danced on the shimmering water, bordered by a hazy skyline of pencil-thin minarets. Every straight-edged cloud in the sky appeared to stretch as my finish line. I had nowhere else to go, nothing more to prove after a caravan of migrations from country to country, person to person.

It would take a long time to decipher what they all meant. But I did feel at that moment the symbolism of culminating my voyage in Istanbul. The city straddles East and West, just as I do in every waking minute, and I was more comfortable about this limbo-land existence. It was no longer a disjointed configuration; the hinges and bolts had been screwed tighter so that I could navigate with ease between my multiple worlds and not have to worry so much about falling through the cracks of my South Asian–Pakistani–Pacific Northwest American–Muslimness. They were all little pieces of a jigsaw puzzle that made up my identity, and now I was beginning to feel them sticking together in a seamless whole.

In the evening, I met Ferhat's thirty-year-old sister, Oznur. She worked as an accountant and made no bones about being a thoroughly modern woman with her maroon leather briefcase, slim-fitting crepe suits, and three-inch stilettos. The *hijab* that I still threw on from time to time purely out of habit was a source of amusement. Oznur was adamantly opposed to wearing the veil. When I asked her why, she said it was a peasant mentality that would revert Turkish society to the Dark Ages. I realized that Oznur represented the polar opposite of what I had been reading about in the local papers—a new generation of young Turkish women, assertive, educated, and politicized, demanding the right to cover their heads as a form of self-expression even as they were studying to become doctors, lawyers, and engineers.

In Turkey, the veiling debate was a potent battleground between personal belief and government ideology. Though the state clamped down on the head scarf out of a dread of totalitarian Islam, the issue at heart for Turkish women was the free will to dress as they pleased. Oznur told me about two friends who had dropped out of medical school rather than remove their head scarves (forbidden by state decree in Turkish government offices and universities). She seemed slightly pained, as if their actions had done her a disservice. Even though Oznur and I were both Muslim women who did not consider veiling to be mandatory in Islam, there was a divergence in our opinions, whereby the freedom of choice to veil was not a bad thing in my book, but to Oznur's way of thinking, a female covered head, in and of itself, was hopelessly backward.

It was hard not to loiter in Istanbul. I fell into a routine of riding the subway from the apartment until Taksim, and then switching to a bus for the older part of the city. Sometimes I would walk to the Galata Bridge, where men sold silvery fish displayed in plastic buckets and others crowded along the rails of the bridge dipping their lines in the water in the hopes of a catch. Farther down at the docks of Eminounou, fishermen stood inside bobbing boats and cooked the fish on steaming grills. I sat on the edge of the Bosporus and munched on freshly grilled mackerel sandwiches for $1 a pop, honoring my father's favorite travel fantasy.

My penchant for mosques flourished in Istanbul. I went to the mosque of Eyup Sultan on a Friday, as highly recommended by Ragib back in Bursa. Worshippers and revelers sprawled on straw mats in the courtyard indulging in little picnics. A mother-and-daughter team befriended me as we scouted out a place in the women's section. Hardly a spare inch was to be found that day, but we managed to find a spot to stand together shoulder to shoulder at prayer time. Every day, I prayed in different mosques, where I observed a visible contradiction in the official rhetoric of Turkey as a secular Muslim state and the strong sense of piety evoked among the masses, as evidenced by the bent knees and bowing heads of the Turkish women beside me. They were living proof of a reality staunchly opposed by the guardians of Atatürk's legacy, in which religion ought not to be on public display.

At the time of my visit in mid-2001, a grassroots Islamic resurgence was challenging the status quo of the government. The party platform had campaigned for social justice and won popular support through elections. Its aim was to improve Turkish lives, to deliver basic health and infrastructure facilities without spurning Islam. Ironically, the counter-campaign to squelch the Islamists appeared to have snagged Turkey's great experiment between Islam and democracy.

At the majestic Suleimaniye Mosque, I met Mustafa, a young, handsome Turk in a stiff starched shirt and tie who was employed as a sort of caretaker. He insisted on showing me a part of the mosque hidden to most visitors. Conversing in broken Arabic and English, we climbed up flights of stairs in narrow little passages and emerged on an open-air balcony with a bird's-eye view of the Bosporus and the domed Ottoman skyline.

Mustafa was a great admirer of Turgat Ozal, the late Turkish president who had died in 1993. According to Mustafa, Ozal did not equate a separation between mosque and state as abandoning religion. He had wanted to synthesize Turkey with business acumen and Islamic morality. He was even known for traveling with the Quran and a laptop. Mustafa laughed appreciatively. He told me to wait in the courtyard while he went home to change clothes, "home" in this case meaning a little fairytale tower at the gate of the mosque. I couldn't help but stifle a knowing smile at Mustafa's makeover. He emerged like the Turkish version of Clark Kent turned Superman in his army fatigue cargo pants with just the right slouch, an orange football jersey, and gel-spiked hair.

The easy switch from East to West seemed natural in Istanbul, and looking at Mustafa beaming at me with those radiant green eyes,

I recalled my own wardrobe changes during high school, when I would slip into the girls' bathroom on balmy spring days to change from baggy sweats to tank tops and Bermuda shorts and then back into a nightshirt-type, knee-length Pakistani tunic with drawstring harem pants at home. It was just part of the chameleon training that I had learned in my teens, just like my comrade Mustafa. He did not consider his Westernized persona in conflict with his Muslim beliefs. I gathered young Mustafa had caught on to Ozal's philosophy.

We went to a neighborhood café where he seemed to know everyone and ordered some light mezes, or appetizers, and *çay*, strong black tea served in little tulip-shaped glasses. I looked up in my dictionary the word *kief*, connoting pleasure or relaxation, which the Turks have perfected to an art form. It just wouldn't be the same back in Seattle. Nonetheless, on my way back to Ferhat's apartment, I finally booked a plane ticket and planned to arrive home in five more days.

My Turkish brother-and-sister hosts were not interested in hearing my rhapsodies over Istanbul. Nor were they inclined to spend any time with me despite my suggestions to go out for dinner or coffee. They would have considered it quite rude if I had used their kitchen unasked, even if the purpose was to cook dinner for the three of us. For the first time since the start of the journey, I encountered an indifferent hospitality where catering to my every need and want was not a matter of monumental concern. I recalled the easy warmth of Um Jasim and her doting daughters back in Aleppo. They had smothered me with attention. Now I longed for it, and my mouth salivated at the thought of eating my mother's home-cooked meals.

I knew she would make all my favorite dishes, from spicy mung beans and potato-filled crepes to shrimp curry with saffron rice and mango pickles on the side. Maybe she would take a day off from retail work on Sundays and stay home so we could cook together like old times. I wanted to hear Ammi call me a mad scientist, which is how I behaved in her Indian kitchen in Seattle. It was hard to believe that I would soon be there, and what a world of difference there was between those two kitchens across the Atlantic.

One morning, Ferhat left home earlier than usual. He hadn't realized that I was still in the apartment, lounging over breakfast in my room, waiting for him to call me on the way out. To my horror, the door was locked from the outside. Even if I had a spare key, it wouldn't have helped much, given the peculiar lock. I started to panic big-time. Today was the deadline to pay in full for my plane ticket. If not, the reservation would get canceled, and I risked the possibility of remaining stuck in Istanbul for weeks on end, waiting for an open flight during the busy summer season.

It wasn't exactly a death sentence, but Istanbul's charms were nearing a limit. I was tired of sightseeing, tired of staying in other people's homes, showering in their bathrooms, living out of a backpack. I had been a traveler long enough. I had done the spiritual warfare against myself and called it a truce. I was satiated with adventures, as one who has gorged at a banquet and could eat no more. Now there was nothing more to do except to get on that plane and fly back to Seattle, which meant that I couldn't remain trapped in Ferhat's apartment all day. I had to find a way out.

There was no phone inside. The brother and sister used their cell phones as the central switchboard. I raced to the balcony adjoining my room and considered climbing down a straggly tree into the apartment below. But the thought of being arrested as an intruder dissuaded me from trying. The panic over losing my plane ticket home mounted. I was desperate to escape. So I did what any desperate, imprisoned person would do. I opened the windows and screamed for help.

The neighborhood slumbered in a sizzling heat. As I continued screaming, my voice caught the attention of two men walking in the street below, and they looked up baffled. A major problem emerged in trying to explain the entrapment situation in my nonexistent Turkish. My mind rummaged through the meager collection of words I had learned. Only *arkadaş,* or friend, seemed relevant. I had no idea how to convey "No key" or "Locked in." So I tried to mime my imprisonment by throwing my legs over the windowsill eight floors up. The men waved their hands, telling me to stop.

Then I had a brain wave and wrote down Ferhat's cell phone number on a piece of paper. I attached the paper with a piece of string to a stone that I took from one of Oznur's flowerpots. The men picked up the paperweight thrown out the window and phoned Ferhat. He must have misunderstood the situation, for his sister walked in the apartment an hour later, fuming like an overheated engine. Tears streamed down her face as she banged dishes in the kitchen. I pleaded with her to settle down and hear my side of the story. She shook her head from side to side. I pleaded again. Oznur refused to listen. Then she blurted out the reason fueling her anger.

Apparently, my strange behavior had caused the men in the street to think that Oznur and Ferhat had kidnapped a foreigner and were holding her hostage in their apartment. The men started hatching conspiracy theories and coarse rumors. Oznur collapsed on the couch and cradled her head in her knees. Her voice spewed flames of bitterness.

"Now the whole neighborhood thinks we are bad people. They think we keep you here for money. And now the landlord wants us to leave. All because of what you did. You make us lose face in front of Turkish people. You bring us so much shame. We are ruined, completely ruined!"

Such heights of imagination would never have occurred to me. I apologized to Oznur and begged her to see the situation as a huge misunderstanding, a cultural/linguistic blunder. Besides, I reasoned, the accusations were not true. So what was the problem? According to Oznur, it did not matter what was true or not true. What mattered was what the public believed. Now that Oznur and her brother were blackballed by the entire neighborhood, they had lost their respect. And it was all my fault. I guess she had forgotten that I was illiterate in Turkish. It was a severe limitation that prevented me from communicating my desperation to leave the apartment. I had so badly wanted to, but not being able to utter the essential words made me feel as if my tongue had been chopped off. I gave up reasoning with Oznur. She rose from the couch and ushered me out the door like an annoying stray cat she was itching to get rid of. I fled to the airline office to secure my precious ticket and freedom.

On the way over, the irony of the situation hit me full force. After all these months and months of dillydallying on the road with no formal schedule or agenda or plans, I had suddenly shifted into a straitjacket mode in which it became the most urgent thing in the world to acquire a piece of paper that would allow me to board a transatlantic flight back to the very place I had once longed to get away from. The thought of not being able to step on that flight, of not getting home at the precise moment I had decided upon, was intolerable. What was the big deal, what why the sudden rush? After all, it was not as if I had a glorious future all mapped out in Seattle. I had in fact not even the remotest clue what I would be doing with my life there, whether I would like it or hate it, but something in me was saying, *Enough, that's just enough.* It was the very opposite of the voice that had told me a year earlier, *The journey isn't over; it hasn't even started.* Listening to both voices was part of my jihad, my inner struggle, first to test my limits and then to know when the results were in. Now I could plainly see that the learning curve was over, at least in this journey.

When I returned to the apartment in the evening, Ferhat asked me to leave right away. Oznur seemed to have softened her attitude and argued with her brother to let me stay for one more night. He refused to budge. According to Ferhat, the whole block knew about the crazy foreigner he and his sister had abducted for a hefty ransom. Now brother and sister risked eviction from the building with their reputations shattered. Then Ferhat said something that really stung. "I only helped you because you are woman." That was it. I went to my room and started to pack, knowing that my leftover money wasn't enough to cover the cheapest of pensions. But pride got in the way of practicality. In the worst-case scenario, I planned to sleep at the airport. An hour later, Oznur came in to inform me that would not be necessary. Ferhat relented on the condition of ignoring my presence.

The following day, I walked around Istanbul in a jangle of thoughts. The unexpected turbulence at the apartment reminded me of how little control I wielded, not just with my travels, but with life in general. "Allah can turn your world upside down in the blink of an eye," my mother always said. Whenever I made grandiose plans or built those castles in the air, she chastised me for forgetting to bracket my dreams with the requisite *Inshallah,* or God willing. It was her way of reminding me that controlling life was an illusion, and I often argued back that in spite of this illusion, we have to go along with the pretence of control so that we don't just sit there and do nothing. But no one is telling you to sit and twiddle your thumbs, was Mom's rationale. She added that it was imperative to exert an effort, to act, to struggle, as long as one had agency in faith. There is a phrase for this in Urdu. *Khudi ki tayari.* It roughly translates as preparing one's self.

For a long time, I had never really understood what this preparation was for. Now I wondered if the goal was to reach an ideal state of self-knowledge, which of course is a lifetime's work. But I had made some headway by having found a truer mirror with which to see and feel myself. Maybe there would be other mirrors in the future, from experiences yet to be had, some just as true, some less so, though for the time being, I valued this mirror, the one I had polished by going on a journey that had been the bravest, craziest, and most rewarding thing I had ever done. All I wanted now was to be anchored in home port because I felt myself as a tired, creaky ship, stripped and refurbished from the inside out and in need of some rest. Having indulged my curiosity of crossing frontiers, both external and internal, I found it immensely satisfying to be able to say that I had seen and felt enough.

A pay phone booth lay ahead. I went up to it and arranged for a cab to pick me up at midnight for the drive to Atatürk airport. My flight to Amsterdam would be departing at 5:00 AM. Back at the apartment, my hosts said cordial good-byes. I gave Oznur a sterling silver ring capped with a blood-red stone. It fitted snugly on her slim finger. She seemed pleasantly surprised that I had guessed the right size.

Epilogue

As far as soul-searching expeditions go, the Middle East is not likely to make the cut on most people's top-ten list. Danger zone, terrorist haven, and religious extremism characterize the region's better-known associations. But if I were to say that this region is also a place where I was the happiest I'd ever been, totally awake and in love with life, where I found a trace of inner peace and serenity, where I met people who showered me with kindness and taught me humility and grace, then chances are that people would think something is amiss. Either I'm not tuned in to reality, or maybe the reality that I seem to be refuting is not concerned with what I saw and felt and experienced.

Exactly two weeks after I landed in Seattle, the events of September 11 sent shock waves around the world. It was a rude welcome home. Before I had even caught my breath and settled into my old comforts, I was facing grief and sadness and anger and not knowing what to do with this memory I had brought back, the memory that you have just read about.

The whole experience of writing this book in a post–9-11 environment was a journey in itself. On one hand, I was reluctant to even begin such a task; I certainly had not traveled with the intent of becoming a writer. I was not a journalist nor a Middle East expert. I was just a girl with a story to share—a story too good to keep entirely to myself. But how to tell this story in the flurry of all the negative news about Muslims, Arabs, and Islam was a far bigger challenge than I had ever anticipated. I was constantly trying to reconcile two different realities: the one spewing from TV broadcasts and daily headlines and the one in my head.

I would finish a paragraph about Leila, the cute Jordanian Muslim teenager in frayed blue jeans with a Valley Girl accent who missed watching *Oprah*, and click on the remote to find Oprah talking to Muslim women who didn't look or sound anything like Leila or my friend Asma in Cairo, who was proud of her veil and her feminist ideology. There were times when I would be thinking of all the fun Bea and I had in Dahab, dancing until dawn with poor old Waheed gaga-eyed over the beautiful Beatrice, and in the next instant there would be a news flash about a bomb blast that had killed foreign tourists in the nearby resort of Sharm el Sheikh. Then I would remember Sharif in Aleppo, his subsistence on faith, his complete sense of surrender to Allah, which is the true practice of Islam, and a couple of mouse clicks away from my desktop, I would read an article describing Muslims as a bunch of deranged sickos prone to violence condoned by their ultrastrict and puritanical religion.

Which of these realities is more real, which should be believed, which should be dismissed? I would say that they are all real, and to believe in one does not necessarily mean to negate the other; it's a matter of having a perspective, a worldview that sees the other side, the side of everyday humans living out everyday lives—maybe not as dramatic or newsworthy as the side that gets most of the media coverage (which in all fairness makes sense, since the business of news is not to show nice pretty pictures of the girl or boy next door—but it wouldn't hurt once in a while to do so).

If you don't want to wait for the news makers to level the playing field when it comes to airing stories about the Middle East, or anywhere else in the world for that matter, that are more positive, that shy away from caricatures, and maybe even throw in a few laughs, then you might as well go see for yourself what's out there. Nothing quite compares to the immediacy of travel as a way of shaping inner knowledge, the kind that must be lived out in your heart and mind. That's why I have never looked upon travel as a frivolous escapade—indulgence, yes—but as a self-investment to simultaneously sharpen our perceptions of the world and lead us toward hidden corners and byways of our interior sanctums that might otherwise go unexplored. The objective is not to have all the answers, but to come up with better questions.

And that is also why I believe that the Middle East I once knew and loved can still be found in spirit if you only take the effort to go there and look. Maybe not in a crazy sort of way that blindly hurls you halfway across the world on a one-way ticket, but given the undeniable dangers in certain places, at least in a way that still is responsible, considerate, and open-minded.

As my life has taken on a newer shape and form, I sit back sometimes, and if I'm still and quiet, I begin to see the hours and moments in which dangers and pleasures, strangers and friends, tears and laughter crafted a journey whose echo does not fade with distance or the ravages of time. The most important thing was just to show up.

Maliha Masood
Kirkland, Washington, USA
October 2006

Acknowledgments

My deepest gratitude is to Allah, who guided me from beginning to end in this journey with infinite compassion, mercy, and wisdom.

I am also indebted to:

My parents for putting up with me at all times and letting me go my own way when I needed to, and especially to my beloved husband for his kindness and support.

Beautiful Beatrice (Bea), my partner in adventure, for her intuitive powers and killer sixth sense.

The wonderful folks at Seal Press for taking a chance on me. Infinite gratitude to my editor, Marisa Solís, for her unwavering enthusiasm and brilliant insights.

Special thanks to John Mifsud and the Jack Straw Writers Program.

Last, I would like to honor the memory of all the exceptional people I met in the Middle East, both friends and strangers, for welcoming me in their lives with open hearts. I owe them a zillion thanks. Without them, this book could not have been written.

Glossary

aamiyah	spoken Egyptian dialect
abaya/aba	ankle-length cloak in a variety of colors and designs, traditionally worn by Muslim women
Abboo	father in Urdu
adhan/azan	the call to prayer in Arabic/Urdu
Ahlan wa sahlan	Welcome in Arabic
ajnabee	foreigner in Arabic and/or stranger in Urdu
alatule	Egyptian Arabic slang for Straight Ahead
Alhamdulillah	Thanks be to God
Allahaismarladik	Turkish good-bye said by the person leaving: I am putting myself in God's hands
Allahu Akbar	God is great

al-Qahira	traditional Arabic name for Cairo, meaning the city victorious
al-Sham	Arabic name for the city of Damascus
Ammi	mother in Urdu
arkadaşh	friend in Turkish
azan/adhan	the call to prayer in Urdu/Arabic
bab	door/gate
baba ghanoush	dip made of pureed roasted eggplant
bawwab	doorman
bazaar	marketplace
Bedu	short for Bedouin
beit	house in Arabic
Bikam	Arabic expression for asking how much something costs
block print	technique of textile design common in India and Pakistan
bukra	tomorrow
bulgar	cracked wheat
burqa	a loose garment that covers the face and body
cacik	Turkish yogurt-and-cucumber dip
cap	cappuccino

çay	tea in Turkish
çok guzel	Turkish expression for Very Nice
Dadi	paternal grandmother in Urdu
darbouka	Middle Eastern hand drum
debke	traditional Middle Eastern dance
deir	monastery
dhikir	Arabic term for remembrance—often a Sufi ritual to recollect and repeat the attributes of God through music and dance
dolma	stuffed grape leaves
dolmuş	small Turkish bus used for local transport, often stuffed with passengers
duas	prayers in Urdu
dupatta	long rectangle scarf worn by women in India and Pakistan as an accessorized shawl or draped over the head
duur	far away in Urdu and Kurdish
Eid al-Adha	the Muslim feast commemorating Abraham's sacrifice of Isaac; it occurs on the tenth day of the month of pilgrimage
ekmek	Turkish bread
Es salaem w'alekum	Traditional Islamic greeting; Peace be upon you
fag	cigarette in British slang

fajr	dawn, first prayer of the day
falafel	ground chickpeas fried into small round or oval pieces, stuffed in sandwiches or served with yogurt and salad
fasoli	hearty bean stew
felucca	a narrow fast sailing vessel
fondouk	hotel in Arabic
fricki	a type of *bulgar,* or cracked wheat
fushah	classical Arabic
fuul	ground fava bean stew commonly eaten for breakfast in Egypt
fuul mudammas	fava bean stew cooked in tomato sauce
galabiya	Egyptian term for traditional full-length gown worn by men and women
gendarme	police officer
ghazal	a prominent form of Urdu poetry and/or lyrical song
GSM	global system for mobile communication—a globally accepted standard for digital cellular communication prevalent in Europe and Asia
güle güle	Turkish good-bye, said by the person seeing friends off: Go happily
gulet	Turkish sailboat
hadith	sayings, doings, teachings of Prophet Muhammad

hajji	term of address for a man who has completed the pilgrimage to Mecca
Halab	Arabic name for the city of Aleppo
halib	milk
hammam	Middle Eastern public bathhouse
haram	forbidden or shameful
hawala	to try in Arabic
hawkawati	storyteller
hewlldan	to try in Kurdish
hijab	head scarf worn by Muslim women
hummus	puree of chickpeas eaten as a dip
hurriya	freedom
ibn al-balad	salt of the earth
iftar	breaking of the fast meal at sunset
ijtihad	a process of inquiry and self-analysis
imam	Muslim leader of the prayer
Inshallah	Arabic expression for God willing
intifada	uprising, used in reference to the Palestinian cause
isha	night prayer, last of the five daily prayers
jama	mosque in Arabic

jandarma	Turkish military unit functioning as a rural police force in Eastern Turkey
jelbab	full-length gown worn by men and women, also known as *galabiya* in Egypt
jihad	Islamic term for inner struggle and/or holy war
Kaaba	Central, cubic, stone structure, covered by a black cloth, within the Great Mosque in Mecca, Saudi Arabia. Also represents the direction Muslims face during prayer.
Kaatiba	female writer in Arabic
kaffiyeh	checkered tasseled cloth worn as a scarf, usually in black and white or red and white
kahve	Arabic coffee
karkaday	tea made of hibiscus flowers
khalas	Enough, no more, finished in Arabic
khamsa	numeral five in Arabic
khan	caravansary, a shelter for trading merchants and their cargo
khubz	bread in Arabic
Khudi ki tayari	Urdu expression for self-awareness
khutbah	Islamic sermon
kibbe	minced meatballs
kief	pleasure or relaxation in Turkish

kilim	tribal rug, usually hand-woven
koshish	to try in Urdu
kunafa	Middle Eastern pastry made with fine shredded wheat stuffed with honey and nuts
kurta	South Asian tunic, usually knee length with side slits
kushari	Egyptian staple dish of rice, pasta, and beans topped with fried onions
labneh	Middle Eastern yogurt cheese
Lavazza	brand of Italian espresso machine and espresso
lesh	Why in Arabic
lokanta	neighborhood Turkish restaurant or bistro
loo	bathroom in British slang
Maasalaama	Farewell or good-bye in Arabic, literally Go in safety and peace
Mabrouk	Congratulations in Arabic
Mafi mushkil	No problem in Arabic
maghrib	sunset prayers
manakeesh	thin crepe soaked in thyme and olive oil, common throughout Lebanon
mashallah	Arabic expression of delight and/or praise
mashi	Okay in Arabic
mashrabiya	traditional wooden carved window screen

maulvi-saab	Urdu term for a male religious scholar
mawdah	place for performing ablutions in a mosque courtyard
medina	non-European part of a North African city; Middle Eastern reference to the old part of the city
meze	small dishes of appetizers, eaten collectively as a light meal
Merhaba	Hello in Turkish and/or Arabic
midan	traffic circle or square
mihrab	a niche set into the mosque's wall indicating direction of Mecca that Muslims turn toward in prayers
min fadlik	Arabic expression for Please, Help Yourself
minaret	mosque tower
misr	Egyptian reference for Egypt, also used for Cairo
moz	banana
muezzin	man who calls the five daily prayers from the minaret of a mosque
Mukhabarat	Syrian secret police
mullah	Muslim cleric (male)
mulukhiyya	Middle Eastern dish of dried spinach leaves cooked with chicken
mussafira	female traveler in Arabic

nadeef	clean in Arabic
nargileh	Middle Eastern term for water pipe, also known as *sheesha* in Egypt
ney	open-mouthed reed instrument
niqab	face veil, usually black in sheer or opaque fabric
noor	light or illumination in Arabic
noria	waterwheel
otogar	Turkish bus station
oud	Arabic lute
pakora	fried chickpea dumpling common in South Asian cuisine
PKK	Kurdistan Worker's Party—Kurdish insurgency group banned as a political party in Turkey
qanun	Arabic zither
Quran	literally, The Recitation and the central religious text in Islam
raki	distilled alcoholic beverage flavored with aniseed common throughout Turkey. Similar to arrack in the Middle East or ouzo in Greece.
raqs/raqs sharki	dance/Oriental belly dance
Ramadan	Muslim month of fasting
Sabah al-kheir	Good morning in Arabic

sabar	patience
sabeel	public water fountain
Sabra/Shatila	Palestinian camps in Beirut
sadiq	friends in Arabic
sahlab	a hot milky concoction flavored with cinnamon and pistachios common during Ramadan
salaam	peace; also a greeting
samosa	deep fried fritter filled with vegetables or meat
sadiq	friend in Arabic
saz	Turkish mandolin
servees	shared taxi
settar	Middle Eastern four-stringed instrument
shai	tea in Arabic
Shangri-la	idyllic place
sharmuta	whore in Arabic
shawarma	thin slices of barbecued meat or chicken often eaten as sandwiches
sheesha	water pipe in Egypt, also known as *nargileh*
sheikh	Muslim male religious and/or spiritual leader; sheikha for woman.
Sheray fay	Cheers in Turkish

Shukrun	Thank you in Arabic
shorba	broth and green lentils
singlet	tank top in British English
souq	Middle Eastern marketplace
Subhanallah	Praise be to God
Sufi	a practitioner of Islamic mysticism or Sufism
suhoor	predawn meal eaten during Ramadan
sukur	sugar in Arabic
sumac	Middle Eastern spice derived from dried berries with a reddish-purple color and sour, tangy flavor
surah	Quranic verse
tabouli	Middle Eastern cracked wheat or *bulgar* salad
taliba	female student in Arabic
tamam	Arabic expression for Great, Perfect, A-okay. Also common in Turkey
taraweeh	special late-night prayer sessions during Ramadan
tasawwuf	Islamic concept of self-improvement and purification; also refers to Sufism
tawhhid	Islamic concept of an uncompromising unity and oneness of divinity
tazbi	Islamic rosary beads in Urdu

Um	Mother in Arabic, traditional expression for mother of (followed by first son's name)
Umrah	Shorter informal pilgrimage to Mecca that Muslims perform year-round
wadi	desert valley
wallah	Arabic expression for "I swear to God" or "Really" or "I'm telling the truth"
Yallah	Arabic expression for Let's go!
zabiba	forehead scar visible among devout Muslims
zakah	alms or charity, obligatory for Muslims
zaatar	herbal mixture of roasted sesame seeds and thyme, often mixed with olive oil and eaten for breakfast

About the Author

© ANTHONY EGIZI

Maliha Masood was born in Karachi, Pakistan, and moved to the United States at the age of twelve. A graduate of Tufts University with a Master's in Law and Diplomacy, she has worked internationally in human rights policy and conflict resolution. Maliha is also an emerging playwright and the founder of Diwaan: Dialogue on Islam, a cultural theater collective based in Seattle, where she makes her home.

Selected Titles from Seal Press

For more than thirty years, Seal Press has published groundbreaking books. By women. For women. Visit our website at www.sealpress.com.

Voices of Resistance: Muslim Women on War, Faith, and Sexuality edited by Sarah Husain. $16.95, 1-58005-181-2. A combination of essays and poetry, this one-of-a-kind book reveals the anger, pride, and pain of Muslim women.

Tales from the Expat Harem: Foreign Women in Modern Turkey edited by Anastasia M. Ashman and Jennifer Eaton Gökmen. $15.95, 1-58005-155-3. Female expats from different countries describe how the Turkish landscape, psyche, people, and customs transformed their lives.

Stalking the Wild Dik-Dik: One Woman's Solo Misadventures Across Africa by Marie Javins. $15.95, 1-58005-164-2. A funny and compassionate account of the sort of lively and heedless undertaking that could only happen in Africa.

The Risks of Sunbathing Topless: And Other Funny Stories from the Road edited by Kate Chynoweth. $15.95, 1-58005-141-3. From Kandahar to Baja to Moscow, these wry, hilarious essays capture the comic essence of bad travel, and the female experience on the road.

Mexico, A Love Story: Women Write about the Mexican Experience edited by Camille Cusumano. $15.95, 1-58005-156-1. In this thrilling and layered collection, two-dozen women describe the country they love and why they have fallen under its spell. Also available, **Italy, A Love Story: Women Write about the Italian Experience**. $15.95, 1-58005-143-X and **France, A Love Story: Women Write about the French Experience.** $15.95, 1-58005-115-4.

Solo: On Her Own Adventure edited by Susan Fox Rogers. $15.95, 1-58005-137-5. An inspiring collection of travel narratives that reveal the complexities of women journeying alone.